Discovering the Mid-Atlantic

Discovering the Mid-Atlantic

Historical Tours

Patrick Louis Cooney

Photographs by Rosemary Santana Cooney

Rutgers University Press
New Brunswick, New Jersey

Library of Congress Cataloging-in-Publication Data

Cooney, Patrick, 1947–
    Discovering the mid-Atlantic : historical tours / Patrick Cooney.
        p.   cm.
    Includes bibliographical references and index.
    ISBN 0-8135-1703-6 (cloth)—ISBN 0-8135-1704-4 (pbk.)
    1. Middle Atlantic States—Description and travel—Guide-books.
2. New York Region—Description and travel—Guide-books.
3. Historic sites—Middle Atlantic States—Guide-books.   4. Historic
sites—New York Region—Guide-books.   I. Title.
F106.C768   1991
917.404′43—dc20   90-23764
                                                          CIP

British Cataloging-in-Publication information available.

For My Wife,
Rosemary

Contents

Preface

There is no shortage of travel books; in fact, every time you visit a bookstore, it seems that someone has published another guide book to compete with Fodor's or Frommer's. There are even other guide books to the New Jersey/Philadelphia area. So why still another one? Because this one is different.

What is unique about this book is its historical—as opposed to geographical—organization. Since most travel books are arranged geographically, the sites usually represent vastly different time periods. For instance, in the mid-Hudson River region you can see a seventeenth-century Dutch settlement, a Victorian mountain house, and the home of Franklin Roosevelt. This mixing of periods can result in a haphazard, jumbled sense of history. This book singles out sites located near one another, but from the same historical period. It helps the traveler put the sites into perspective and gives a glimpse into the lives and activities of the people who occupied them.

This book is especially helpful for parents. It gives them the opportunity to involve their children in the region around them. It is my hope that you will use the information provided here to bring an early settlement or a battlefield and its generals to life. Too many people see battlefields as boring places simply because they do not know what really happened there.

I have been a lifelong history buff, and I wanted to write a guide book that answers the major questions inquisitive travelers (like me) ask about the places they visit. That goal kept me going over the six years it took to research and write *Discovering the Mid-Atlantic*.

Sometimes it is hard to tell from travel guides and state pamphlets whether or not a site is worth visiting. I used many different travel books in preparing *Discovering the Mid-Atlantic*, but found them usually too brief for my taste in their descriptions of the historical, political, social, and technological contexts in which the sites existed. Often these books raised more questions than they answered. The research I did in preparing this book has convinced me even more of the need for such a travel guide.

There is no substitute for actually visiting the sites. At each site, I took notes on what was said and recorded my impressions, gathered any pamphlets available, and purchased the local area or site histories. I also did extensive library research. Biographies were useful in adding color and detail to the lives of historical figures. Specialty books covering such subjects as architecture, furniture, art, railroads, and ironmaking helped me to understand the humanistic and the technological changes that occurred. General histories added further insights into political and social trends.

How to Use This Book

The book provides maps, directions to the sites, and a geographic cross-reference that lists *all* sites in a given area, regardless of their historical place in time. Many areas—such as the city of Philadelphia—have sites from several different time periods. This book provides options. You can either take separate day trips and visit places within one period, or you can stay several days, use the geographic cross-reference, and see many or all of the sites at one time.

Although the book covers American history as revealed in the mid-Atlantic region, area sites do not exist for every important trend or event in American history. Also, the historical attractions that do exist unevenly cover different periods of time. For instance, there are proportionally more sites dealing with the Revolutionary War in general, and George Washington in particular, because many of the battles took place in this region. In contrast, most Civil War battles occurred in the South, so only one northern battlefield is listed. I have tried to find places representative of most of the major historical periods—sites you might otherwise overlook because of their out-of-the-way location.

Before you leave on any trip, you may want to purchase your own maps of the area. Even though the book gives directions, there is no substitute for a highly detailed map.

If overnight expenses present a problem, consider purchasing a tent and a guide to the campgrounds in each state. Even if you take just a few weekend trips, the tent will quickly pay for itself through the savings on motel or hotel bills.

Although I have listed visiting hours, these times are always changing. In addition, new sites become available for viewing through restoration or reconstruction. For lesser-known sites, it is always a good idea to telephone ahead. Current state travel guides, available free of charge from the state travel bureaus, are invaluable. The state travel agencies will also send listings of planned events for the different seasons. Here are the addresses:

> Delaware Tourism Office
> 99 Kings Highway
> Box 1401
> Dover, Delaware 19903
> Toll free: (800) 441-8846

Division of Travel and Tourism
State of New Jersey
20 West State Street
Trenton, New Jersey 08625
(609) 292-2470
Toll free: (800) JERSEY 7

Division of Economic Development
Division of Tourism
New York State Department of Commerce
99 Washington Avenue
Albany, New York 12245
(518) 474-2121
Toll free: (800) CALL NYS

Travel and Marketing Division
Department of Commerce, State of Pennsylvania
453 Forum Building
Harrisburg, Pennsylvania 17120
Toll free: (800) VISIT PA; for Philadelphia (800) 321-9563

The information in the book is correct to the best of my ability and to the time of publication. The reader should note that dates for social trends are approximations. For example, the Jacksonian Age runs from 1828 to 1860, but both starting and ending dates are debated in scholarly circles. If you find any of the information inaccurate, please contact me by writing to

Patrick Cooney
c/o Rutgers University Press
109 Church Street
New Brunswick, New Jersey 08901

A Personal Note

Over the past six years, my family and I have taken hundreds of one- or two-day trips in preparing this book. We have had a great deal of fun, and we have learned the basics of architecture, literature, painting, technology, transportation, and politics. As a result of your travels, you too may find your family becoming more well rounded and appreciative of our regional history and landscapes.

I would like to thank my wife, Rosemary, for her invaluable assistance and interest, especially in nature and photography, and my son, Carl, for his kid's eye view of things. Our friends Judy Nelson and Al Williamson often traveled with us, making the trips more enjoyable. I would also like to thank Neil Soderstrom for his editorial advice and encouragement. Leslie Mitchner of Rutgers University Press was very helpful and patient, and I thank her very much for believing in the larger purpose of the book. Kate Harrie provided valuable services in editing the text for grammatical and substantive improvements. And I cannot forget a special thank-you to the workers and volunteers at all the historical sites that help preserve the region's and the nation's heritage.

MAPS

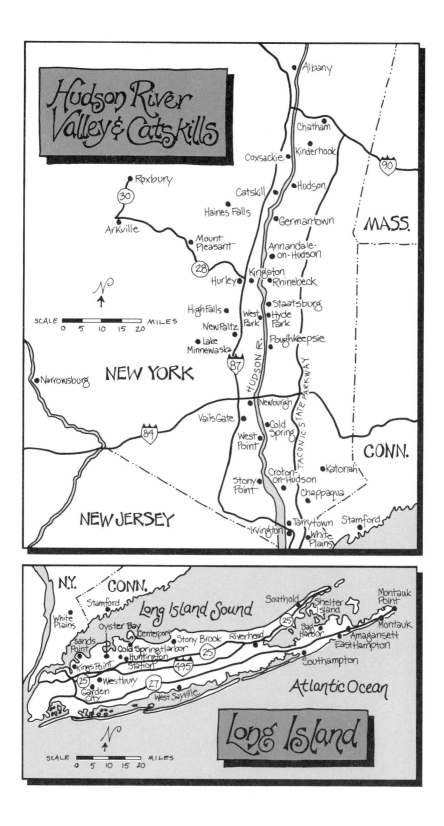

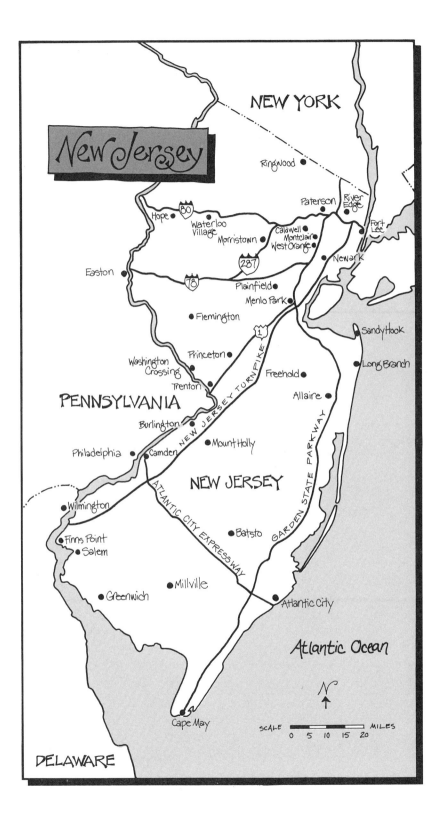

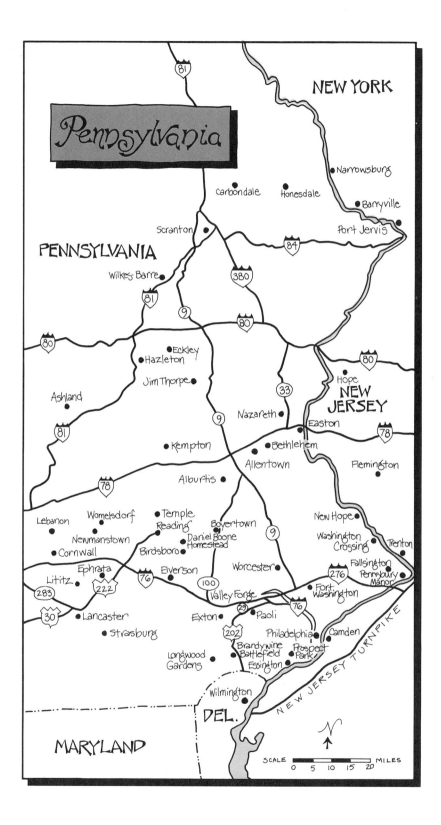

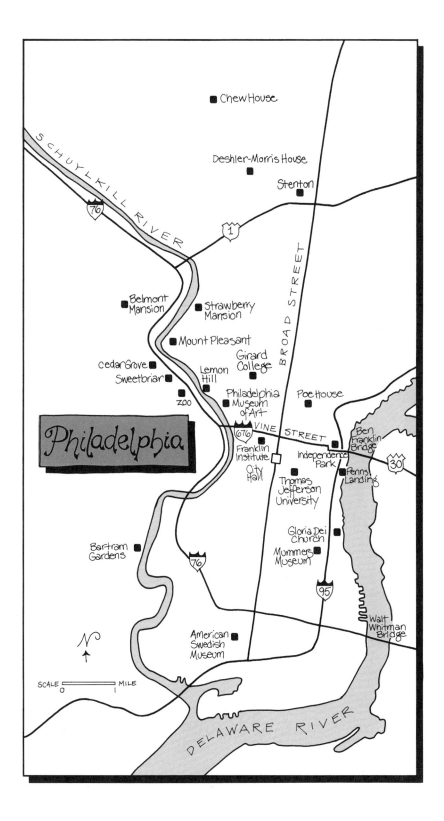

Discovering the Mid-Atlantic

PART

ONE

The Early Settlements

The tours in part 1 cover the earliest settlements in the region—Dutch settlements in the Hudson River valley and Swedish settlements in the Delaware River valley—and the English manorial system in the Hudson River valley. Just as families can trace their roots back in time, you can trace the ethnic roots of a region. There are a number of museums and villages to visit to aid this investigation.

The story begins with the Dutch because they were the first to settle in the area. Colonization began in 1614 with a trading post in the Albany area and in 1624 with the founding of the settlement that grew into New York City. There are very few Dutch houses left in these two cities, but in Kingston there is a concentration of houses showing Dutch influences.

In 1638 the Swedes settled in present-day Wilmington, Delaware. However, the Scandinavian colonists built mostly with logs, which have long since decayed. They did not have time to build more substantial structures because the Dutch took control over the Swedish areas in the 1650s. This makes it more difficult to find Swedish-American places to visit. There are, however, a few sites in an arc along the Delaware River from Wilmington to Philadelphia.

On eastern Long Island the English established a number of early settlements: Gardiner's Island (1639), Southold and Southampton (1640), East Hampton (1648), Shelter Island (1652), Huntington (1653), and Brookhaven (1655). In 1650 a line, corresponding to the present Nassau-Suffolk county border, was drawn across the island to separate the Dutch on western Long island from the English on the eastern end. These settlements are not included in the tours, because they really belong more to the history of New England than to that of the Mid-Atlantic region.

After a tour of the early settlement sites, the next visit is to those places historically associated with the period after the English (who had settled Massachusetts, Connecticut, and eastern Long Island) seized control of all Dutch territory (1664). Traveling up the Hudson River, through Sleepy Hollow territory to Livingston Manor, one finds reminders of the once powerful lords of the manor.

1

Dutch Settlements

The directors of the Dutch East India Company, seeking a shorter route to India, in 1609 hired the Englishman Henry Hudson to search for a northwest passage. In the ship the *Half Moon*, the explorer sailed up the river that now bears his name to a point near Albany. Dutch colonization of what became Albany and New York City, and of the Delaware and Connecticut river valleys, laid the basis for their claims of ownership to today's New York, New Jersey, Delaware, and Connecticut.

To encourage further colonization, the directors of the Dutch company adopted a quasi-feudal system of land ownership known as the patroonship. The patroon received a grant of land in return for a promise to settle at least fifty colonists within four years. Three patroonships were established: Pavonia, New Jersey, across from Manhattan; Swanendael, located on the west bank of Delaware Bay near the present Lewes, Delaware; and Rensselaerswyck in the Albany area. Other patroonships were later established, but of all of them, the only economically successful one was Rensselaerswyck.

Although the English took control of the entire area in 1664, by no means did Dutch influence end. The Dutch influence led to the establishment of greater tolerance. In terms of personal ethics, the people of the New York area were less "puritanical" than those of the New England states. While it is true that most Dutch were Calvinists, they had established settlements primarily to gain profits, not to set up religious communities. In the seventeenth century, the Netherlands was a relatively tolerant country and a haven for persecuted religious groups. The Dutch transmitted these tolerant attitudes to the New World.

The trip to Kingston will reveal a great deal of Dutch influence. The visit will be enhanced by some knowledge of Dutch architecture, which is actually a mixture of many different national styles: Dutch, Flemish, Belgian (Walloon), and French (Huguenot). Dutch exteriors often include the following features: the gable (the area immediately under a pitched roof) usually extends above the roofline, and the edges of the gable may be straight, crow-stepped (like stairs), or some variation of this; in the towns, houses are often placed gable end to the street; Flemish houses often have flaring eaves (overhanging lower edges of a roof); Dutch houses often are of ample proportions, reflecting the combination of the house and the basement barn in one dwelling; and the Dutch door—a double door (cut horizontally in the middle and with both halves independently opening and closing).

Some aspects of Dutch interiors are Delft tiles (decorated with a white opaque glaze and a blue overglaze) around the fireplace; use of the *kas* (a wardrobe—a tall, upright free-standing cabinet used to store clothes or linens), instead of a closet; fireplaces that are often jambless (without side walls); and the use of cupboard beds or bed boxes (with doors that close) instead of free-standing beds.

Kingston is an interesting place to visit because of the high concentration of eighteenth-century stone houses built of native Ulster County limestone. The original houses consisted of one room with a staircase leading to a cellar and a half-story loft. Later, the owners built an attached structure that was either the same size or larger than the original.

Most visitors enjoy the rough appearance and varied colors of the stones. The town is especially pleasing in the fall when the trees and vines have turned colors, providing a vivid contrast between the bright leaves and the whites and browns of the houses. Touring the town will take around three-quarters of a day. If time is limited, be sure to see the Senate House. The second Saturday of each October the town holds an open house. Call ahead (914-331-9506) for the latest information.

While the Dutch landlords liked the patroonship system, their subjects did not. A group of colonists, unhappy with life at Rensselaerswyck (now Albany), left that area and in 1653 settled Esopus (renamed Wiltwyck and later called Kingston).

Friction between Dutch colonists and the Esopus Indians began at once. The so-called Peach War (or First Esopus War) began in New Amsterdam (New York City) when, in 1655, a Dutchman killed an Indian woman simply for taking a peach. For revenge, the Esopus seriously wounded the Dutch offender with an arrow. They then descended on New Amsterdam and caused some property damage. The city itself got off lightly; not so, the outlying settlements. The Indians killed fifty people in raids on Pavonia and Hoboken in New Jersey and on Staten Island. The trouble then spread to Indians on both sides of the Hudson. The residents of Kingston fled as a precautionary measure.

In 1658 the Dutch governor of New Amsterdam, the peg-legged Peter Stuyvesant, organized the construction of a wooden palisade around the town. The settlers enlarged the stockaded area several times, eventually enclosing about forty acres. Perhaps the stockade gave the residents a false sense of security, for a group of them viciously attacked a party of four reportedly drunken Indians gathered around a campfire, killing one. The Indians responded by placing the fort under constant siege. Stuyvesant had to return to protect the town.

Kingston Visitors' Center

308 Clinton Avenue, near the Stockade area and directly across from the Senate House Museum, Kingston, NY (Open in the summer)

Pick up a walking-tour map here (In order to get to the Stockade area, most drivers will use the Kingston exit of I-87, drive south on I-587 to its end, turn right onto Albany Avenue, and bear right to Clinton Avenue.)

Academy Green

Between Albany Avenue and Maiden Lane, near the Stockade area, Kingston, NY

Ending the First Esopus War, in 1660 Stuyvesant signed a treaty with the Indians on what is now the Academy Green. On the green itself are statues of Stuyvesant, Henry Hudson, and Governor George Clinton (the first governor of New York State and father of DeWitt Clinton, the builder of the Erie Canal).

The treaty did not bring permanent peace to the area. In 1663 the Second Esopus War broke out. Esopus Indians again attacked the village. This time they killed twelve men, four women, and two children and burned twelve houses and part of the stockade. The following year, a peace treaty ended the hostilities. Thereafter, the Esopus peacefully retreated, slowly selling more and more of their lands to the white settlers.

Colonel Wessel Ten Broeck House
(Senate House)

269 Fair Street, Corner of Clinton Avenue and North Front Street, Kingston, NY (Open Wed–Sat 10–5, Sun 1–5, Apr–Dec; Sat 10–5, Sun 1–5, Jan–Mar)

In 1676 Colonel Wessel Ten Broeck built this two-and-a-half-story brick and limestone house. By marriage it came into the hands of Abraham Van Gaasbeek, who lived here in 1777 when Kingston became the temporary capital of New York State. The house is set up as the home of a middle-class Dutch-American merchant with authentic eighteenth-century furnishings, mostly from the Hudson Valley. Van Gaasbeek had a store in one section of the house. To supply his store he owned a sloop that sailed back and forth to New York City, bringing supplies the locals could not make themselves: molasses, salt, tea, codfish, window glass, and bolts of ribbon.

The house became intimately involved with the history of New York State. During the Revolutionary War, the New York Senate fled from White Plains to Fishkill to evade the encroaching British. They had to leave Fishkill, not because of further British advances, but to avoid a smallpox epidemic. The senators knew that the Kingston Dutchman was a local patriot, and so they asked him if they could use his house. He quickly assented. An interesting question is, why would he take such a risk, especially with British troops so close?

The answer is related to Abraham Van Gaasbeek's personal history. In 1775 he lost his daughter and granddaughter during childbirth. The next year his wife died. Moreover, his son, Peter, joined the American army and became a spy. (James Fenimore Cooper based his book *The Spy* on Peter's adventures.) Abraham was also being squeezed financially, because he could no longer import goods from New York City. Moreover, he held many worthless continental dollars. And, finally, the senate offered to rent his store, thereby providing him a much-needed source of income. Given these conditions, the man with nothing to lose quickly agreed to offer his place to the senate. The senate met at the house on September 9, 1777, while the assembly met in a tavern.

Kingston did not long remain the temporary capital. The state government adjourned on October 7, upon learning of the British capture of Forts Clinton and Montgomery near Bear Mountain on the Hudson River.

The British under General John Vaughn began a cannonade of the town at nine o'clock on the morning of October 16. They then landed a force of four hundred men. The American militia fled rather than face the much stronger force. The enemy then began to pillage and burn the Kingston homes. The British also burned the Senate House on that October day. (Van Gaasbeek restored the house sometime prior to his death in 1794.) Of the 116 houses, the only one spared was that belonging to Tobias Van Steenbergh (located at the southwest corner of the intersection of Wall and Franklin streets). There are two different stories explaining this. The first one says that the servants rolled barrels of rum in front of the house and served the soldiers to distract them from their destructive task. The other says that General Vaughn knew the father of the pretty Dutch girl who lived in the house.

General George Clinton arrived with the American militia just after the invaders had departed. Many of the town's citizens had to spend the winter in lean-to structures built against charred stone walls.

The neighboring museum, associated with the Senate House, has paintings by the artist John Vanderlyn (1775–1852), a Kingston native who painted landscapes in the Hudson River school tradition. Aaron Burr was his patron and painter Washington Allston his intimate friend. There is a monument to him in Wiltwyck Cemetery.

Old Dutch Church

Corner of Main and Wall streets, Kingston, NY

Founded in 1659, the present building, designed by noted architect Minard Lafever in the Renaissance Revival style, dates from 1852. In the interior is a Tiffany window (1891) behind the pulpit and a framed letter from George Washington wishing the congregation success in teaching their religion to posterity. A plaque on the entrance wall commemorates Washington's visit to the church on November 16, 1782. Visit the church museum, which contains the oldest continuing record of marriages and baptisms in the United States. Also visit the church cemetery, where George Clinton is buried.

Court House
Corner of Main and Wall streets, Kingston, NY

On this site two famous New Yorkers were sworn into office: Governor George Clinton and John Jay (as the state's first chief justice). On the courthouse lawn is a marker dedicated to Sojourner Truth (ca. 1797–1883), who worked for abolition and women's rights. She was born and worked as a slave in Hurley, not far from Kingston. In this courthouse she won the first lawsuit ever by an African-American parent, when she saved her son from slavery in Alabama.

Dr. C. Elmendorf House (private)
Southwest corner of Wall and Main streets, Kingston, NY

This prerevolutionary house was the home of the old Dutch church conferentie family leader, 1754–1772. (Under the leadership of Theodore Frelinghuysen, in 1755 the Dutch Reformed church declared its freedom from the mother country. A small group of ministers, wishing to remain tied to the homeland, withdrew and formed the conferentie.) The house's other claim to fame was the founding here in 1806 of the Ulster County Medical Society.

Cornelius Tappen House (private)
Crown Street between John and Green streets, Kingston, NY

Cornelius Tappen was the deputy county clerk in 1777 and saved many records when the British burned Kingston. This is supposedly the oldest house in town. It was also the first post office.

Cornelius Tappen House, Kingston, New York

Henry Sleight House

Across the street from the Cornelius Tappen House at the pie-shaped junction of Green and Crown streets, Kingston, NY

Travelers can tour this home, the earliest part of which dates from the late 1600s, by calling the Wiltwyck chapter of the Daughters of the American Revolution.

Lucas Elmendorf House (private)

111 Green Street, Kingston, NY

This house dates from around 1790. Elmendorf was a judge in Ulster County and served in Congress from 1797 to 1803. He was an associate and great admirer of Thomas Jefferson.

Anthony Hoffman House (private)

Southeast corner of North Front and Green streets, Kingston, NY

Martinus Hoffman, a Swede, came to New Netherland in 1657, eventually settling in Kingston. The house, built about 1660, came to be owned by Anthony Hoffman, a descendant. Nine generations of Hoffmans have lived in the house.

Other Sites to Visit

For other sites in Kingston see the sections on steamboats and railroads. Across the river is the Old Rhinebeck Aerodrome (see the introduction to the Jazz Age). Other towns with Dutch elements are Hurley, New Paltz, and Schenectady. In New Paltz be sure to see the Jean Hasbrouck House (located at Huguenot and North Front streets), which many consider to be one of the finest examples of Flemish architecture in the United States.

There are also many individual Dutch houses spread throughout the Hudson River valley. For instance, close to New York City is the recommended Von Steuben House (Main Street) in River Edge, New Jersey. It is filled with many Dutch items.

When on eastern Long Island, visit Southfolk, which has a number of old English houses. For instance, tour the Southold Historical Society Complex (Route 25/Main Road), which includes the Thomas Moore House with rooms dating from before 1653.

2

Swedish Settlements

In 1623 Captain Cornelius Jacobssen May, sailing for the Dutch, established a trading settlement on the east bank of the Delaware River near Gloucester Point, New Jersey. He also built a fort named Fort Nassau in Gloucester. The Dutch, however, were not the only ones with their eyes on the Delaware River area. Peter Minuit, former director-general of New Netherland, proposed to Swedish associates that they found a New Sweden Company to take advantage of the many natural resources in America.

What would cause a former Dutch director-general to help a competitor nation? The explanation is straightforward. Minuit had favored the establishment of private manors in America by executives of the Dutch East India Company. Bitter quarrels developed over the issue, and the directors recalled him to a hearing at the main office in Amsterdam. It is not known whether the company dismissed him or he resigned. Either way, the end result was negative for the Dutch; the embittered man offered his services elsewhere.

In 1638 the Former Dutch director-general guided two ships up the Delaware River and established Fort Christina at what is now Wilmington. He named the fort in honor of Sweden's Queen Christina. As already mentioned, the independence of the new settlement did not last long, as first the Dutch and then the English took control.

Swedish influence on American life continued; neither Dutch nor English ownership had much impact on the average citizen. One of the Swedes' greatest contributions to America was the log cabin. Other colonists modified this Nordic structure to produce the log cabin as we know it. Look for the following exterior features in the Swedish version: both ends of the logs are cut either with the saddle-notch or V-notch and crossed at the corners of the building; the ends of the logs are often slanted to aid in the runoff of rain; the chimney is set to one side rather than on top of the roof ridgeline; and thin, overlapping roof boards are used. The interior of the Swedish log cabin might include a corner fireplace; a log bed filled with straw, using animal skins for blankets; and floors of packed earth.

The tour of the Wilmington sites will take less than half a day, and the Philadelphia sites will take an entire day. These Wilmington sites are modest ones, and visitors may wish to combine this tour with visits to the much more impressive mansions of the Du Pont family (see the appropriate sections). The Philadelphia sites are more impressive, especially the American Swedish Historical Museum.

Old Swedes' (Holy Trinity) Church, Wilmington, Delaware

Fort Christina State Park

East Seventh and Church streets, along the northern bank of the Christina River (driving north on Route 9, which is the first exit after crossing the Delaware Memorial Bridge), Wilmington, DE (Open Tues–Sat 10–4:30, Sun 1:30–4:30, all year)

This small park contains a monument to the Swedish settlers, a gift from the people of Sweden. The monument consists of a shaft on which are various sculptures by the famous Swedish artist Carl Milles. One is of the *Kalmar Nyckel*, the vessel that brought the first settlers to the New World. Near the monument is a log cabin brought here in 1962 from Price's Corner, Pennsylvania.

Old Swedes' (Holy Trinity) Church

Seventh and Church streets, Wilmington, DE (Open Tues–Sat 12–4, all year)

A short walk from the Fort Christina monument is the oldest surviving church in the Delaware River valley. Swedish colonists built this fieldstone structure in 1698. The south porch was added in 1750 and the gallery with outside stairs in 1774. The brick bell tower was added in the early 1800s, when the church became Episcopalian. In the church interior, don't miss seeing the oldest pulpit in the United States, made of native black walnut. Also note that there are at least eight known burials in the floor of the church (but only three are marked). Surrounding the church is the original burying ground of Fort Christina.

Hendrickson House

Across from Old Swedes' Church, Wilmington, DE (Open Tues–Sun 12–4, all year)

This structure was brought here from Crum Creek in Ridley Township, Pennsylvania. It was unusual to build a house of stone for a farmer, but there was plenty of freestone on the property. In 1690 John Hendrickson built it for his brother, Andrew, a young Swedish farmer, and his bride, Brigitta, daughter of Morton Mortonson, Sr. (see below). Three generations of Hendricksons lived here. Armegott, daughter of Swedish Governor Johan Printz, knew the family well.

The house serves as a small library and museum of Delaware Swedish life, as well as a church office. Especially interesting is the hatchway through the kitchen wall, where wood could be thrown directly into the huge fireplace area. When not in use, an outside wooden shutter covered it.

Governor Printz Park

Taylor Avenue and Second Street, Essington, PA (not far from Philadelphia International Airport)

In 1642 Johan Printz, a 400-pound career army officer, became the governor of New Sweden. The Delaware Indians called him "large stomach." Printz was an able administrator, though a trifle despotic.

In 1643 he made the first settlement ever within the borders of Pennsylvania, at Tinicum Island. The governor wanted to move the capital of the Swedish colony from Fort Christina to this site, which was then an island. He asked for and received personal title to the land. The Swedish leader never really said why he chose the location, but he did want to move his family away from the residents of Fort Christina, whom he regarded as rather coarse.

On Tinicum Island, the governor built Fort New Gothenburg, some two hundred yards to the west of the present Corinthian Yacht Club, at Essington. He also built a two-story mansion of hewn logs, which he called the Printzhof. Adding a homey touch, he constructed a traditional Swedish *badstu* where his family could take saunas. A religious man, Printz soon built a chapel. A stone step from this church is now the doorstep of the nearby yacht club.

The Swedish colonists considered Printz to be a brutal autocrat, guilty of avarice and arbitrariness. Many of the settlers fled to Maryland. The governor was also unhappy with life in New Sweden. According to his contract, he could retire from service after three years in America. He asked repeatedly to return, but was forced to stay on for a total of nine years.

Fire destroyed the Printzhof in 1645. A careless sentry had started the blaze to keep warm, but it had gotten out of control. Printz sent the sentinel in irons back to Sweden. By the same ship, Printz sent a note saying he needed Swedish women to marry his twenty-six love-starved men. Sweden sent the women, but they never reached their destination. Shipwrecked off Puerto Rico, they were seized by the island inhabitants. The unfortunate women had to perform servant duties for two years, after which they gained their freedom. Tragically, the French captured the ship bringing them to New Sweden. The governor of the Virgin Islands then turned them over to his soldiers.

A second Printzhof, built on the old foundations, stood for 160 years, after which it also burned. Subsequently, stones and bricks of the church were used in the construction of Gloria Dei (Old Swedes') Church in Philadelphia.

Hearing nothing from Sweden for his last six years of service, Governor Printz decided on his own initiative to return to his native land. When he arrived in Sweden, his superiors did not punish him, but promoted him to full colonel and made him a district governor. He died in his native land in 1663.

Following the governor's departure, his son-in-law and his daughter, Armegott, ruled the colony. The daughter proved to be one of the most courageous and determined of all colonial women. When the newly appointed governor, Johan Rising, arrived in New Sweden, she continued to serve as first lady, since the new leader was a bachelor. And when her husband returned to Sweden, she remained behind managing their properties and four sons.

In 1662 she sold the holdings on Tinicum Island and sailed for Sweden. Stopping in Holland to collect part of the money due, she learned that payment had been refused. This dauntless woman was not going to be cheated by anyone. She turned around and sailed directly back to New Sweden. It took her ten years to achieve justice, but she finally won the court battle. The achievement is even more remarkable because she acted as her own lawyer. In 1665 her husband sued for divorce. This feisty woman was able to refute most of the charges brought against her, even bringing suit against the judge for his behavior.

Armegott returned to Sweden in 1676. Her husband had died in the interim, and she inherited his estates. This story has a happy ending, as the well-deserving pioneer eventually retired to a castle of more than two hundred rooms.

The foundations of the Printzhof have been excavated at the small park, but have since been covered to protect what remains. On the grounds is a statue of Governor Printz.

Morton Homestead

Not far north of Governor Printz Park, off PA 420, just north of the Tinicum Natural Environmental Center and Darby Creek, Prospect Park, PA (Open Tues–Sat 10–5, Sun 10–5, all year)

Morton Mortonson, Sr., was a Swedish settler and great-grandfather of the Declaration of Independence signer John Morton. In 1654 he built a one-story oak log cabin on the property. Around 1698 Mortonson's son, Mathias, built two structures and connected them with a dog-trot, as is common to houses in the American South. Later, the two cabins were joined by a stone section that replaced the dog-trot.

This homestead was long thought to be the birthplace of John Morton, but his only connection to the house is that his great grandfather built a log cabin on the site. In the Continental Congress, Morton's affirmative vote on the adoption of the Declaration of Independence came at a time when both the Pennsylvania delegation and the Congress were deadlocked.

The house is an excellent example of early Swedish architecture. There is a large corner fireplace, a bed with animal skins for blankets, and a *bordstol*, which in Swedish translates as table-chair (the chair converts into a small table). The interior looks very plain and well-used, which adds to the charm of the place. The house exterior is black because of the creosote used in the 1930s.

American Swedish Historical Museum

1900 Pattison Avenue, Franklin Delano Roosevelt Park, Philadelphia, PA (Open Tues–Fri 10–4, Sat 12–4, all year)

This museum is so large and has so many exhibits that it is an excellent place to learn more about the entire history of Swedish-American relationships. Displays cover the earliest settlement at Wilmington to the latest visit to America by the king of Sweden. Among the many exhibits, there is a model of the *Kalmar Nyckel*, often called the Swedish Mayflower, and a Swedish coin that weighs seven pounds. With this one coin a man could buy a good horse.

Gloria Dei (Old Swedes') Church

Swanson Street, between Christian and Water streets, Philadelphia, PA (Open daily 9–6, all year)

This one-and-a-half-story English-style brick building is the oldest church in Philadelphia. The first Swedish Lutheran congregation vacated the church on Tinicum Island and (in Philadelphia), between the years 1698 and 1700, converted a 1669 Swedish blockhouse into a new church. As mentioned previously, the builders used stones and bricks from the Tinicum Island church.

Remaining relics from Tinicum include two winged cherubim, brought from Sweden in 1643 and now attached to the west end of the gallery, and a stone baptismal font. The church has been Episcopalian since the late eighteenth century. In the churchyard is a monument to John Hanson, president of Congress under the Articles of Confederation, 1781–1782. Around the base of the memorial are bas-reliefs of other famous Swedish-Americans.

Other Sites to Visit

Check the Geographic Cross-Reference for the sections on Wilmington and Philadelphia for other sites to see in the area. In Wilmington stop at the Old Town Hall, which has changing exhibits. A recent exhibit honored the 350th anniversary of New Sweden with a large display on the treasures brought up from the shipwreck of the Swedish vessel *Kronan*. Upstairs there are three paintings by native son Bass Otis, who painted mostly in the 1840s. In the basement is the old jail, which is available for touring. The solitary-confinement cell is particularly frightening; the prisoners had to sit on the floor in total darkness.

3

English Lords of the Manor

As discussed earlier, the English took control of the Dutch territories in North America in 1664. The large Dutch landholders were naturally anxious about their futures. But as it turned out, they need not have worried quite so much. The English perpetuated the Dutch semifeudal system by setting up a manorial system. As was the case with the patroon, the power of the lord of the manor was similar to that of the English nobleman of the Middle Ages.

The British established the same system among the large landowners of English Long Island. Those interested can visit, for instance, the Sagtikos Manor (located off Montauk Highway, West Bay Shore); the Henry and Joseph Lloyd manor houses (Lloyd Harbor Road, Lloyd Harbor); and the Manor of Saint George (Neighborhood Road, Mastic Beach).

Most of the patroonships had failed, but the manors proved successful. They succeeded, in part, because they were extensions of already prospering businesses such as breweries, fur trading posts, shipyards, and wholesale and retail operations.

The manorial system had several negative consequences for New York colony and state. First, the quasi-feudal conditions slowed the population growth of the upstate area. Many settlers left the colony; others avoided it altogether, for who wanted to be a peasant? Second, the dominance by a few powerful men led New York to take a very conservative stance, at least in the initial stages, on the issue of independence from Great Britain.

The Crown believed that the large landholders would create a class of conservatives supporting the status quo. Actually, the British created similar systems in all the middle colonies. Like that colony, New Jersey's early history is filled with conflict between landowners and tenants, and some of this tension spilled over into mob violence. Likewise, the early story of Pennsylvania revolves around the tension between the proprietors and tenants. The situation in New York was just worse, not different, from that in the other middle colonies. For instance, while New Jersey had a number of proprietary estates, they did not come close to matching the large size of those on the Hudson River.

The manors in the Hudson River valley included, from north to south, Rensselaerswyck (Albany), Livingston (Tivoli area), Van Cortlandt (near Croton-on-Hudson), Philipsburg (Yonkers), Scarsdale (in Westchester County), and Pelham, Fordham, and Morrisania (in the Bronx). The tours in this chapter cover sites associated with three of these manors: Philipsburg, Van Cortlandt, and Livingston. The sites are divided into two geographical areas: Sleepy Hollow territory and the mid–Hudson River valley.

The architectural style of the period is known as Georgian. This style dominated American building for almost the entire eighteenth century. Borrowing classical details from the Italian Renaissance, its emphasis on balance and harmony is seen in the symmetrical composition of the buildings. Windows are aligned horizontally and vertically in symmetrical rows. There is often a pedimented projecting pavilion with columns or pilasters (half columns attached to a wall). The windows often have double-hung sashes with many small windowpanes that open upward, as opposed to outward and to the side (as in earlier casement windows). A term frequently encountered is Palladian window. This is a large arched window flanked on both sides by a smaller arched window.

The idea of balance also appears in Georgian interiors. There are matching rooms on either side of a central hallway. Balance is even seen within the individual rooms themselves. For instance, there are often matching mirrors exactly lined up on either side of the room.

This period encompassed many interior styles. The William and Mary style (1700–1725) had wainscoted (wood-paneled) walls and raised panels, painted walls, and bold curved ornamentation. Some characteristics of the furniture are trumpet legs (resemble a trumpet turned upside-down); curved stretchers (crosspieces or rungs connecting legs of chairs, tables, etc.); Spanish feet (rectangular ribbed feet enlarged at the base); and japanning (where black lacquer is painted on a surface and then polished to a mirror-smooth finish).

The Queen Anne style (1725–1760) had wainscoted walls with recessed panels. The distinguishing characteristic of the furniture is the use of the cabriole leg. The name originated from the Spanish word for goat, because the furniture leg resembled the bent rear leg of this animal. The leg is shaped in a double curve, with the upper part bending out and the curve swinging in toward the foot.

Finally, the Chippendale style (1760–1790) stemmed from the application of French rococo ideas to Queen Anne furniture. The French style, using elaborate ornamentation emphasizing curves, dominated during the reign of Louis XV. Favorite decorative forms were shells and rocks. Some of the characteristics of Chippendale furniture are the addition of a ball-and-claw foot (an eagle's claws clasping a ball) ending to the cabriole leg; the use of acanthus leaf (resembles a many-lobed maple leaf) decoration on the Queen Anne leg; pierced splats on chair backs; and latticework (a crisscross pattern formed by narrow bars) in the Chinese style (a result of the increasing trade with China).

Sleepy Hollow Territory

The area along the east bank of the Hudson River in Westchester County is known as Sleepy Hollow territory. Washington Irving, who lived in what is now the town of Irvington, made the area famous through his authorship of Dutch folk tales. Visitors can see the Dutch flavor of the area by visiting sites connected with the county's Dutch and English settlers.

It will take about a day and a half to see all the Sleepy Hollow sites. Children especially like the Philipsburg Manor house in North Tarrytown because of its farm animals and implements. The Van Cortlandt Manor has a good colonial herb garden. If you like slow drives, see the area by traveling up Broadway (Route 9). There are many beautiful towns along the way and occasional glimpses of the Hudson River and the cliffs of the Palisades.

Philipse Manor Hall

Warburton Avenue and Dock Street (take the Yonkers Avenue exit off the Saw Mill River Parkway, drive west on Yonkers Avenue, turn right onto Ashburton, and turn left onto Warburton), Yonkers, NY (Open Wed–Sun 12–5, end of May–Oct)

This manor hall was the social and administrative center of Philipsburg Manor, created by Frederick Philipse I. His career is quite the success story. He trained as a carpenter, but slowly worked his way up the ladder to become the wealthiest man in New York City. He built his fortune in shipping, but marriage to a wealthy widow, Margaret Hardenbroeck, also helped.

Along with Stephanus Van Cortlandt of Van Cortlandt Manor, Philipse voted for the execution of Jacob Leisler (who in the aftermath of the Glorious Revolution of 1688, had taken over New York City's government in support of the new monarchs, William and Mary). He resigned from political office after learning that the English authorities had concluded that he had been too intimately involved with the illegal trade activities of Captain William Kidd. Upon the death of his wife, in his mid-sixties he married a Van Cortlandt, bringing these two wealthy families closer together.

Through a series of purchases, the ambitious merchant gradually acquired land extending from the northern tip of Manhattan to the Croton River and inland to the Bronx River. In 1693 he obtained a royal patent creating Philipsburg Manor.

The former carpenter built two main centers to help administer the large manor. One is the Georgian manor house in Yonkers, built and extended between 1682 and 1758. The other is located in North Tarrytown. Gristmills were built at each administrative center.

Frederick Philipse III, eldest son of Frederick Philipse II, inherited the entire manor. He sold the northern part and contented himself with living in the Yonkers mansion. In the Revolutionary War, he sided with the Loyalists. As punishment, the authorities confiscated and later sold his land at auction to 287 different individuals.

At one time the mansion here was used as Yonkers' City Hall. This oldest building in the city is constructed of brick (imported from Holland) and stone. It has a colonial porch that is ten feet wide and six feet deep. There is some period furniture in the building, but the interior is mostly empty. On the positive side, the manor hall does offer changing local history exhibits.

Philipsburg Manor: The Upper Mills
381 Bellwood Avenue, off U.S. 9, not far north of the Tappan Zee Bridge, North Tarrytown, NY (Open daily 10–5, all year; closed Tues, Dec–Mar)

This is the northern center of what was once Philipsburg Manor. Between 1680 and 1682 the first lord of the manor constructed a gristmill and a dwelling on the property. Some forty families milled the grain. The grain was then shipped to the Philipse bolting house in New York City, where it was finely ground, packaged, and distributed. Part of the finished product was sent back to be consumed by the farmers who had produced it in the first place.

The manor house is relatively simple considering the wealth of Philipse. Nevertheless, it became his favorite dwelling. The manor house was primarily for business and not luxury, and this is probably the reason why Frederick stayed here. About 1720 Adolph Philipse doubled the size of the house. The land and house were, in turn, owned by Frederick II and Frederick III, after which it passed from Philipse family hands.

At the Visitors' Center the guests see a film narrating the history of Philipsburg Manor. The guide then leads a tour of the house, mill, millpond, and farmhouse. Be sure to walk over the bridge spanning the Pocantico River on the west side of Route 9. Parallel to the highway bridge is a reconstructed span. It is said that Ichabod Crane rode over this bridge to escape the Headless Horseman (see the section on Washington Irving).

Old Dutch Church
U.S. 9, North Tarrytown, NY (call for tours, 914-631-1123)

A short distance north up the hill from Philipsburg Manor, Upper Mills, is the Old Dutch Church. It is popularly known as Sleepy Hollow Church in reference to Washington Irving. Frederick Philipse I had this Dutch colonial church built about 1697, so the tale goes, in an attempt to stop floodwaters from washing away his dams. One of his slaves dreamed that the dams would not hold until a church was built nearby. The church bell bears the inscription If God Be For Us, Who Can Be Against Us?

Reminders of the family are the weather vane bearing the Philipse symbol in the shape of a flag and a silver baptismal bowl and beaker bearing their name. Be sure to see the nearby graveyard where Washington Irving, industrialist Andrew Carnegie, publisher Whitelaw Reid, and labor leader Samuel Gompers are buried.

Old Dutch Church, North Tarrytown, New York

Van Cortlandt Manor

South Riverside Avenue (off U.S. 9 on the northern bank of the Croton River), Croton-on-Hudson, NY (Open Mon–Sat 10–3, Sun 12–5, all year; closed Tues, Dec–Mar)

In 1638 Oloff Van Cortlandt arrived in New Amsterdam as a soldier with the West India Company. From this humble start he became the fourth wealthiest individual in New York by the time he died in 1684.

Detail of Van Cortlandt Manor, Croton-on-Hudson, New York

His eldest son, Stephanus (1643–1700), married well—Gertrude, daughter of Philip P. Schuyler of Albany. In 1677 he became the first native-born mayor of the city of New York. As a political leader of the city, he fought against the rebellious group under Captain Leisler—even being forced to flee for his very life. Once back in power, with the support of Frederick Philipse, he pushed for the prosecution and execution of Leisler for treason. Upon the rebel's execution, the former mayor finally got his revenge.

Stephanus bought extensive amounts of land in the Hudson River valley and in 1697 had this chartered as Van Cortlandt Manor. Its boundaries extended from Philipsburg Manor on the south to the present Westchester-Putnam county line on the north, and from the Hudson River on the west to the New York–Connecticut boundary on the east.

Stephanus started building the manor house, but the exact date is unknown. At this time it was little more than a hunting lodge and tenant office. Pierre Van Cortlandt (1721–1814), grandson of Stephanus, expanded the house in 1749 and 1760. The double-tiered porch was added in the early nineteenth century and is an architectural anomaly (but this one is too lovely to remove). The interior has rooms with a great many different furniture styles. For instance, the parlor has Queen Anne, Chippendale, and Federal pieces.

Pierre's wife, Joanna Livingston, designed the "long walk" that leads from the house to the tavern and ferry landing. Here she planted many beautiful gardens. (Your guide may stop by the herb garden to point out a spearmint plant.)

Life at the manor was relatively self-sufficient. Much of the work was done by slaves, and tenants and hired hands managed the dairy and crops. The only disturbance of this lifestyle, other than the Revolutionary War, was the 1760s upsurge in tenant resentment over not owning their own lands.

During the Revolutionary War, Pierre and his son Philip became officers in the Continental army. The family moved out of the house when Westchester became neutral ground between the British in New York City and the Americans above the county line. The house was plundered after the family left. During the conflict, Philip saw a great deal of action: he was at Valley Forge; he cooperated with the Sullivan-Clinton expedition against the Iroquois; and he was brevetted brigadier general for conspicuous bravery at Yorktown. Following the war, his father became the first lieutenant governor of New York State and held that position periodically for eighteen years. The bachelor Philip inherited the manor house upon his father's death in 1814.

In addition to touring the manor house, visit the reconstructed tenant farmers' house and the ferry house. The ferry house, located on the old Albany Post Road, served passengers crossing the Croton River.

Other Sites to Visit

Visit the Hudson River Museum (511 Warburton Avenue between Glenwood Avenue and John F. Kennedy Memorial Drive, Yonkers) for changing exhibits, many dealing with the Hudson River valley. Also visit Washington Irving's house off Route 9 in the village of Irvington. Just north of the Irving house is the beautiful Lyndhurst mansion.

Mid–Hudson River Area

In this section we explore two of the many Livingston mansions. As mansions go, Clermont is not one of the prettiest, but it does have lovely grounds, formal gardens, and beautiful views of the Hudson River. And, of course, Clermont has many interesting historical tales to reveal. Montgomery Place, on the other hand, is absolutely gorgeous and has a very interesting history. The two houses can be toured in little more than half a day.

The Livingston dynasty dominated the mid–Hudson River area. A visit to their Clermont mansion illustrates interesting aspects of the Dutch/English quasi-feudal system. First, it was here that the great landowners saw in the antirent agitation a precursor of Shays' Rebellion (a revolt of western Massachusetts farmers against foreclosure hearings occurring after the American Revolution). Second, leading families intermarried and thereby perpetuated their wealth. The Livingston offspring married into such wealthy families as the Beekmans, Schuylers, Duanes, Van Rensselaers, Van Cortlandts, and Ten Broecks. Even more startling is the tendency for Livingstons to marry Livingstons.

We start with an introduction to the main characters in the family, because it will help prevent confusion when the guides at both mansions talk about these people. This is especially true at Clermont, where there are many portraits of family members.

Robert Livingston (1654–1728) founded the dynasty, the power of which becomes apparent when one realizes that the party of the large landowners in New York was referred to as the Livingston party. In the state the rise of this party was the most important development of the 1750s. Robert married extremely well—to Alida Schuyler Van Rensselaer, the widow of the patroon of Rensselaerswyck. In 1686 he obtained a manorial patent for his estates on the Hudson River and in the Taconic Mountains. The 160,000 acres now became the Manor of Livingston.

With three-quarters of the colony of New York in the hands of perhaps a dozen men, trouble was bound to come. The first tenants of Livingston manor were German refugees from the Palatinate. They arrived in 1710. Finding themselves badly treated, they rebelled. They had to be forced to work under military guard. Many fled to the Schoharie Valley. In the 1750s there were revolts against the Van Rensselaer and Livingston estates, this time aided by Massachusetts authorities, who were in a boundary dispute with New York. In 1766 there was another antirent rebellion, which presaged the similar disputes of the 1840s.

Robert Livingston (1688–1775), one of the sons of the first lord of the manor, built the Clermont mansion, a Georgian brick house. This second lord of the manor had only one offspring, Robert Robert, who in 1763 became judge of the supreme court of New York. The judge married Margaret Beekman, daughter of the great Dutchess County landholder, Colonel Henry Beekman. This act increased Livingston landholdings by 240,000 acres.

Robert Robert's eldest son was Robert R. Livingston, who had a very distinguished career indeed. He was a law partner for a short time with John Jay; a delegate to the Second Continental Congress, where he served on the Committee of Five to draft the Declaration of Independence (although he did not work much on the actual document itself); a member of the committee that wrote the first New York Constitution; and New York's first Chancellor (the state's highest legal office.). After the war, he became the first United States minister of foreign affairs (equivalent to secretary of state), worked on the drafting of the United States Constitution, and administered the presidential oath of office to George Washington.

Clermont State Historic Park

Woods Road, off NY 9G, Germantown, NY (sixteen miles south of the town of Hudson) (Open Wed–Sun 10–5, May 1–Labor Day; Wed–Sun 12–5, Labor Day–Oct 31)

Since Clermont was his parents' home, in 1773 the future chancellor built his own house next-door. He named it Belvedere. The British burned both mansions in 1777 in the same campaign in which they destroyed Kingston. Clermont was rebuilt by 1782 and Belvedere by 1793. (The remains of Belvedere are visible at the south end of the parking lot at the state park.) The mansard roof was added in the 1870s and looks totally out of place on the mansion.

Besides his interest in political endeavors, the chancellor was also interested in inventions. As early as 1797 he thought seriously about the possibility of building a steamboat. His brother-in-law, John Stevens, famous in his own right in New Jersey industrial history, helped him. They put a steamboat on the river, but it just would not move.

As minister to France, the chancellor negotiated the Louisiana Purchase. While abroad, he met Robert Fulton. With Livingston's backing, the great inventor built the first practical steamboat. The men decided to test it on the Hudson River, inviting a number of guests from the Livingston clan. The travelers were highly skeptical of the whole idea, and when the boat stopped soon after it was underway they felt their negative attitudes justified. The persistent inventor begged their forbearance for one-half hour and fixed the boat within this allotted time. The vessel then proceeded up river without incident. The women passengers slept overnight on cots in the cabin, while the men slept on deck. The boat must have been an unusual sight, for one riverbank villager rushed home, locked the door, and shouted to his family, "The devil's going up to Albany in a sawmill!"

The boat stopped at Clermont, where Livingston announced the engagement of his second cousin's daughter, Harriet Livingston, to Fulton. (Harriet's brother married the chancellor's daughter.) By the Hudson River is a plaque noting that at one o'clock in the afternoon of August 18, 1807,

Robert Fulton's *North River Steamboat* anchored off the dock here on its maiden voyage from New York City to Albany. The steamboat later became known as the *Clermont*. The mansion has a museum room with a few highlights of the owner's career, including his relationship with Fulton.

Because of their pioneering activities, the two entrepreneurs were given a monopoly over all steamboat services on the Hudson River. Naturally, others resented this and did all they could to get around it. The monopoly was opposed by a steamboat captain whose descendants would one day be neighbors of the Livingstons: Cornelius Vanderbilt.

It was not until the Supreme Court decision in the *Gibbons v. Ogden* case (1824) that the monopoly was declared illegal. Mr. Gibbons started running a ferry service from Elizabethtown Point to New York without having purchased a license from the monopoly. His line was in direct competition with that of Mr. Ogden, who had purchased such a license. Cornelius Vanderbilt himself was the captain of Gibbon's ship, the *Bellona*. John Marshall was the chief justice of the Supreme Court, and Daniel Webster was the lawyer for the antimonopolists.

Today, the Clermont mansion represents the time when John Henry Livingston, a great-grandson of the chancellor, lived here. John Henry's father was angry with him for his second marriage to a woman of whom the father did not approve. The family atmosphere became so heated that the son moved to Philadelphia, staying at Clermont only during the summer months. The father, in turn, altered his will, leaving the estate to his disobedient son's daughter. The daughter eventually deeded the estate over to her father. And yet, something must have been wrong, for the daughter changed the spelling of her name and moved with her family to England. After her father's third marriage, she cut off all communication for the next fifteen years. They finally reconciled when John Henry visited her in England.

Clermont is a mixture of styles: classical porch, mansard roof, and constructed of brick and stone painted white. On the river side of the house, be sure to see the pair of lions, one with eyes open and the other with eyes shut. It is said that one of the pair is always awake guarding the mansion.

Montgomery Place

Annandale Road, off NY 9G, Annandale-on-Hudson, NY (south of Germantown and just north of the Hudson River Bridge to Kingston) (Open Wed–Mon 12–5, all year)

About 1800 the widow Janet Livingston Montgomery built this twenty-three-room mansion. Architect Alexander Jackson Davis later remodeled it in the Classical Revival style. Janet was the sister of Robert the chancellor and the widow of Revolutionary War hero Richard Montgomery. Her husband was born in Ireland and immigrated to America when he felt that future mobility in his army career had been blocked. He took over the command of

Montgomery Place, Annandale-on-Hudson, New York

the American attack against Canada when his superior officer, Philip Schuyler, fell ill. He captured Montreal, but died in the assault on Quebec. The mansion's Montgomery Room contains a portrait of the general along with some of his belongings (for instance, telescope and army trunk).

Upon Janet's death in 1828, her brother Edward inherited the mansion. Edward had a distinguished career. He was a courier and advisor to Andrew Jackson during the Battle of New Orleans in the War of 1812, secretary of state in Jackson's cabinet, and minister to France. His wife was Creole and added a French touch to the house.

The look of the mansion, with its cream colors and green shutters, is especially pleasing. In the front is a circular portico with four large columns. Also pleasing are the many decorations on the walls, the stucco of which is painted to look like stone. The mansion sits on more than four hundred acres of land with beautiful views of the Hudson River. Leave enough time to visit the gardens or hike the trails.

Other Sites to Visit

In the town of Staatsburg, New York, is the Mills mansion, associated with another Livingston, Gertrude. She was a sister of Robert the chancellor, Janet, and Edward. Kingston is also nearby.

PART

TWO

Later Settlements

Part 2 covers sites connected with the history of three immigrant groups: Quakers, Pennsylvania Dutch, and Moravians. Of these later immigrants, the Quakers came first, settling in New Jersey and Pennsylvania. In 1674, soon after the Society of Friends was founded in England, the Quakers began to colonize the New World. They settled in southern New Jersey in the towns of Salem and Greenwich, and we follow them there in chapter 4. If you think of the New Jersey Turnpike or the urbanized northeastern section when you think of New Jersey, you will be surprised by the beauty of south Jersey. Quakers, under the direction of William Penn, also settled Pennsylvania in the 1680s. William Penn's home, Pennsbury Manor, is not far north of Philadelphia, where Quaker sites abound in the city itself.

William Penn, the great Quaker leader, encouraged religious groups in Germany to emigrate to Pennsylvania to populate his colony. These religious immigrants, including the Amish and Mennonites, came to be referred to collectively as Pennsylvania Dutch. Lancaster County, Pennsylvania, is a favorite of tourists because of the presence of these people who have retained many of their traditional ways. Chapter 5 has tours of the Lancaster area to learn more about their heritage.

Some observers also consider the Moravians to be Pennsylvania Dutch, but they are sufficiently different to be discussed in a separate section. In the 1740s they settled in the area of Allentown-Bethlehem, Pennsylvania. This religious group retained its traditional ways for many years.

Touring these areas reminds us that much of the United States was settled by religious groups. Many of these groups were considered extremist in their countries of origin and were subject to religious persecution. Some groups left their home countries of their own free will, while others were pushed out. The settlement of America by these people has given the country a set of values that still exists today. On a number of important issues the United States is the most conservative of the advanced industrial societies, and this is largely the result of the religious character of the nation. One has to understand the country's religious origins, if one is truly to understand the attitudes of modern-day Americans.

Quaker Settlements

Before proceeding to the Quaker sites, a little background is necessary. The Englishman George Fox, apprentice to a shoemaker, left home at the age of nineteen to travel around England. In 1647 he had a spiritual experience, one of many to come, that convinced him that God speaks directly to people. Each person, therefore, has an inner light, which is the Divine speaking through the individual.

In 1652 Fox formed the Society of Friends. The name Quaker was at first a derogatory term. The story is that when a follower of Fox told a judge that the authorities would quake before God, the judge responded: "You will be the only one quaking here." The Friends attracted many people from the more extreme of the religious groups of the day, such as the Levellers, Diggers, Ranters, and Seekers. They themselves were regarded as religious radicals and became the target of much persecution in England.

Protestant England frequently accused the Quakers of being Catholics and of plotting to overthrow the government. The Puritans regarded the Doctrine of the Inner Light as blasphemous and anarchic. They believed that God had revealed his final word in the Bible, which should be strictly obeyed and not reinterpreted by each individual. As many as fifteen thousand Quakers were in prison by 1689, when England finally passed the Act of Toleration. George Fox himself was in and out of jail eight times.

Persecution also existed in the New World. When two Quaker women arrived in Boston in 1656, the authorities imprisoned them, searched them for signs of witchcraft, and then transported them to the Quaker colony on the island of Barbados. The Boston authorities passed a law imposing a fine of one hundred pounds on any master of a sailing vessel bringing Quakers into the colony. In 1660 Mary Dyer, a friend of Anne Hutchinson, was hanged on Boston Common for being a Quaker. She was just one of four to be killed for fighting the discriminatory Boston laws.

Nor were the Dutch hospitable. They passed an anti-Quaker act to help combat Quaker settlement on Long Island. In spite of this, the settlement continued to grow. In 1662, four citizens of Barbados bought Shelter Island on Long Island and made it a Quaker sanctuary. Religious liberty finally became a reality when the English took over from the Dutch. (In 1672, during his visit to America, George Fox stayed at the Sylvester Manor on Shelter Island.)

After the takeover, King James II gave the area that came to be known as

New York and New Jersey to his brother, the duke of York. The duke subsequently gave modern New Jersey to two friends, Sir George Carteret and John, Lord Berkeley.

In 1673 Lord Berkeley, faced with serious money problems, sold his half of New Jersey (referred to as West Jersey) to Major John Fenwick, a Quaker. The dividing line between East and West Jersey extended from Little Egg Harbor on the Atlantic coastline to the most northwestern point of New Jersey.

Quakers began settling West Jersey in great numbers starting in 1675 with the establishment of Salem and then Greenwich. By 1681 there were 1,400 Friends in the new province. Other Friends settled in Burlington and Mount Holly.

When touring South Jersey, look for the many Quaker meetinghouses. These are very simple buildings. There are usually separate doorways for men and women on the long side, with a covered porch over the entrances. In the interior there is often a stairway leading to a second-story balcony. Note the absence of a pulpit. Anyone may stand and testify at a Quaker meeting.

Greenwich

It should be possible to see both Greenwich and Salem in one day. There are only a few house tours available, but there is a great deal to see on foot. You should enjoy touring South Jersey. The terrain is very flat, but there are many farms and open spaces. Overall, driving in the area is a treat. Often the only sign of clustered life is at the crossroads where a general store exists.

Getting back to the main story, Fenwick had been a major in the army of Oliver Cromwell. After he left the service he became a Quaker. Excited by the idea of future success, he jumped at the chance to buy Lord Berkeley's West Jersey. And then his life got complicated. The evidence suggests that much of the money for the purchase came from a group of Quakers led by Edward Byllinge. A dispute arose between the two over just who owned the land. The English courts investigated the purchase and ruled that Fenwick was a front for Byllinge. William Penn stepped in as umpire. He decided that Fenwick could have only his promised one-tenth of the West Jersey land. But before feeling too sorry for the major, note that this one-tenth today embraces modern Salem and Cumberland counties.

The great opportunist was boiling mad over the decision. In his bitterness, he decided to colonize his lands quickly. His wife stayed at home, but his two married daughters and their families, his son, and another daughter traveled to New Jersey. With them went fifty to two hundred settlers.

Under the great white oak that still stands in Salem, Fenwick bought the land from the Indians for a few guns, rum, and articles of clothing. To attract other settlers, he advertised his new colony in the most glowing terms (as a "terrestrial Canaan . . . where the land floweth with milk and honey"). More English Quakers soon arrived.

The other Quaker leaders were highly suspicious of Fenwick's motives and began to harass him. He brought this on himself to a great extent, because his real motivation was monetary gain. Furthermore, the story goes that Fenwick tried to establish himself as a lord of the manor in Salem. Indeed, he called himself the Lord Proprietor of Fenwick's Colony and tried to have the colony declared a separate English Crown colony, rather than a private Quaker colony.

The arrogant man's claim to be a governor infuriated Lord Edmund Andros, royal governor of New York and New Jersey. Twice, in 1676 and 1678, he sent soldiers to Salem to bring Fenwick to New York City in chains to answer charges of impersonating a royal governor. Both times the major wound up in jail for short periods.

These actions and others caused trouble in Fenwick's colony. Many settlers wondered whether the leader had any right to sell land, and they started to desert him. Finally, in 1682, the major had to sell all but 150,000 acres of his land, first to mortgagees, and then to William Penn. He died six months after the close of the last deal an impoverished, broken-hearted, bitter man who thought himself a failure. Today no one even knows where his grave is. However, he made a real contribution to American history by interesting Penn in settlement in the New World.

In addition to founding Salem, Fenwick planned the town of Greenwich, which is located along the Cohansey River, not far from Delaware Bay. In 1701 the town became the official port of the province of West Jersey.

Fenwick planned the town's main street, called Ye Greate Street, to be one hundred feet wide for an entire mile. This has left the town with a marvelously wide main street. The open feeling adds to the pleasure of a walking tour. There are also many fascinating houses lining this beautiful street.

While touring Salem and Greenwich, also notice how some of the houses use special brick patterns to create designs or write dates in the walls. The patterns are created by inserting *headers* (bricks with the small end out) among the *stretchers* (bricks with the long side out). Also note the use of glazed brick ends to create decorative patterns.

The Gibbon House

Ye Great Street, Greenwich, NJ (Open Sat–Sun 2–5, Apr–Nov)

From a relative, the brothers Nicholas and Leonard Gibbon received a large tract of land in the vicinity. It is said the two almost single-handedly built Greenwich. These merchants engaged in trade with both the West Indies and New York City. Their ships carried three-quarters of all their home town's imports and exports. Among other items, they exported hides.

In 1730 the bachelor Nicholas had this Georgian Colonial brick building constructed. Not long afterward, he married Ann Grant Hedge, the widow of his business partner. She brought two children to the marriage and had six more with her new husband.

In 1740 the family moved to Salem to the Alexander house, which Mrs. Gibbon had inherited. The guide told us that Richard Wood, owner of thousands of South Jersey acres, lived in the Greenwich house for a while.

The residence now houses the headquarters of the Cumberland County Historical Society. Note the Flemish bond pattern of bricklaying, with alternate red stretchers and blue headers, on the house's exterior. The museum contains some beautiful glass in the dining room, a tea set belonging to the fifth justice of Delaware, a bust of Richard Wood, Civil War items, and a toy collection.

Behind the house is the Red Barn Museum, which displays craft tools. Also here is the Swedish Granary (ca. 1650), moved from Lower Hopewell Township. This is perhaps the only surviving farm building of the Swedish settlers in the Delaware valley.

Richard Wood Mansion
Bacons Neck and Ye Greate streets, Greenwich, NJ

In 1795 Richard Wood built this mansion. His son, Dr. George Bacon Wood, used it as his summer home for many years and allowed his peacocks to strut about in the garden. The house is now a museum.

Richard Wood Store (commercial)
Bacons Neck Street, Greenwich, NJ

This is one of the oldest retail stores in the country. Today the Wood family own the Wawa convenience store chain.

Friends Meeting House
Ye Greate Street, Greenwich, NJ

This is a 1771 red brick structure.

Sheppard's Ferry House (private)
Cohansey Wharf, end of Ye Greate Street, Greenwich, NJ

A section of this house dates back to the founding of the town. The wings were added in 1734 and 1900. The vessel known as the *Greyhound*

Friends Meeting House, Greenwich, New Jersey

anchored here on December 12, 1774, and unloaded its cargo of taxed tea. The ship's captain transported the cargo to the cellar of a local Tory, Daniel Bowen. Several days later, twenty-three men emerged from the home of Richard Howell near Shiloh (about four miles from Greenwich) and rode to the home of Phillip Vickers Fithian in Greenwich, where they donned Indian costumes. They then went to the Bowen house and carried the huge tea chests out onto the street. The boxes were soon aflame. Thus, did Greenwich have its own tea party to match those of Boston and Annapolis.

Several attempts at prosecuting the "Indians" were made, but they proved futile because the majority of the grand jury secretly approved of the rebels' actions. A monument to the tea burning on Ye Greate Street contains the names of the participants.

Phillip Vickers Fithian House (private)
Sheppard's Mill Road, near Molly Wheaton Road, Greenwich, NJ

Phillip Vickers Fithian attended Princeton, where two of his classmates were the Revolutionary poet Philip Freneau and Aaron Burr. After graduation he became a teacher, then changed to preaching. The tea-burners met at his house to don their Indian disguises.

Fithian married his boyhood sweetheart in October 1775. Princeton president John Witherspoon, a radical Revolutionary, performed the ceremony. The newlywed went on missionary journeys (alone), and the diary he kept has proved very helpful to historians. He also became a soldier in the Continental army. Participating in the Battle of Long Island, he caught dysentery and died at the young age of twenty-nine.

Other Sites to Visit

Combine this tour with one of nearby Salem. The Robert Gibbon Johnson House (90 Market Street) is the home of a relative of Nicholas Gibbon, who, before a gathered crowd, actually ate a tomato on the courthouse steps. This was a radical feat at that time. People believed the tomato to be poisonous because it belongs to the same plant family as the poisonous nightshade.

Tour the 1734 Hancock House near Salem (NJ 49 and Front Street, Hancock's Bridge). On one of the end walls is an outstanding example of chevron brickwork. The initials HWS stand for William and Sarah Hancock, the original owners of the house. This is just one of the many examples of patterned brickwork available for viewing in Salem County. The house was the scene of a bloody massacre of American patriots by the British during the Revolutionary War. Also tour nearby Fort Mott and Finns Point, where there are Spanish-American gun emplacements and a Civil War cemetery.

Pennsbury Manor

Pennsbury Manor, the home of William Penn, is a beautiful mansion that sits on spacious grounds by the Delaware River. A visit to the manor will give you a great chance to learn more about this fascinating man, his family, and their way of life. The mansion's forty-five acres are also very interesting to walk through. If you combine this outing with one to nearby Fallsington, where Penn worshiped, you will have an interesting day trip. Since so much of this section revolves around the great Quaker leader, it seems best to start with a brief biography.

Born in 1644, William was the son of Sir William Penn, an admiral in the king's navy. At the age of twelve he heard a speech by Quaker Thomas Loe— a speech that deeply moved him. The effect must have stayed with him, for when he entered Oxford University, the administrators soon expelled him for religious nonconformity. Upon his return home, his father beat and then banished him. His mother interceded, and he was sent on a European tour. He then went to Ireland to manage the family's estates.

In 1667, at the age of twenty-three, Penn became a Friend. The authorities quickly responded by imprisoning him several times for a total period of about two years. Looking for an escape from persecution, the future leader and other Friends turned toward the New World. King Charles II owed Penn's father, who died in 1670, a large sum of money. In 1681 the king settled the account by granting William's request for land on the west bank of the Delaware River. Charles himself named the new land Pennsylvania, meaning Penn's woods. Thus did the founder of Philadelphia receive title to the Province of Pennsylvania, consisting of forty-five thousand square miles of land. The duke of York, later James II, added the three counties of Delaware to the royal grant.

Penn wrote pamphlets to promote the new land among the German dissenting sects. His advertisements must have been effective, because by the time he himself set sail for Pennsylvania in 1682, eighteen ships filled with immigrants had already departed for the new colony.

Pennsbury Manor

Located on the Delaware riverfront, 400 Pennsbury Memorial Lane, near the intersection of Bordentown and New Ford Roads, Morrisville, PA (Open Tues–Sat 9–5, Sun 12–5, all year)

Penn's first cousin and deputy in Pennsylvania, William Markham, selected the house site and purchased from the Indians the necessary lands. Work on the mansion may have begun even before Penn came to Pennsylvania. When he did arrive, he concerned himself with the most intimate details of the building's construction.

Large-scale immigration ensured the rapid growth of Philadelphia. By 1685 nearly ninety ships had brought in some eight thousand immigrants. Although the new colony prospered, Penn did not. He came into conflict with the settlers, because they wanted him to relinquish some of his political power. Many colonists refused to pay him rent, which made it impossible for him to make a profit. Further difficulties arose when the Maryland claim to ownership of Delaware forced him to return to England in 1684 to plead his case before Charles II and Parliament. The Pennsbury mansion was still under construction at this time.

Penn and his family had been great supporters of the Stuart kings. While they were in England, Charles II died. Catholic King James II fled to France in 1688 when the Glorious Revolution brought the Protestants William and Mary to the throne. Unfortunately for Penn, rumors spread that he had plotted with King James. He found himself accused of treason and in and out of prison several times, beginning in 1689. In 1692 William and Mary revoked his charter for Pennsylvania, but restored it two years later after forcing the Quaker leader to promise he would support any royal military efforts in the colonies.

In England, Penn's first wife died. He remarried and took his new wife and a daughter from his first marriage to Pennsylvania. He arrived in 1699 after a fifteen-year absence. Apparently, the founder of the City of Brotherly Love was very disappointed in his own creation. However, this was only natural for a man who condemned sports, frivolity, and any type of unproductive play. The founder could have tolerated the vices of the city, but he could not tolerate the noise. He needed peace and quiet and so looked forward to staying at his country manor. Once the workers had readied the mansion, he stayed there for the rest of his time in America. This was, however, for only two more years. At the mansion, his daily routine was to study in the morning and to ride around the estate on his great white horse in the afternoon. He had always loved good food and began to put on considerable weight.

While he may have been happy, his wife and daughter were not nearly as pleased, even though some said they lived ostentatiously at the mansion. The mansion had a household staff of seven (mostly indentured servants)—the utopian dreamer had always lived in the grand style. Despite this, the women missed the excitement of the city.

When Penn arrived in Philadelphia he was deeply in debt. He had been defrauded by his steward, and the Crown wanted various rents from him. The leader tried to get the money by imposing quitrents (rents paid by tenants in lieu of services), but he received no cooperation. In fact, he soon realized he was proprietor in name only.

Nothing seemed to be going his way. About this time, the people of Delaware forced Pennsylvania to grant them independence. Furthermore, his enemies made it imperative that he return to England to fight an attempt to take Pennsylvania away from him and make it a Crown colony. The great leader never returned to America. Following two strokes, he became an invalid for the last six years of his life. He died in England in 1718.

His son, William Penn, Jr., visited America for a short while, making Pennsbury his home for an even shorter period. Even while the elder William had lived, his country mansion had begun to fall into ruin, the estate slipping from family hands altogether. The manor house was rebuilt between 1932 and 1938, but is not a faithful reproduction. It contains only a few objects owned by the great man, but has the largest collection of seventeenth-century furnishings exhibited in Pennsylvania. Don't miss the replica of the barge Penn used to go back and forth to Philadelphia. Also tour the other buildings on the grounds: the icehouse, smokehouse, plantation office, bake and brew house, and seventeen other structures.

Other Sites to Visit

While residing at Pennsbury Manor, Penn would travel the five miles to worship at Falls Meeting (now Fallsington), established in 1683. The town derived its name from the falls located three miles away. The inhabitants built log cabins in the Swedish mode with no nails. Some two dozen eighteenth-century houses survive in this quaint little village, many of them with pent roofs in the Germanic tradition. A visit here will give you a better idea of an early Quaker settlement.

Tours of the village are available Wednesday through Sunday 1–5,

March 15 through November 15. Stop at the Gillingham Store at Yardley Avenue and Lower Morrisville Road, Fallsington for a tour. The tour starts with a slide show on the entire history of the village. This trip is mostly a walking tour in which you can enjoy the atmosphere of a small settlement. The second Saturday of October is Fallsington Day, when many of the private homes are open to the public. Also tour the nearby cities of Trenton and Burlington. And, of course, see the next section on Quaker Philadelphia.

Quaker Philadelphia

To really get a feel for the Quakers and their influence, tour the Quaker sites in Philadelphia. The city itself is relatively easy to drive in, and parking is readily available. Philadelphia has saved many of its historic buildings and is, quite frankly, a history buff's dream come true. The visit here will take all day.

In September 1681 William Penn sent three commissioners to the New World to supervise the settlement of Pennsylvania and to set up a city there. The final site selected extended about a mile along the Delaware River between the city's present South and Vine streets. When the leader himself arrived, he decided to expand the city westward. He obtained a mile of land along the Schuylkill River, paralleling the Delaware River mile previously selected. The center of activity for the new city was around the area where City Hall now stands. Here Penn built the meeting, state, market, and school houses.

Welcome Park

Across the street from City Tavern at the northwest corner of Walnut and Second streets, Independence Park, Philadelphia, PA

This park marks the site of the Slate Roof House, Penn's residence and Pennsylvania's seat of government from 1700 to 1701. In the center of the tiled park is a statute of the great Quaker leader.

Atwater Kent Museum

15 South Seventh Street, between Ranstead and Market streets, Philadelphia, PA (Open Tues–Sun 9:30–4:45, all year)

To learn more about Philadelphia's early days, visit this museum. It has an excellent exhibit on Penn and a diorama of Elfreth's Alley showing how an early Philadelphia street looked. The museum also has exhibits on the city's industries and many ship and boat models. Displays cover the nation's Centennial Celebration of 1876, which took place in Philadelphia. In fact, the many exhibits take you through the entire history of the city. Upstairs are the children's toys. Children have a special liking for Smilin' Sam from Alabam, the Salted Peanut Man. At one time you could drop a coin in the slot, hold a cupped hand under his tongue, and be rewarded with a shower of peanuts.

Free Quaker Meeting House

Fifth and Arch streets, Philadelphia, PA

During the Revolutionary War, the Quakers divided into those who wanted to maintain their pacifist principles and those who wanted to aid the American cause. Those who took part in the war effort were "read out" of their monthly meetings.

In 1777 the Philadelphia Meeting read out weaving manufacturer Samuel Wetherill. This outstanding American had supported the movement to establish an American manufacturing sector free of British control. Furthermore, his timely shipment of supplies to the troops at Valley Forge saved the camp from virtual disbandment.

Wetherill and seven other Friends formed a new meeting called the Free Quakers. Unable to use any of the existing meetinghouses, they constructed this one in 1783. When the war ended, the need for the meetinghouse faded. Wetherill and Elizabeth Claypoole (Betsy Ross) were the last members.

At the meeting house is a mannequin wearing a Quaker wedding dress. Members of this faith liked to use subdued colors, such as soft gray, sage green, and somber brown. Here also is an old piece of folded paper given to Wetherill by Betsy Ross. Ross showed Washington how she could fold a piece of cloth and with one snip of the scissors make a perfect five-pointed star. She demonstrated this to Wetherill, and he put the piece of paper in his safe, which was not opened for another 150 years.

Arch Street Meeting House

302–338 Arch Street between Third and Fourth streets, Philadelphia, PA (Open Mon–Sat 10–4, all year)

In the 1820s the Quakers split into liberals and conservatives. This division occurred over the ideas of Elias Hicks from Long Island. He emphasized the Doctrine of the Inner Light as the most essential teaching of the Bible. According to his view, Jesus was essentially human, but was a prophet of the highest order. As prophet, Jesus spiritually revealed that God, and therefore Christ, is in all humans. The Quaker poet Walt Whitman frequently heard Hicks speak and was greatly influenced by his religious ideas.

The ideas of Hicks were most popular in Philadelphia, where the first split occurred in the so-called Great Separation of 1827. The division within the ranks of the Friends did not heal until the two groups reunited in 1955.

The two Quaker branches had separate meetinghouses. The Orthodox Friends kept the Arch Street Meeting House, and the Hicksites first erected a meetinghouse on Cherry Street, followed by a larger one on Race Street. For one hundred years people knew the two groups of Friends as the Arch Street Friends and the Race Street Friends.

The two groups of Philadelphia Friends even built separate institutions of higher education. The Orthodox Friends established Haverford College in 1833, and the Hicksite Friends established Swarthmore College in 1864. Bryn Mawr (near Haverford) was established by a Quaker physician, Joseph Wright Taylor, a former member of the board of Haverford College.

The Arch Street Meeting House is a major Quaker landmark. Inside this red brick building, attributed to Owen Biddle, are exhibits explaining the Quakers' many past and present humanitarian activities. Also here are dioramas depicting the main events of William Penn's life. In addition, the Society of Friends' Yearly Meeting convenes here.

Race Street Meeting House

Independence Mall at the corner of Arch and Fifth streets, Philadelphia, PA (Open Tues–Sat 10–4, Sun 12–4, Memorial Day to Labor Day)

The Race Street Meeting House was home to the Hicksite Friends. In 1856 this group erected the double meetinghouse west of Fifteenth Street, with space for the Society of Friends Monthly Meeting on the Cherry Street side and a larger room facing Race Street for Yearly Meeting.

Other Sites to Visit

Many Philadelphia homes of famous Quaker individuals are described in other sections (see the sections on Germantown, Federal Philadelphia, and Fairmount Park). When in the vicinity of Chester, Pennsylvania, stop to see the Caleb Pusey House at 15 Race Street. Pusey arrived on Penn's ship in 1682 and set up a gristmill and sawmill. It is believed that this is the only extant house Penn visited. It is also the oldest surviving English-built house in the state.

5

Pennsylvania Dutch

William Penn's colony proved attractive to many sufferers of religious persecution on the European continent—not only native Germans, but also people from Switzerland, the Netherlands, and Czechoslovakia who had come to Germany as refugees. When these people settled in Pennsylvania, they were referred to collectively as Pennsylvania Dutch—*Dutch* was a corruption of the German word for *German*, which is *Deutsch*.

When most people think of the Pennsylvania Dutch, they think of the plain dress and way of life of the Amish. The Pennsylvania Dutch population, however, can be divided into three groups. The first group, that of the "plain people," includes the Mennonites, the Amish, the Dunkards, and the River Brethren. The second group, the "church people," includes Lutherans, the Reformed, the United Brethren, the Schwenkfelders, and Evangelicals. Sometimes this group is called the "gay people," because they are more modern in their lifestyles. The church people constitute 90 percent of the Pennsylvania Dutch. The Moravians, with their own distinctive culture, constitute a third group.

Even though there are many different types of Pennsylvania Dutch, the tourist emphasis in Lancaster County is on the Amish and the Mennonites. In keeping with this, the next two sections take a more intimate look at these groups. The Moravians are discussed in the next section.

Both the Amish and the Mennonite faiths stem from the Anabaptist movement. Anabaptism was the most radical of the three main streams of the Protestant Reformation (the other two streams were Lutheranism and Calvinism). We can draw a religiopolitical spectrum with the Anabaptists on the left, the Lutherans in the center, and the Calvinists on the right.

The Anabaptists believed only in adult baptism, reasoning that infants could not know the ceremony's purpose. They insisted on their own interpretation of the Bible, had no clergy, and disapproved of military service and the taking of oaths. Protestants and Catholics saw these views as extremely radical and united to suppress this faith in the 1530s after a group of Anabaptists took control of the German town of Münster.

Since the Amish split off from the Mennonites, we tour the Mennonite sites in Lancaster first and then the Amish sites. This will then be followed by a discussion of some of the places to visit that deal with Pennsylvania Dutch culture in general. You can easily spend several days in this area and still not see everything.

Pennsylvania Dutch Farmers, Strausburg, Pennsylvania

While traveling, notice the houses of German origin. Some of the characteristics of German architecture as seen in the area are a steeply pitched roof; the pent roof, which is a hood around the house between the first and second stories; the frequent use of field stone; the German gambrel roof, which is bell-shaped with a break midway down the roofline and a flare at the eaves; and long, wooden shingles attached with only one nail. German parlors often include a heavy, carved dining table because Germans frequently dined in the parlor. Early German furniture and pottery are often covered with floral and animal motifs. The stove in the parlor is often a five-plate stove; the back sixth plate is missing because the back of the stove opened into the kitchen fireplace.

Lancaster County is, undoubtedly, one of the major tourist attractions in the region. And as such there are myriads of tourist type activities such as putt-putt golf, wax museum, water slide, amusement park, etc. But there are also many historical sites.

Pennsylvania Dutch Culture

Here we include some of the places where the traveler can learn more about Pennsylvania Dutch culture in general.

Heritage Center Museum of Lancaster County

Center Square and Queen Streets, Lancaster, PA (Open Tues–Sat 10–4, May–mid Nov)

This museum features arts and crafts made locally, including furniture (often decorated in the Pennsylvania Dutch style), wood carvings, and tinware.

Folk Craft Center and Museum

Mt. Sidney Road (off PA 340, east of the intersection of U.S. 30 and PA 340), Witmer, PA (Open daily 10–5, April 1–Nov 1)

Visitors start their tour with a twelve-minute slide and tape presentation on the culture of the Pennsylvania Dutch people. In the museum don't miss the displays on Dutch fractur, which are pen drawings inspired by the illuminated manuscripts of the Middle Ages. Also displayed are old tools, housewares, paintings, and clocks. Here also is a 1762 log cabin.

Other Sites to Visit

A good deal of the attraction of the Pennsylvania Dutch area is the wonderful food available. There are many all-you-can-eat, buffet-style places to satisfy one's appetite. Try the chocolate pecan pie. Don't miss visiting the places where they make some of the foods for which the Pennsylvania Dutch are famous. One such place is the Anderson Pretzel Bakery at 2060 Old Philadelphia Pike in Lancaster, where they make pretzels. To see how pretzels were made the old-fashioned way, visit the Julius Sturgis Pretzel House at 219 East Main Street in Lititz. With pretzels goes beer, so visit A. Bube's Brewery and Catacombs at 102 N. Market Street in Mount Joy. This is the only remaining brewery of the over twenty that once existed in nineteenth-century Lancaster County.

It is ironic that the "plain people" by their very plainness have attracted so much glaring commercialization. In fact, there are so many attractions that the visitor should write to the Lancaster Tourist Bureau (Visitors' Official Information Center, 1800 Hempstead Road, Lancaster, Pennsylvania, 17601— include fifty cents for postage and handling).

The Ephrata Cloister is located on 632 W. Main Street in Ephrata, which is north of Lancaster. This cloistered community is neither Amish nor Mennonite, but rather Seventh-Day Adventist. The German Pietist mystic Conrad Beissel, a somewhat shady character because of his sexual shenanigans, founded the community in 1732. He separated the community into two distinct groups: the solitary and the householders. The solitary were single men and women, who belonged to separate religious orders, while the householders were the married couples. Beissel ruled over both groups with an iron fist.

The enchanting green-tinged buildings of this community are not to be missed. Among the houses open to the public are the community house, the residence for celibate sisters, Beissel's log home, and a householder's cabin.

While in the area, visit the home of President Buchanan in Lancaster and the Moravian town of Lititz (see the appropriate sections). Also available is Rock Ford, the residence of General Edward Hand, who delayed Cornwallis's approach to Trenton during the Revolutionary War.

If you have children, they will convince you to take them to Hershey Park. There is a large amusement park here, but for the more serious adult they also have an interesting museum and a ride through Chocolate World, where they tell you how chocolate is made. And, of course, you will spend too much time shopping for candy and Hershey souvenirs. The Hershey Gardens are also worthwhile to visit.

Mennonites

The term Mennonite is derived from Menno Simons, a Catholic priest who converted to Anabaptism in 1536. He became an important leader and worked for twenty-five years among the widely separated groups of Anabaptists, converting them to his faith.

The Mennonites took part in the planting of the first German colony in America. This was in Germantown (now a suburb of Philadelphia), where the first Mennonite church was built (see the section on the Battle of Germantown for more information).

Other Mennonites followed and settled in what are now the Pennsylvania counties of Montgomery, upper Bucks, and Lancaster. In the New World the Mennonites splintered into many different groups, including the Funkites, Herrites, Stauffer Mennonites, Weaver Mennonites, Evangelical Mennonites, Brennemans, Old Order Mennonites, Wislerites, Martinites, and Wengerites. Obviously, with so many different groups of Mennonites it is virtually impossible to make any universal statement about the ways of life of these people.

Mennonite Information Center

1849 Hans Herr Drive, Willow Street not far from the intersection of U.S. 222 and PA 272, southeast of Lancaster, PA (Open Mon–Sat 9–4, Apr–Oct; Mon–Sat 10–3, Nov–Dec & Mar; Mon–Sat 10–3, Jan–Feb)

Swiss Mennonites claim to be Lancaster County's first permanent settlers. In 1710 they established a Mennonite community near Willow Street. Nine years later, Christian Herr built this stone farm/meetinghouse for his father, Bishop Hans Herr. The house is a wonderful example of medieval Germanic architecture.

The Mennonites used this house as a place of worship for more than a century. In the meetinghouse room is Christian Herr's Bible. Here also is a book called the *Martyr's Mirror*, which tells of the many persecutions the Mennonites suffered in Europe. The nearby Visitors' Center has displays providing even more information about the history of the Mennonites.

Amish

In 1693 Jacob Amman, a Mennonite preacher in the canton of Bern, Switzerland, insisted on the strict enforcement of the doctrine of shunning (that rule violators be ostracized by the religious community). The group that followed Amman's teachings became known as the Amish.

The first large group of Amish to come to America arrived in 1737 and settled in Berks County, Pennsylvania. This early settlement failed. In the latter 1700s the Amish began to migrate slowly down the Conestoga Valley.

The leading settlement of Amish is in Lancaster County. The House Amish, who have no churches but worship in houses or barns, settled near the towns of Intercourse and Bird in Hand. The Church Amish, who have Quaker-like meetinghouses, settled along the Conestoga River from Morgantown to Blue Ball. They also settled in the southern part of the county near Gap and Honey Brook. There is another group of Amish known as the Peachey Amish, named after an Amish preacher. The Peachey Amish split into the King and the Stoltzfus people. Both of these groups use electricity, and the Stoltzfus people even use automobiles.

How do you distinguish between the Amish and the Mennonites? Mennonite buggies are flat-roofed and black. Amish buggies, on the other hand, have rounded roofs and are painted gray. The Mennonite dress is usually more sedate than that of the Amish. They dress in black, gray, or tan or in a quiet print, whereas the Amish will use, at least for their children, bright blues, violets, reds, and greens. But you can learn more about this by visiting the various sites dealing with the Amish.

Start at the Visitors' Official Information Center of the Pennsylvania Dutch Tourist Bureau, where you can see a film on the Amish. The visitors' center is located east of Lancaster on U.S. 30 (bypass) and Hempstead Road Interchange.

There are a number of Amish farm houses tourists can visit. It probably does not make a great deal of difference which one you choose. None of the places are actually run by the Amish, since they do not believe in commercialization. However, you still learn a great deal about the ways of these mysterious people.

Amish Farm and House

2395 Lincoln Highway East (U.S. 30), just east of the intersection with Witmer Road, Lancaster, PA (Open daily 8:30–5, spring and fall; 8:30–8 summer; 8:30–4, winter)

You can tour this ten-room stone farmhouse built in 1805 along with the farmyard.

The Amish Homestead

2034 Lincoln Highway East (U.S. 30), just west of the intersection with PA 283, Lancaster, PA (Open daily 9–8, summer; 9–5, spring and fall; 9–4, winter)

Part of this farmhouse can be toured—the other part is being used by an Amish family. A farmyard tour is also included.

Amish Village

Route 896 (not far south of its intersection with U.S. 30), two miles north of Strasburg, PA (Open daily 9–5, spring and fall; daily 9–7, summer)

Here is not only a farmhouse and farmyard tour, but a tour of an Amish store, blacksmith shop, and one-room school house. The guide tells visitors about the old-order Amish. These people do not have electricity and believe it is sinful to have their picture taken. The children attend school only through eighth grade, and science is not taught. The community votes on their ministers by lot and goes to church every other Sunday in a different member's house. The benches for the services are transported on special bench wagons.

Green, blue, and white are the only colors allowed for house interiors. The kitchen, usually the largest room, is where the family spends the most time. The Amish use blue, purple, and black for everyday clothing and white for church.

Moravians

The Renewed Church of the United Brethren (its followers known simply as the Moravians) began as an evangelical branch of the Hussite movement. This movement flourished in Moravia and Bohemia in Czechoslovakia. The teachings of John Huss (1369–1415) were a precursor of the Protestant Reformation, ca. 1520. This religious leader fought against clerical abuses and asserted Czech nationalism by demanding an end to the domination of the Catholic church in Bohemia by German prelates.

In 1415 the Conciliar Movement of the Catholic church condemned him to death in an unsuccessful attempt to stamp out the Hussite movement. What an execution did not accomplish, a war did. In the Thirty Years' War, the Bohemian Protestants were defeated at the Battle of White Mountain in 1620. This forced the Moravians underground or into exile.

Christian David led a few of the survivors to a place of refuge on the Saxony estate of Austrian nobleman Count Nicholaus Ludwig Zinzendorf (1700–1760). Here they settled in 1722. Zinzendorf originally intended to convert his guests to his version of German Pietism (i.e., a movement, originating in the Lutheran Church in the seventeenth century, that stressed personal piety over religious formality and orthodoxy). Instead, they converted him to their faith. The Count even became a bishop of the Church of the United Brethren and one of the leaders of the resuscitated Moravian Church.

Fearing that they would one day be banished from their new homes, a group of Moravians led by Augustus Gottlieb Spangenberg came to America and in 1734 settled in Georgia. The settlement failed, and the remaining members of the group, under Peter Boehler, left for Pennsylvania. The famous preacher of the Great Awakening, George Whitefield, provided passage for many of the Brethren to a place that came to be known as Nazareth.

The Brethren was the most important of the pietistic sects in America. Gillian Gollin has delineated some characteristics of the Moravian religion in his book *Moravians in Two Worlds*: a focus on Jesus Christ, especially on his crucifixion wounds; an emphasis on religious feeling rather than dogma; a stress on communal living; a sense of being God's chosen people and, therefore, the need to be separate from non-Moravians; and a stress on good works, hence the importance of missionary activities among the Indians. In 1747 about fifty of four hundred Moravians were performing missionary duties.

One of the more intriguing aspects of the original Moravian way of life was their communal living pattern. These good people divided themselves into groups known as choirs, which formed along lines of sex, age, and marital status. Choirs grew out of bands or classes that were formed for religious purposes. Each choir—single men, single women, married families, and widows—had its separate building.

Choir members would attend weekly choir "speakings," where each person discussed his or her actions with the choir supervisor. The supervisor would give advice and guidance. The system was backed up by access to considerable punitive powers, including the power to reduce a person's pay or deny someone religious or social privileges. Troublesome cases would be turned over to the Community Helpers' Conference and Judiciary Council, which had the authority to arrest people.

When the Moravian communities first began, the communal living arrangements were relatively economically efficient, since communal living lowered the cost of housing. But as the economic status of the community improved, the choir system became relatively inefficient. This led to the eventual abandonment of communal living patterns. As early as 1760, individuals demanded the right to set up private households in Bethlehem. However, the Single Brethren's choir did not formally disband until 1817, and the Single Sisters' choir held on until 1841.

To learn more about the Moravians, tour the towns of Bethlehem and Nazareth near Allentown, Pennsylvania, in the Lehigh Valley. This trip will easily take a day. Then there is a side tour of Lititz in the Pennsylvania Dutch territory of Lancaster County. This should only take half a day.

Whitefield's attempts to convert the Brethren at Nazareth proved unsuccessful and so he ordered them to leave his land. They eventually moved on to a new settlement in Bethlehem, not far from Allentown.

The town of Bethlehem began in 1740 when a group of Moravians bought five hundred acres of land on the Lehigh River from William Allen (of Allentown fame). Count Zinzendorf arrived in Philadelphia in December 1741. He spent Christmas at the new settlement and named it Bethlehem in connection with the celebration of Christmas Eve vigils. With the successful establishment of the new town the Moravians eventually bought the town of Nazareth from Whitefield.

A tour of Bethlehem can take up to a full day if you want to see everything, including the interesting Lehigh University campus set on a hillside. Start your tour at the Eighteenth-Century Industrial Area.

Eighteenth-Century Industrial Area

Entrance at South Main Street and Ohio Road, Bethlehem, PA (from U.S. 22, take Bethlehem Exit 378 South to the last exit before going over the Lehigh River, and head north on Main street) (Open Tues–Sat 10–4, Sun 12–4, Jul–Aug; Sat 10–4, Sun 12–4, Tues–Fri by appt., Apr–June and Sept)

In the restored 1869 Luckenback flour mill, pick up a walking-tour guide of the city. Here also is an orientation center for visitors to the Industrial Area, as well as displays on the mill and local crafts. In the Industrial Area itself you can see the entire process of tanning hides. Also on the grounds are the waterworks, miller's house, and springhouse.

A short walk up a set of steps will bring you onto Bethlehem's Main Street. The first place to visit is the Gemein House. Here you will learn a great deal about Moravian history and culture.

Moravian Museum (Gemein House)

Located in the Gemein House at 66 West Church Street at the intersection with Heckewelder Place, Bethlehem, PA (Open Tues–Sun 1–4, Feb–Dec)

This 1741 one-time house of worship is the oldest building in Bethlehem. From 1780 to 1834 it was home to Lewis David de Schweinitz, a botanist. The house is now home to the Moravian Museum, through which you are given a guided tour. The museum has a collection of early Moravian furniture, clocks, silver, and musical instruments.

After the tour, guests partake in a mini love feast. The love feast is a celebration wherein the participants sing hymns or chant a liturgy and are served coffee and bread or rolls. This ceremony is performed quite often on many different occasions, such as the finishing of a work project. (Don't worry, they won't ask you to sing. Rather, the guide offers you different types of sweet rolls.)

On the walking tour of the various buildings of the choir system, please notice the interesting brick window arches forming a pattern that looks like a connected series of the letter *H*. This pattern also exists in other Moravian towns, such as Nazareth and Hope, New Jersey.

Please do not miss the Moravian cemetery, located between Market and Church streets, first laid out in 1742. Here all the stones lie flat on the ground, indicating that, if people are not always equal in life, they are equal in death. Illustrating the power of the choir system, the graves are arranged not by families but by choir system.

Annie S. Kemerer Museum

Around the corner from the Moravian Museum, 427 North New Street, Bethlehem, PA (Open Mon–Fri 1–4, second and fourth Sun, Feb–Dec; Sat 10–4, Apr–Dec)

Annie S. Kemerer (1865–1951) was married to a wealthy real estate man. She left her collection of antiques to the town upon her death. The collection contains furniture, oriental rugs, Bohemian glass, and many other items. The collection is very eclectic, so be prepared. There is a gallery with Pennsylvania-German and Moravian objects. Also here are some interesting paintings of the Delaware River and vicinity in the Hudson River school style. One of the artists, Gustavus Grunewald, was an instructor from 1836 to 1868 at the Moravian Seminary for Young Ladies in Bethlehem.

John Sebastian Goundie House

501 Main Street at the intersection with Market Street, Bethlehem, PA (Open Mon/Sat 10–4, all year; Sun 12–4, Apr–Dec)

A brief self-guided tour will take you through the home of John Sebastian Goundie, a Moravian brewer, fire inspector, and mayor. This Federal-style building is thought to be the first brick residence in Bethlehem. The dining room is decorated in the Federal style with Federal and early Empire furniture made of mahogany and cherry. There is a gift shop in one of the parlors of the house.

There is a special Christmas Night Light Tour of Bethlehem. The bus tour leaves on the hour from 5:00 to 9:00 P.M. from December 1 to 30, except Christmas Eve and Christmas Day. The tour goes past the Nativity scene, Advent wreath, colonial Moravian district, parade of lighted trees on the Hill-to-Hill Bridge, Victorian houses on Wyandotte Street, and up to South Mountain. Be sure to call ahead to the Visitors' Center (215-868-1513) for details.

George Whitefield House

214 E. Center Street (PA 191), Nazareth, PA (Open Tues, Fri–Sat and second Sun of each month, 2–5, Apr–Nov)

Construction of this home for black orphans began in 1740 at the behest of George Whitefield. Moravian carpenters, under the leadership of Reverend Peter Boehler, built the large stone structure. Whitefield had financial problems and eventually sold the building to his guests.

The building now serves as the headquarters and museum of the Moravian Historical Society. On the second floor are many items dealing with the history of the Moravian church, including a collection of musical instruments, a hymnal from 1501 (the Moravians were the first to introduce congregational singing), and paintings by John Valentine Haidt, which emphasize the wounds of Jesus on the cross.

The Gray Cottage

Located on the grounds of the Whitefield House, Nazareth, PA (Open Tues, Fri–Sat and second Sun of each month, 2–5, Apr–Nov)

This is a 1740 log house built by the Moravians as a temporary shelter before beginning construction of the Whitefield House.

Zinzendorf Square

Zinzendorf Square, Nazareth, PA

The buildings of the Moravian choir system are located around Zinzendorf Square. Pick up a walking-tour pamphlet at the craft shop on the square. Many of the buildings have been converted into apartments.

Johannes Mueller House

137–139 East Main Street, Lititz, PA (Open Mon–Sat 10–4, Memorial Day–Columbus Day)

In 1741 John George Klein acquired 296 acres of land in Lititz, located seven miles north of Lancaster. Zinzendorf needed a tract of land for the establishment of a religious community. Luckily for him, his preachings converted Klein, and the landowner turned his then 491 acres over to the count's planned community. The town of Lititz was founded in 1756. The village with its square surrounded by religious buildings can be toured in less than half a day.

In 1792 Johannes Mueller, a printer and dyer of linen, built the main portion of this stone house. At one time, as many as nine people lived here—the parents, four children, and three apprentices. The house now contains hundreds of items from the area. There a number of pieces that once belonged to General John Augustus Sutter (see below). The house also serves as a gift shop. Pick up a walking-tour pamphlet here.

Sturgis Pretzel House

219 East Main Street, Lititz, PA (Open Mon–Sat 9–5, all year)

Here's an interesting success story involving a homeless person of the 1850s. A man in need of a good meal stopped in the town and struck a deal with baker Ambrose Rauch. In exchange for the meal, he gave the baker a recipe for hard pretzels. The baker got the better of the deal, for the recipe led to the success of the first commercial bakery in America.

Rauch gave the recipe to his young apprentice, Julius Sturgis, who used it in 1861 when he started his own bakery. The pretzels were an immediate hit, and the bakery's future was assured. This was the first bakery to sell pretzels commercially.

Sturgis lived in this 1784 house with his wife and fourteen children. He did not actually bake the salted treats in this building, but rather next-door. As in the old days, when milk was delivered to homes, the baker had a regular route of customers as far away as a day's travel by wagon.

At the house the workers show visitors how pretzels were made the old-fashioned way. Did you know that the pretzel's original shape represented folded arms in prayer and that in the year 610 a monk in northern Italy or southern France used them as an educational tool to teach children about the importance of prayer? You will learn this and other things about the background of the pretzel here. The kids especially love this place, because they actually roll their own pretzels.

Moravian Square

Across the street from the Sturgis Pretzel House, Lititz, PA

On the square is the Brethren's House built in 1759 and the Sister's House built in 1758, as well as the more recent Moravian Church (1786). General Washington commandeered the Brethren's House for a military hospital (December 1777 to August 1778). Treated here were as many as 1,000 troops, of whom 110 died. They are buried in a plot to the east of the village.

Archives and Museum

Moravian Square, Lititz, PA (Open by appointment)

This building holds a collection of old musical instruments. The Moravians hold dear the trombone choir, and the museum has a good collection of these instruments.

General Sutter Home (private)

19 East Main Street, Lititz, PA

This is the former home of General John Augustus Sutter (1803–1880), an immigrant from Switzerland who made his way west to California. He convinced the Mexican authorities to let him establish a colony in the Sacramento area. He built a baronial estate for himself and continued to prosper when the Americans took over California. In 1848 the discovery of gold on his estate was his undoing. His farm hands and workers deserted him, and squatters settled on his land. He went bankrupt by 1852. In 1871 he settled in Lititz, but spent his winters in Washington, D.C.

Other Sites to Visit

Close to Bethlehem is the town of Easton, which has an excellent canal museum. The town of Jim Thorpe is a little further away. When in Lititz, tour the Pennsylvania Dutch sites in Lancaster County.

Another Moravian town is Hope, New Jersey, settled in 1769. Fourteen Moravian structures still exist. The old church is now a local bank. The town is very small, but does have a historical society museum (not Moravian) where the tourist can obtain information about the Moravians.

P A R T

THREE

The Fight for the Continent

In 1689 the English and French began a series of conflicts that some historians have referred to as the Second Hundred Years' War. Since both nations had settlements in North America, the wars naturally brought French and English America into conflict. Using the American names, the wars were: King William's War (1688–1697); Queen Anne's War (1701–1713); King George's War (1745–1748); and the French and Indian War (1754–1763).

In this protracted struggle both nations wooed the Indians. The French made great progress with certain Indian nations, such as the Huron, but the Iroquois were the real power in the area. In 1608 the Frenchman Samuel de Champlain made a terrible diplomatic blunder when he helped some Algonquin Indians defeat a group of Iroquois. This won his nation the enmity of this powerful confederacy. The Iroquois fought on the side of the English—that is, they did until they realized they were losing a great many braves. They then decided to take a neutral stance and play off one European power against the other.

Even though the Iroquois never had more than a maximum strength of 2,500 warriors, they gained control over other tribes extending north to Hudson's Bay, south to the Carolinas, west to the Mississippi, and east to the white settlements. More important for our story, they dominated the tribes on the Pennsylvania frontier.

William Penn's generous policies toward the local Delaware Indians kept the peace on that colony's frontiers. Following Penn, his successor, James Logan, largely determined Indian policy. To carry out his plans, Penn's former secretary employed a resident of the Reading area, Conrad Weiser. The first chapter of this section describes the home of Weiser, who helped keep peace on the Pennsylvania frontier with the Iroquois and Delaware Indians. The following chapter includes a tour of Fort Delaware on the New York–Pennsylvania border to gain still more insight into Indian/settler activities in the area.

6

The Pennsylvania Frontier

This chapter covers three sites connected with the Pennsylvania frontier. It will take a full day to see all three places. To be honest, these sites are rather modest ones. The houses are relatively plain and sparsely furnished. They are more likely to appeal to the committed history buff.

Sometimes good things arise from bad things. The abuses of the landlord system in New York chased many settlers and potential settlers away from that colony. One such settler was Conrad Weiser (1696–1760), who fled to Pennsylvania in 1729. This German immigrant proved to be an important reason why Pennsylvania maintained peace with the Indians on its frontiers while other colonies faced burning towns. He settled his family in the Tulpehocken Valley at what is now the town of Womelsdorf, Pennsylvania (west of Reading). There he became the justice of Lancaster County courts.

As a lad he had learned the Iroquois language when he spent a winter and spring as the adopted son of an Iroquois chief. This skill enabled him to become the interpreter for Shikellamy, who was the representative of the Six Nations to the Iroquois-dominated Indians of the Susquehanna Valley area, mainly Shawnee and Delaware Indians. At this time he met James Logan, who played such a crucial role in pushing the local Indians into the Ohio Valley to make way for the advancement of white settlements.

Weiser participated in many conferences that reaffirmed peace with the Iroquois. In 1737 the Iroquois Confederacy prepared for war with Virginia. Logan ordered Weiser to travel to the Iroquois Onondaga Council to negotiate for peace. Shikellamy and a plant hunter, John Bartram, accompanied the peacemaker. Traveling in the winter, Weiser would have died of starvation if not for the help of his Indian friend. Once at the council, the German-American convinced the Iroquois to stop their preparations for war.

In this same year, the brothers John and Thomas Penn hoaxed the local Indians out of a great deal of land. They told the natives that, according to a previous treaty, the whites had land coming to them to the extent that a man could walk. In the so-called Walking Purchase, the whites had three athletes speedily walk as fast and as far as they could. The Indian observers and two of the white runners dropped out of the race, but the third one covered sixty miles. Surveyors then added even more land.

It is said that Weiser was so upset over the Walking Purchase that he joined the Ephrata Cloister (see the section on Pennsylvania Dutch territory). He had been baptized there a couple of years earlier. The man with

Conrad Weiser House, Womelsdorf, Pennsylvania

five children became a celibate known as Brother Enoch. He later quarreled with the leader of the religious group, Conrad Biessel. Apparently, the recent convert was incensed at being punished for having four children by his wife during his supposed period of abstinence. Nevertheless, he returned to the group and found himself consecrated as priest.

If Weiser was upset over the Walking Purchase, you can imagine how the Delaware Indians felt. They wanted the situation redressed, but their Iroquois superiors sold them out at a peace conference held in Philadelphia in 1742. Weiser helped negotiate the treaty that enforced peace on the buffer-zone Delawares. He also helped negotiate a treaty ceding Iroquois land in the Ohio Valley to the English colonies.

Upon the death of his Indian friend in 1748, Weiser's influence diminished and he was superseded by New York's Sir William Johnson and George Croghan. This must have been painful for the Pennsylvanian, since he had very little respect for Johnson. He even helped the Iroquois stay neutral in King George's War, thereby resisting Johnson's efforts to get them involved.

During the war, Pennsylvania suffered little from Indian depredations. The Quakers must have felt pleased with their pacifist policies. However, during the French and Indian War, the colony felt the wrath of the Indians for the first time. Naturally, the frontier colonists, many of them Scotch-Irish, felt betrayed by the pacifist Quakers. Benjamin Franklin led the attack on the Quaker Indian policy and was able to have a series of frontier forts built. Weiser commanded a Pennsylvania regiment that helped hold these forts. This rebellion against the Quakers' Indian policies marks the final demise of the dominant position of this religious group in Pennsylvania.

The leader of the Delaware Indians in the Wyoming Valley at this time was Teedyuscung, an overweight, drunken man who had been baptized into the Moravian faith. Thinking the French would win, the chief sided with them and attacked settlements on the Delaware River. Then, when the English started winning, he switched to their side. Pennsylvania honored him at several peace conferences held at Easton. To further please him, the governor even sent carpenters to build European-style houses for the chief and his people.

In 1758 the Iroquois, tiring of the chief's shenanigans, agreed to attend a peace conference in Easton. Weiser served as translator. The conference can be seen as a confrontation between the policies of Johnson, who backed the Iroquois, and the Pennsylvania Quakers, who backed Teedyuscung. Unfortunately for the Quakers, their man showed up in a drunken condition. The conference attendees did not appreciate the Indian alcoholic's shouted curses. Johnson's viewpoints won out, and the Iroquois reasserted control over the Delaware Indians. This was the most important Indian conference ever held in Pennsylvania, for it marked the formal shift of the Native Americans away from the French.

Conrad Weiser Park

Fifteen miles east of Lebanon on U.S. 422 near its intersection with PA 419, Womelsdorf, PA (Open Tues–Fri 8:30–5, Sun 1–5, daylight savings time; Tues–Fri 9–4:30, Sun 1–4:30, winter)

In 1729 the future diplomat built a one-room stone house after settling in the Tulpehocken Valley. He expanded the dwelling in 1751 to a two-room dwelling to accommodate his growing family. Can you imagine two parents and fourteen children living in this small house? There is, however, more room in the attic. The owner led a frugal life, and the house interior attests to this. The house museum has a few of Weiser's belongings, such as a money belt, silver spoon, and a copy of his will. One unique interior feature is the bake oven in the main house. Also here is a linen Bible in the German language.

As mentioned earlier, the diplomat participated in the experiment at the nearby Ephrata Cloister for a year and a half. He also worked closely with the Moravians. Count Zinzendorf hired him to promote the Moravian religion among the Indians. During this period, the great negotiator saved the count's life. He returned to Lutheranism when one of his daughters married Henry Melchoir Muhlenberg, who is considered the father of the Lutheran church in America.

On the grounds is a statue of the Indian ambassador Shikellamy. Also here are the graves of Conrad and his wife.

Zeller's Fort

Route 1 (from I-78 travel south on Route 419 through Newmanstown, turn right at the last intersection onto Fort Zeller's Road), Newmanstown, PA (Open by appointment; the fort is located on a working farm)

This 1745 house served as protection from the Indians during the French and Indian War. It is thought to be the oldest private fort in Pennsylvania and is of medieval German architecture (compare it to the Hans Herr house in Lancaster). This house museum, located on a working farm, displays various antiques with a large variety of clocks.

Daniel Boone Homestead Site

Daniel Boone Road (located off Route 422 southeast of Reading near Baumstown), about two miles north of Birdsboro, PA (Open Mon–Sat 8:30–5, Sun 1–5, summer; Mon–Sat 9–4:30, Sun 1–4:30, winter)

If you expect to see and learn many new things about Daniel Boone, you might be a little disappointed in this site. There is very little left of his boyhood home. But don't let this discourage you. The grounds are immense, making for a nice country feeling.

When Americans think of the early frontier, one of the first names that comes to mind is that of Daniel Boone, the great pathfinder. Boone was born on this site in 1734 and lived here for the first sixteen years of his life. All that remains of the cabin in which he was born is the original foundation, now incorporated into the east end of the cellar wall in the present house.

To get a better idea of the way the Boone cabin may have looked, examine the Bertolet Cabin (ca. 1735) on the property. Other interesting buildings are the blacksmith shop, sawmill, bake oven, and smokehouse. This park could benefit from a slide show on the importance of Daniel Boone and better Boone exhibits. When we visited, they only had a Pennsylvania rifle exhibit along with some old tools.

Other Sites to Visit

There are several sites to see around Reading, Pennsylvania. A few of these are the Duryea auto museum at Boyertown and the canal park in Reading (see the appropriate sections). Lebanon County is known for its bologna, so be sure to visit one of these places if touring on a weekday. Also visit the iron furnace in Cornwall (see the section on the iron industry).

When in Philadelphia, be sure to see the Bartram Gardens, located at Fifty-fourth Street and Lindbergh Boulevard. It is unfortunate that space is limited, for it would have been interesting to cover the plant-collecting activities of John Bartram and his son, William. Their lives nicely illustrate how Philadelphia at this time was the leading center for the sciences, especially botany. The pair also reveal that the frontier was not just a place of conflict, but an area to be searched for new plants to serve agricultural and horticultural goals.

7

Fort Delaware and Minisink Battlefield

In this chapter we tour two sites connected with the history of the New York/Pennsylvania frontier: Fort Delaware and Minisink Battlefield. It takes less than a day to see both sites. The children will really enjoy Fort Delaware. You don't have to travel to the West to find a fort that looks like something out of the wild west. As a matter of fact, it is not that easy to find such a western fort, since most of them were not palisaded. Therefore, this fort near the Delaware River is a visual treat. It is a reconstructed colonial settlement enclosed within a stockade. Children can walk on the ramparts, imagining Indian sightings. And then they can visit a battlefield park where real Indian fighting took place.

Adding to the joy of this trip is the great natural beauty of this section of the Delaware River. Hawk Nest Drive runs along the northern bank of the valley, which at times is very steep. Canoeing is available and this adds further to the enjoyment of the area's natural beauty.

Fort Delaware

Route 97, Narrowsburg, NY (Open daily, end of June–Labor Day; plus weekends, Memorial Day–June)

The colony of Connecticut was running out of land, and so its people looked to settle elsewhere. One of the new areas for possible settlement was the Wyoming Valley in Pennsylvania. The Pennsylvanians, of course, were very upset about this. To discourage the New Englanders, they moved Teedyuscung and his followers into the area. Despite threats and harassment, the stubborn immigrants just kept coming. This eventually led to what is known as the Pennsylvania-Connecticut or the Pennymite Wars.

Fort Delaware is located near the community once known as Cushetunk. The original site of the settlement was six miles north of the present fort. Connecticut men started the settlement in 1754, the year the French and Indian War began. About seven years later, the Cushetunk settlers erected a stockade around their houses. There was another rough fort around the house of settler Moses Thomas.

In the dispute between the Delawares and the New Englanders, someone set Teedyuscung's house ablaze; he died in the fire. This was not a smart thing to do. The Indians believed in revenge and they took it. Moreover, the French and Indian War was already in progress, which meant there were fewer soldiers available to respond to further Indian attacks. Captain Bull, Teedyuscung's son, went on the warpath, killing many white settlers. Iroquois friendly to William Johnson finally captured him.

At the Moses Thomas fort, settlers held off an Indian raid. Following the American Revolution, the old stockade was no longer needed and it soon decayed. The settlement lives on in the family farms of the vicinity.

Minisink Battleground Park
Located off Route 97, Minisink Ford, NY

The Battle of Minisink occurred during the American Revolution, but it is discussed here as it can be seen as the natural extension of the relations between the Iroquois and the whites in the area. The loyalty built up between these Indians and their old friend William Johnson led a large portion of them to back the British during the Revolution.

During the war, Iroquois and Tory raiders from Canada did a great deal of damage to outlying settlements. In fact, the damage was so severe and the fear so extensive that settlers virtually abandoned the frontier. This hurt the colonial cause because the army needed food and clothing. In 1779 Washington sent Major General John Sullivan on an expedition from Easton, Pennsylvania, through the Wyoming Valley to link up with Brigadier General James Clinton coming south from the Mohawk Valley. The Americans were then to attack Fort Niagara, where many of the Tory/Indian raids originated.

To divert some of Sullivan's forces, the British told Chief Joseph Brant of the Mohawk Indians to create a distraction. Brant was the equivalent of William Johnson's brother-in-law, since the famous Indian superintendent lived with Joseph's half-sister, Molly Brant. On July 20, 1779, the Iroquois chief led a party of twenty-seven Tories and sixty Indians in an attack on Minisink in the Port Jervis area. The local militia at Goshen, under Lieutenant Colonel Benjamin Tusten, pursued the raiders and attempted a surprise attack. Unfortunately, it failed and the militia retreated to the high ground where the battlefield park stands today. Finding a weak spot in the defensive perimeter, the enemy poured in amongst the militia and a massacre began. Between forty-five and fifty American revolutionists died that July 22 day. Brant reported losing only eight men.

An interesting sidelight is that the Indian chief occupied the Cushetunk fortifications after a Minisink raid in 1778. The fort was abandoned after its settlers learned of the Wyoming Massacre of July 3, 1778, in Wilkes-Barre.

In spite of Brant's efforts, General Sullivan's troops destroyed forty Indian towns. The Iroquois crowded into Niagara and suffered miserably that winter. The next year, Brant sought revenge, burning a great number of white farms and houses. Needless to say, the suffering on both sides was tremendous.

Pick up a brochure at the park and take the walking tour of the battle sites. The walk is not long, as the battlefield was not that large. A highlight is the cliff site of the makeshift hospital, where the raiders killed many of the wounded soldiers.

Other Sites to Visit

Read about the Delaware and Hudson Canal in the chapter on canals.

PART

FOUR

The American Revolution

A great many battles of the American Revolution took place in the Mid-Atlantic region, and most of these battlegrounds are available for touring. In fact, there are so many of these sites that they cannot all be covered in this book. However, this part does cover the more important ones, following the action from 1774, when the First Continental Congress met in Philadelphia, to the end of the war. With a few exceptions, the battles and winter quarters are arranged chronologically. The material is also largely arranged geographically because the armies fought a series of battles constituting a campaign, such as the one in and around Philadelphia, in a concentrated area.

8

A Declaration of Independence

Revolutionary Philadelphia

The Revolutionary War began with the Battles of Lexington and Concord in April 1775, which took the Continental Congress by surprise. The Second Continental Congress did not meet until May 1775. And when it did assemble, the delegates were still very cautious about promoting actual independence for the colonies. Fourteen more months would pass before the Continental Congress officially declared independence. The writer Thomas Paine provided the crucial thrust toward independence by providing a well-reasoned ideological justification for revolution.

The steps toward freedom were delayed for over a year because three middle colonies—New York, New Jersey, and Pennsylvania—plus Maryland refused to support the move to independence. The Continental Congress appointed General George Washington commander in chief and sent Colonel Benedict Arnold to Canada to make it the fourteenth colony. Washington made his way to Boston to counteract the British thrust there, but he arrived after the Americans had won a strategic victory at the Battle of Bunker Hill (June 1775), which naturally aroused great enthusiasm in the nation.

The American thrust at Canada collapsed in December 1775 at Quebec. This disappointment was partially balanced by the British abandonment of Boston in March of the following year. The Americans had set up an impressive array of cannon, recently captured by Ethan Allen and his Green Mountain Boys from New York's Fort Ticonderoga, atop Dorchester Heights overlooking the enemy position.

Before and during the Revolutionary War, Philadelphia functioned as the unofficial capital of the thirteen colonies. In this city the Continental Congress met to declare independence from Great Britain and the revolutionary government functioned (except during the British occupation, 1777–1778). Because the city holds so many Revolutionary War sites, you can spend several days seeing them. Needless to say, this is one of the nation's outstanding national treasures and should be visited by every American. The best place to start is Independence Park.

Independence Park Visitors' Center

Chestnut and Third streets, Philadelphia, PA (Open daily 9–5, all year)

At the Visitors' Center, a film establishes the historical mood. More practically, arrangements can be made for tours of some of the buildings, such as Independence Hall, the Bishop White House, and the Todd House. (The latter two houses are discussed in the tour of Federal Philadelphia.)

Carpenters' Hall

310 Chestnut Street (in the middle of the block bounded by Third and Fourth streets), Philadelphia, PA (Open daily 9–5, all year)

This Georgian brick building takes its name from the Carpenters' Company, one of the earliest American crafts guilds (founded 1724). In September 1774 the First Continental Congress met in this building to support Massachusetts in its efforts to resist the British punishment for the Boston Tea Party (December 1773). Virginia took the lead by instructing its committees of correspondence to poll the other colonies on whether to call a continental congress.

Fifty-six delegates from twelve colonies (Georgia was not yet included) met in Carpenters' Hall. Among the more notable delegates were Samuel and John Adams, Patrick Henry, John Jay, and George Washington. The Continental Congress supported the Massachusetts declaration that the Intolerable Acts were unconstitutional and void; issued the Declaration of Rights; adopted the Articles of Association (a forerunner of the later Articles of Confederation); and agreed to cut off imports from Britain.

At that time a central passageway divided Carpenters' Hall into two sections. The Continental Congress used only one-half of the hall. Inside the hall are an exhibition of carpentry tools and a small display on the historic meetings that took place here.

This First Continental Congress lasted for almost two months. Before departing, the members agreed to meet again in May of 1775 if their efforts did not meet with a satisfactory British response. Events ran ahead of them, however. Fighting began in April 1775.

Independence Hall

Chestnut Street between Fifth and Sixth streets, Philadelphia, PA (Open daily 9–5, all year)

Independence Hall is now surrounded by buildings that did not exist when the Second Continental Congress met here in 1775. Congress Hall (to the right of Independence Hall as you face the front of the building) was constructed in 1787; Old City Hall (to the left of Independence Hall) in 1791;

Behind Independence Hall, Philadelphia, Pennsylvania

and Philosophical Hall (behind Old City Hall) between 1785 and 1789. So, if you want to return to 1775, imagine the buildings surrounding Independence Hall as not here.

Andrew Hamilton, the Penn family's favorite lawyer and the free-speech defender of New York's John Peter Zenger (a newspaperman whom the British unsuccessfully tried for libel and who laid the groundwork for freedom of the press) designed the hall in Georgian colonial architectural style. The building served as the State House of the Province of Pennsylvania. In

May 1775, the Second Continental Congress convened in the hall. The Continental Congress used the building until 1783 (except for the period when the British occupied the city).

The ground floor is divided by a central hallway into two meeting rooms. On one side the Pennsylvania Supreme Court met, and on the other, the Continental Congress. This latter room has been recreated to look as it did in 1776. Windsor chairs are set by tables covered with green cloths. Each table has an inkwell and a candle. Upstairs is the impressive Long Gallery, which is 120 feet in length. It has white walls with blue wainscoting and window trim. The governors of Pennsylvania would entertain guests here. Off the gallery are two rooms: the governor's room with council chamber and the legislative room.

On June 11, 1776, the Continental Congress appointed a committee of five to prepare a Declaration of Independence. The committee members were Thomas Jefferson, John Adams, Benjamin Franklin, Roger Sherman, and Robert R. Livingston. Jefferson wrote most of the document, with Adams and Franklin making a few changes. To authenticate it, President of Congress John Hancock and Secretary Charles Thomson signed the document July 4, 1776. Hancock made his signature very large, commenting that King George III should be able to see it without using his glasses. The committee of five then saw to its printing. On July 8, Colonel John Nixon, a member of the Committee of Safety, read the document in the yard of Independence Hall from a circular platform that had been erected by the American Philosophical Society for astronomical observation. The audience was not large, and commentators noted that it was not composed of the "most respectable class" of citizens. The huge Liberty Bell, then in the steeple of the hall, was rung to celebrate the event. On July 19, the Continental Congress voted to engross the document on parchment. The delegates finally signed the Declaration of Independence on August 2.

Liberty Bell Pavilion

Independence Mall, Market Street between Fifth and Sixth streets, Philadelphia, PA (Open daily 9–5, all year)

The Liberty Bell, cast in England in 1751, was brought to Philadelphia in 1752 for the (belated) celebration of the fiftieth anniversary of the Pennsylvania Charter of Privileges, which William Penn had granted in 1701. It cracked during testing and was recast by two Philadelphians, John Pass and John Stow (whose last names are on the bell itself).

The bell was hung in the steeple of Independence Hall. In 1835 the bell cracked again during the funeral tolling for Chief Justice John Marshall. This is not surprising, since the bell tolled for thirty-six hours. The bell was again repaired, and in 1846 it was rung in honor of George Washington's birthday. Unfortunately, another crack developed.

At that time the bell was known as the Bell of the Revolution. It did not become a national symbol of liberty until much later, when Boston abolitionists used the words printed on the bell, Proclaim Liberty Throughout the Land, in their campaigns.

You can actually touch the bell. In keeping with its recasting, it feels rough to the touch—not nice and smooth. Notice how the word *Pennsylvania* is spelled.

Graff House

Market Street between Seventh and Eighth streets, Philadelphia, PA (Open daily 9–5, all year)

Thomas Jefferson wrote the Declaration of Independence in his second-floor apartment in this reconstructed building. The house itself had been owned by bricklayer Jacob Graff, Jr. The first floor contains exhibits, including a short film on the drafting of the document. Jefferson used the bedroom and parlor on the second floor, and these have been recreated. The rooms contain period furnishings.

Franklin Court

Market Street between Third and Fourth streets, Philadelphia, PA (Open daily 9–5, all year)

Here is the site of Benjamin Franklin's Philadelphia house, built 1763–1765. Today a steel outline of the house frame hovers over the site. An underground museum, a special treat for children, tells more about this immensely talented man, who first came to Philadelphia in 1723 from Boston (where he was born in 1706). The young egalitarian did not care for the more restrictive environment of that Puritan city and felt more at home in the more diverse society of Philadelphia.

Franklin accomplished so many things and his story is so well known that it will not be covered here. The sociologist E. Digby Baltzell did not exaggerate when he said that Franklin was a "one-man city," starting a multitude of institutions from the first firehouse to the first hospital.

Franklin resided in many different places in Philadelphia before actually owning his own house—the one portrayed here. In 1764, even before his residence was completed, he sailed for London to petition George III for royal, rather than proprietary, rule for Pennsylvania. He did not return to America until 1775, arriving just in time to be appointed the first postmaster general and to help draft and sign the Declaration of Independence.

In 1776 he was sent to France as a diplomat to help secure that nation's assistance for the cause of American independence. He proved successful in this effort, but did not return to America until 1785. Upon his arrival, he expanded his house. He died in the house in 1790.

City Tavern

Corner of Second and Walnut streets, Philadelphia, PA (Open daily 11–11, all year)

This reconstructed tavern was first built in 1773 by a group of Philadelphians who thought the city needed a tavern that matched the town in prestige. Members of both the First and Second Continental Congresses, the Constitutional Convention, and the 1790–1800 federal government gathered at the tavern. (Now it serves lunch and dinner daily.)

Betsy Ross House

239 Arch Street between Third and Bread streets, Philadelphia, PA (Open daily 9–5, all year)

This is the restored two-and-a-half-story brick town house where Betsy Ross lived. She was born in Philadelphia in 1752, the eighth of seventeen children in a Quaker family. She was a bit of a rebel, for she eloped with John Ross to New Castle. The Friends disowned her for marrying out of meeting.

She attended Christ Church for a number of years, but with her husband became a member of the Society of Free Quakers. She also helped to run her husband's upholstery shop. Unfortunately, her spouse died in a gunpowder explosion while on guard duty for the militia.

Betsy Ross continued the business, part of which was to make flags. There is no documentary evidence that she actually sewed the stars-and-stripes flag, which Congress adopted as the national symbol in June 1777.

Her bad luck with husbands continued. She remarried, but her new spouse died as a prisoner of war in England. She did no better with her next marriage, to John Claypoole. He had been a fellow prisoner of war with her second husband. Claypoole had the unpleasant duty of informing Ross of the fate of her second husband. They married in 1783 and together had five daughters before Claypoole's death in 1817. Ross lived on until 1836.

The first room visitors enter is the Flag Room, where they say Betsy Ross met with George Washington. Visitors also see the upholstery shop room, the bedrooms, and the kitchen (in the basement), along with the storage room for the upholstery material. One can easily tell this is the shop of a small merchant because the rooms are tiny and the general feeling is one of being cramped.

Christal Church

Corner of Commerce and Second streets, Philadelphia, PA (Open Mon–Sat 9–5, Sun 1–5, all year)

This is the second church on this site. The first church was erected in 1696. Historically, Christ Church is very important in Philadelphia and Pennsylvania history because the founders had broken away from, and hence weakened, the Quaker dominance of the city. Dr. John Kearsley oversaw the construction of the present Georgian structure, built between 1727 and 1747. The famous architect Thomas U. Walter made extensive interior changes in 1832. Be sure to look inside the church, which is absolutely gorgeous. Hanging over the center aisle is a twenty-four-branched chandelier made in London in 1774. In 1769 Philadelphia cabinetmaker John Fowell designed the wine-glass pulpit.

Washington, Jefferson, Franklin, and other founding fathers worshiped here. Two signers of the Declaration of Independence, Robert Morris and James Wilson, are buried in the churchyard. Also buried here is Major General Charles Lee, court-martialed for insubordination at the Battle of Monmouth in the Revolutionary War.

Christ Church Burial Ground

Corner of Fifth and Arch streets, Philadelphia, PA (Open Apr 15–Oct 15)

Five signers of the Declaration of Independence are buried here: Benjamin Franklin, Francis Hopkinson, Dr. Benjamin Rush, George Ross, and Joseph Hewes.

Elfreth's Alley

Second Street between Arch and Quarry streets, Philadelphia, PA (Museum open daily 10–4, all year)

For a glimpse into urban life in colonial Philadelphia, take a stroll through cobblestoned Elfreth's Alley, which is only six feet wide. Thirty extant two- and three-story brick houses, built between 1728 and 1836, line the alley, making it the oldest residential street in the United States. Here were homes and shops for carpenters, printers, and other craftsmen. The Mantua Maker's House Museum, number 126, displays some of the items made by the residents. (A mantua is a capelike cloak.) Open-house tours are held the first Sunday in June.

Other Sites to Visit

You can also take the tour of Federal Philadelphia, which concentrates on the period when Philadelphia was capital of the new nation.

Thomas Paine

If ever Americans had a love-hate relationship with one of their own, that person was Thomas Paine. On the one hand, they praised him for providing ideological justification for revolution. On the other, they despised him as an atheist (even though he was really a deist—that is, one who believes in a supreme being but does not believe that God intervenes in human affairs) and a revolutionary republican. The country's attitude toward Paine reflected the basic conflict of a conservative nation engaging in revolutionary activity. In this section we visit the New Rochelle cottage of this interesting man to learn more about him. This visit should take less than half a day.

Paine was born in 1737 in Thetford, England. He came from a Quaker family of humble origins—his father was a corsetmaker. Until he met Benjamin Franklin in London in 1774, he had led an uneventful life, jumping from job to job and in and out of two marriages. The great man sent him to Philadelphia with letters of introduction, but it was Franklin's son-in-law, Richard Bache, who helped him secure the editorship of the *Pennsylvania Magazine*.

All around town, conversations buzzed about how unfair the British were to the Americans. The new immigrant, however, had not seriously considered American independence until the Battles of Lexington and Concord jolted him into new ways of thinking. In January 1776 he published a fifty-page pamphlet called *Common Sense*. As late as the spring of 1776, most Americans still did not believe independence was possible or even thinkable. Paine's book changed this situation drastically. Suddenly, the idea of independence became widely accepted. The pamphlet became a bestseller—perhaps the greatest seller in American history in terms of the proportion of the population who purchased it. It is often included, and rightfully so, in discussions of books that have changed the world.

Paine also participated in the Revolutionary War. Shortly after the Americans declared their independence, the British commander, Lord William Howe, moved against New York City. Via a flanking movement, Howe defeated Washington at the Battle of Long Island in August 1776. The American forces had to retreat north to White Plains in Westchester County. In October the Continental army stopped the enemy at the Battle of White Plains, forcing the British to retreat to New York City.

The British completed their hold over New York City by inflicting a near-disastrous defeat on the Americans, under General Nathanael Greene, holding Fort Washington, located on upper Manhattan Island. It is said that Washington, with tears in his eyes, watched the collapse of the American defenses from Fort Lee, New Jersey. Paine had joined the revolutionary army and become an aide-de-camp to General Greene. He served during the British capture of both Fort Washington and Fort Lee and was even cited for personal bravery. The Americans abandoned Fort Lee when the British crossed the Hudson River and landed their troops at today's Alpine Boat Basin. The enemy pulled their artillery and supplies up the trail to the top of the Palisades. American campfires were still burning when the British occupied the New Jersey fortification.

Congress appointed Paine secretary of the Committee of Foreign Affairs in April 1777. While he held this position, Silas Deane, American diplomat to the French court, was accused of pocketing American payments for what were really French gifts of supplies. In this messy affair, Congress blamed Paine and he had to resign. He then served as clerk of the Pennsylvania Assembly, after which he went to France with Colonel John Laurens. There he helped obtain a $6 million loan for the revolutionary cause in 1781.

Following the end of the war, at Washington's request, Congress voted the revolutionary a small sum of money for his services. In 1784 New York State also rewarded him with 277 acres of land and a mansion in New Rochelle confiscated from a Loyalist who had fled to Halifax. With other lands added to the gift, he actually now had a total of 10,000 acres. One would gather that the great republican was not embarrassed at suddenly becoming a large landowner, for he did not return any of the acreage. However, he must have felt a little uneasy, for he spent only one or two weeks at the mansion, concluded it was too big for him, and went back to his New Jersey home. He rented the farm to others and left for England in 1787 to visit his parents. He did not return to the United States until fifteen years later.

While in England, he wrote the book *The Rights of Man* in defense of the republican form of government. He also managed to make himself extremely unpopular in Britain by advocating the abolition of the monarchy. With arrest imminent, in 1792 he escaped to France. Republican France greeted the author as a hero, even electing him to the National Assembly. While there, he worked on his last book, *The Age of Reason*.

In the madness of the aftermath of the French Revolution, the paranoid French government arrested Paine. He spent almost a year in prison because the American minister to France showed no interest in obtaining the release of the controversial man. When James Monroe became minister, he demanded and obtained the prisoner's release. The great republican finally returned to the United States in October 1802.

Thomas Paine Cottage

20 Sicard Avenue off North Avenue (take Exit 8 off I-95), a short distance north of Iona College, New Rochelle, NY (Open Wed–Sun 2–5, all year)

While the great writer was in Europe, his mansion had burnt down and been replaced by a tiny dwelling. (Its original location was on top of the hill on Paine Avenue.) This was unfortunate, for he suddenly needed more room. In France he had been befriended by the Bonneville family. In an attempt to return their hospitality, he invited them to come to America and stay with him. To sweeten the offer, he added that he would leave the bulk of his estate to them upon his death. Madame de Bonneville separated from her husband and decided to accept the American's offer, bringing her two sons with her. Paine's New Jersey quarters were just not large enough.

The host of the French family arranged for workers to expand the small New Rochelle dwelling. They all moved into the shingled saltbox cottage in the early summer of 1804. If he thought this was going to be easy, reality suddenly hit him between the eyes. For one thing, Madame de Bonneville had always had her own servants. Not only did she not pitch in around the house, she actually complained about the accommodations. She finally returned to New York, visiting her boys only on weekends.

To make matters worse, Paine did not know anything about farming. Frankly, he was like a duck out of water. Because of his inexperience, he received no income from his farm. To make matters worse, he had to discharge his troublesome farmhand. The former employee got drunk one day and shot at the founding father through the living room window. Although the man was arrested, Paine did not press charges. That portion of the press hostile to his ideas picked up the story and concluded that Paine was so thoroughly despised in his native land that he was not safe anywhere in the entire country.

He made things a little easier for himself by selling sixty-one acres of his land and hiring a woman as a cook and her husband as a farmhand. This enabled him to stay in the cottage until 1806, although he did spend some of the winter in New York City.

In July 1806 he suffered an attack of apoplexy (today simply known as stroke). His health declined, and he once again rented his farm to others. He lived for a while at the Bayeau Tavern, then located just across North Avenue from where the Paine Cottage now sits. Beginning in July 1808, he lived in New York City. He died in June 1809. Only a few people attended his New Rochelle funeral.

In the cottage the Paine Room contains two chairs used by the writer when he boarded at Bayeau Tavern and a stove presented by Benjamin Franklin. The wax figure of the famous man is very lifelike and is sure to engender a spooky feeling in the viewer.

Paine Monument

Corner of North and Paine avenues, New Rochelle, NY

This monument is just north of the Thomas Paine Cottage. It was originally erected in 1839 and was repaired and rededicated in 1881. A piece of the author's skull and a lock of his hair are under the monument.

Why just pieces of the man? The answer is involved, but very interesting. The Englishman William Cobbett dug up the grave and took the coffin to his native country in order to place it in a splendid monument. He did this to atone for his former attacks on the author. He also had the harebrained scheme of using the body to incite the populace into a frenzy in order to force a change in the British government. Tragically, the monument was never erected. Cobbett willed the coffin to his son. Some sources say the container was auctioned off. At this point, history loses track of the coffin. No one knows what happened to Paine's body.

Thomas Paine Historical Association Museum

983 North Avenue, corner of North Avenue and Valley Road, New Rochelle, NY (Open Fri–Sun 2–5, all year; or by appointment)

This building houses the Huguenot–Thomas Paine Historical Association's collection of items dealing with the Huguenot settlement of New Rochelle and with Thomas Paine. A few items owned by the writer are on display. The museum also has information on onetime resident Jacob Leisler, discussed in the section on the lords of the manor.

Other Sites to Visit

See the section on Sleepy Hollow territory and visit Washington's Headquarters for the Battle of White Plains (Virginia Road just north of the intersection with Washington Avenue in North White Plains). Visit Fort Lee Historical Park located at Hudson Terrace, south of the George Washington Bridge, Fort Lee.

Low Point and Return

The loss of Forts Washington and Lee tarnished George Washington's reputation. At this low point he was vulnerable to others vying for his position. Major General Charles Lee tried to take advantage of the situation by asking New England authorities to send reinforcements directly to him rather than the commander in chief. This opportunist was a former officer in the British army who had just recently immigrated to America. He considered himself a military genius much better qualified than Washington to lead. Furthermore, he felt that only his recent immigrant status kept him from his rightful place. Looking something like Ichabod Crane, he was a strange man in his personal habits. His clothes and body were always dirty and his language similarly so. His pack of yelping dogs always closely followed him.

While at Fort Lee, Washington had ordered Major General Lee to bring his forces to New Jersey. The junior officer disobeyed, reasoning that he could damage the British if allowed to stay in New York. Failing to inflict any damage, the ambitious Lee finally brought his troops across the Hudson. Fortunately for Washington, the British captured Lee in Basking Ridge, New Jersey. The great egotist had stepped out from the protection of his forces for a night on the town, flirting with a local tavern woman.

With or without Lee, the American forces gradually had to retreat across New Jersey and into Pennsylvania. The Delaware River became a blessing, because the Americans took the precautionary measure of gathering everything that would float on the Pennsylvania side of the river. When the British arrived shortly afterward, they could find no boats at all.

Now that his troops had a respite from battle, the commander in chief pondered his situation. He knew he had to have a bold victory immediately because most of his men's enlistments would end on December 31, 1776. He also knew that the country's commitment to continue the war would wane without some battlefield success. So, he decided to hit the Hessian troops stationed in Trenton when they would least expect battle: the day after Christmas.

A visit to Trenton itself is easily an all-day trip. Besides the battle sites, there are the state capitol building and the state museum to see.

Battle of Trenton

Following Washington's famous crossing of the Delaware, there were actually two battles at Trenton. The first battle involved completely encircling Trenton; the second was a defensive battle to fend off the encroaching British. The encirclement of Trenton was not as difficult as it may sound. The town only had two main streets, King and Queen (present-day Broad and Warren) streets, which both ran north-south. General Nathanael Greene had the responsibility for securing the north end of town, and General John Sullivan the south end.

At the north end General Hugh Mercer, coming from the northwest, would attack the Hessian headquarters located halfway down Broad Street. General Henry Knox was to set up his artillery at the north end of the two streets. And William Alexander Stirling, Adam Stephen, and Matthias Fermoy were to work their way to the northeast side of town to cover any possible escape via the apple orchard on the east side of town.

At the south end General Sullivan would attack the Old Barracks, located at the end of Broad Street, while John Glover was to proceed across Assunpink Creek at the southern end of town to cover the southeast escape routes.

The Americans took the Hessians completely by surprise. The Germans had celebrated Christmas Day with light drinking and card playing. They did hear firing as the Americans pushed in the pickets, but by the time they started preparing for battle, the Americans were already on top of them.

The Hessian commander, Colonel Johann Rall, had drunk a great deal of wine while attending a grand dinner at Trenton Tavern. He then played cards all night at the home of Trenton's leading merchant. During the evening, he received a note from a local Loyalist farmer saying that the Americans were planning an attack, but slipped it into his vest pocket without reading it. On the morning of December 26, 1776, a Hessian lieutenant awakened the commander with the report of gunfire. Just as Rall was mounting his horse, an American cannon blasted forth at the head of Broad Street where Battle Monument now stands.

Battle Monument

Five Points intersection of North Broad and Warren streets and Brunswick, Pennington, and Princeton avenues (take U.S. 1, head west on Perry Street, turn right on North Broad Street driving north), Trenton NJ (Open Wed–Sun, all year, with elevator service to the observation platform)

Battle Monument is a tall column surmounted by a statue of Washington and an observation platform. Thomas Eakins, the great Philadelphia realist painter, made the monument's bronze plaques.

This is the spot where the Americans under the direction of Henry Knox set up their artillery. From here the cannon raked the two main streets. The artillery fire was devastating, mowing down the Hessians as they tried to organize themselves.

St. Michael's Episcopal Church

Warren Street, near Perry Street, Trenton, NJ

This church is easy to spot because of its crenellated roof in Norman architectural style. Buried here is Pauline Joseph Ann Holton, the child born to the exiled Joseph Bonaparte and his beautiful Quaker mistress, Annette Savage.

The Hessian commander tried to form his troops behind this church, away from the raking fire of the cannon. But he also had to contend with musket fire from American infantry under General Mercer. Mercer's force came into town just behind Rall's own headquarters (across the street from St. Michael's). The embattled commander decided the only way to get away from the firestorm was to move his troops to the apple orchard on the east side of town. He hoped the orchard would offer some cover and a possible escape route via the road to Princeton. However, this route was cut off by the troops of Stirling, Stephen, and Fermoy.

St. Mary's Cathedral

157 North Warren Street, Trenton, NJ

A great deal of the fighting occurred on this spot. Hessian soldiers moved the wounded Rall to a house that formerly stood here. He died from his wounds with the still-unread note about the coming American attack in his vest pocket.

The Hessians sought a southern escape route at the bridge over Assunpink Creek, but this route was also blocked—this time by Sullivan's forces. With all possible escape routes covered by the Americans, the enemy finally surrendered.

Old Barracks

Corner of Barrack Street and West State Street, immediately south of the New Jersey State House, Trenton, NJ (Open Mon–Sat 10–5, Sun 1–5, all year)

American forces under Sullivan had the task of taking the southern end of Trenton. Their main target was the Old Barracks, where Hessian troops were quartered. This U-shaped fieldstone building, erected in 1758, was the sole survivor of five barracks erected in five different New Jersey towns because of citizen objections to quartering troops in private homes. The barracks housed up to three hundred men.

Sullivan's men emerged from behind the barracks and encountered Lieutenant General Wilhelm Freiherr von Knyphausen's regiment on the north yard. The Hessians got off only one volley before running for safety.

Old Barracks, Trenton, New Jersey

Forced east of town, they found themselves caught in the same trap as the Rall forces. They surrendered shortly after Rall's troops capitulated. In all, the Americans took nearly a thousand prisoners.

The Old Barracks is now a museum. You can see many interesting exhibits on the Battle of Trenton in particular and the Revolutionary War in general. The museum has one of the Washington triumphal arches—one of thirteen placed along present West Front Street to honor Washington as he rode to New York City for his presidential inauguration.

The British now thought they had the Americans in a trap. General Charles Cornwallis felt certain he could pin Washington up against the Delaware River and finish off the rebels. If anyone could do it, it would be Cornwallis, the best English general in America. He was a serious, hardworking, devoted family man, who was very humane to his troops (for which they loved him). If he had a serious flaw, it was his tendency not to press the initiative.

To trap the Americans, he moved 5,500 troops from Princeton to Trenton. He met stiff resistance from a delaying force under Colonel Edward Hand (visit his house in Lancaster, Pennsylvania). Arriving in Trenton on January 2, 1777, he unsuccessfully tried to cross Assunpink Creek three times to get at the enemy defending the south side of the small stream. With nightfall nearing he called off the attack, confident he would defeat the Americans in the morning.

Douglass House

Intersection of Front and Montgomery streets, Trenton, NJ (Open Mon–Sat 10–4, Sun 1–4, all year)

The original site of this house, built around 1766, was on South Broad Street, where a Lutheran church now stands. Here, on the evening of January 2, Washington conferred with his officers and decided to escape the British trap. Present at the meeting were John Sullivan, Nathanael Greene, John Cadwalader, Hugh Mercer, James Ewing, Arthur St. Clair, Philemon Dickinson, Joseph Reed, Edward Hand, John Stark, Thomas Mifflin, Adam Stephen, and Henry Knox. The British delay gave Washington the chance to escape. The commander in chief left a detachment to keep the campfires burning, while the main army slipped away towards Princeton.

Behind the Douglass House is a statue of Washington, and behind the statue is Assunpink Creek. A sign indicates that the Second Battle of Trenton, January 2, 1776, was fought on the creek banks.

William Trent House

15 Market Street, near the intersection with South Warren Street, close to the Delaware River at Bridge Street, Trenton, NJ (Open Mon–Sat 10–4, Sun 1–4, all year)

This two-story brick Georgian house is the city's oldest. It was built in 1719 by William Trent (for whom Trenton is named). Trent was a Scottish immigrant who became a wealthy Philadelphia merchant and Speaker of the Pennsylvania General Assembly. He tried to develop the town of Trenton, but died in 1724 leaving it very incomplete. The guide told us that he owned a ship in partnership with William Penn and James Logan and that for a short time he owned Philadelphia's Slate Roof House, in which Penn once resided.

Lewis Morris, the first royal governor of New Jersey, lived in the mansion for the last four years of his service. During the battles of Trenton, the house was owned by Dr. William Bryant, a Loyalist, who lived here from 1769 to 1778. He had tried to warn Rall of the impending attack. Later, he treated the wounded of both sides at the Old Barracks. Generals Washington, Greene, and Sullivan were just a few of the guests at the Trent house.

A later owner of the house (1778–1782) was Colonel John Cox, who came here after selling the iron works at Batsto (see the section on iron villages). Mrs. Cox was a friend of Mrs. Washington's. General Wayne stayed here in 1781 while negotiating with Pennsylvania Line troops from Morristown to end their mutiny. Judge Philemon Dickerson made the house his home from 1835 to 1838. He was elected governor in 1836. From 1854 to 1857 another governor lived here, the former Navy man Rodman Price.

In the parlor and dining room of the house there are many beautiful examples of English William and Mary–style furniture. You can climb into the cupola on top of the house. When we were there it was so foggy we could not see much. We could barely make out the Delaware River to the west. The view to the east is blocked by a huge office building.

Other Sites to Visit

While in the capital of New Jersey, visit the State House. Also be sure to see the New Jersey State Museum at 205 West State Street.

You can follow the action of Washington's famous crossing at two Delaware River parks, one on the Pennsylvania side (Washington Crossing Historic Park, along PA 32 between Yardley and New Hope), and the other on the New Jersey side (Washington Crossing State Park, County Route 546, eight miles above Trenton).

Battle of Princeton

In this section we visit Princeton Battlefield Park and the older part of Princeton University. This tour will take a full day, especially if you take the time to walk along the main street (Nassau Street) and partake in the wonderful college-town atmosphere.

In the previous section we followed Washington as he slipped away from the British trap at Trenton. The commander's next move was against British forces in Princeton.

The town began with another name. The site, settled by Quakers in the 1680s, was originally called Stony Brook after a small stream south of the town. The name of Prince's Town was adopted in 1724. Located midway between New York and Philadelphia, it prospered as a popular stopover for travelers.

Princeton Battlefield

500 Mercer Street just north of the intersection with Quaker Road (reachable off U.S. 1 at the Quaker Bridge Road exit heading north, then a right turn onto Quaker Road, and another right turn onto Mercer Street), Princeton Battlefield State Park, Princeton, NJ

Walk to the flagpole to find the tile map of the battle. This will help orient you to the battlefield. If you draw a battle clock (without the hands) with 12:00 at due north, you will more readily be able to follow the action. Place the apple orchard at 1:00, the William Clark barn at 1:30, Moulder's guns and the main American army at 5:00, the Thomas Clark house at 6:00, the Quaker Meeting House at 7:00, Mercer's troops at 8:00, the bridge over Stony Brook at 10:30, and the British attack at 12:00.

Now for a description of the battle. Washington escaped from the trap at Trenton by way of what is now Hamilton Avenue. He headed along Quaker Road toward Princeton. On the morning of January 3, the American forces were southeast of the present battlefield park. Before marching into Princeton, Washington talked with General Hugh Mercer. Mercer was the son of a Scots minister and had studied medicine in Aberdeen. He came to America and met Washington when both men served in the French and Indian War. The Scotsman then moved to Virginia and established himself as a pharmacist and doctor.

The American commander ordered Mercer to follow the course of Stony Brook and destroy a bridge across that stream so the British in Princeton could not use it as an escape route. Ironically, just moments before, British troops under Lieutenant Colonel Charles Mawhood had crossed this very bridge on their march away from Princeton. They spotted the main body of Washington's forces heading north toward Princeton. They turned around to head back to town, still unaware of the existence of Mercer's troops.

Mercer, heading along Stony Brook, saw Mawhood's forces and tried to intercept them. Finding he could not catch them, the general marched through the apple orchard, hoping to link up with the main American force.

Mawhood, now informed that American troops (under Mercer) were behind him, sent part of his force ahead to catch up with the main American army, while he led his troops against the smaller rebel force. The engagement started in the apple orchard with the British firing on Mercer's men. A bayonet charge forced the Americans (few of whom had bayonets) to to flee.

Mercer himself retreated to a point about fifty yards from a barn belonging to William Clark, whose home was adjacent to the apple orchard. There he found himself surrounded by British troops. They ordered the general to surrender, but he only slashed at them with his sword. The troops then bayoneted him and left him for dead.

At this time, American troops under Cadwalader approached from a wooded ridge where the Thomas Clark house stands. In addition, Captain Joseph Moulder, returning from the main army, got two cannons in position near the house and opened fire. This bought the Americans just enough time for Washington to arrive with the main body of troops. The tall Virginian rode to the front to rally the troops. An American officer reported that, as the enemy prepared to fire, he closed his eyes to avoid seeing his commander shot from his horse. When he opened his eyes, he was thrilled and amazed that the general was still on horseback urging his men forward. Reinforced by fresh troops, the Americans attacked. This time the British lines broke and the British soldiers ran from the battlefield.

A few of Mawhood's troops who had headed back towards Princeton took up positions in Princeton University's Nassau Hall. American Lieutenant Alexander Hamilton and Captain Moulder wheeled up several cannons

Room in which General Mercer died, Thomas Clark House, Princeton, New Jersey

and began firing at the building. Several troops broke down the door, and the British inside surrendered.

The bayoneted General Mercer was taken to the Thomas Clark house. Washington sent his nephew, Major George Lewis, to help attend him. A British surgeon examined the wounded man and declared that he would recover. However, the wounded general had been an army surgeon himself and knew the diagnosis to be incorrect. According to Frederick English, author of *General Hugh Mercer: Forgotten Hero of the American Revolution,* the general told Major Lewis: "Raise up my right arm, George, and this gentleman will there discover the smallest of my wounds, but which will prove the most fatal. Yes, sir, that is a fellow that will very soon do my business."

The famous Philadelphia patriot Dr. Benjamin Rush arrived to examine him. It was useless. No doctor could help him. It took nine days, but he finally died on January 12, 1777. At the house his bloodstains are still visible.

The general's body was used to arouse the people of Philadelphia to a pitch of war fever when it was exhibited in an upper room of City Tavern. The mutilated corpse had seven bayonet wounds, five in the chest and abdomen and two to the head.

In all, eighty-six British were killed or wounded and about two hundred were captured. Only forty-four Americans were killed. From the low point of being pushed all the way into Pennsylvania, Washington had now rallied and won two quick victories. Now he could retire to winter quarters at Morristown and rest a bit easier.

A short walk from the Thomas Clark house brings you to the Stony

Brook Quaker Meeting House, which was used as a temporary hospital for the wounded. In the cemetery nearby is a monument to Richard Stockton, who you will meet below.

Princeton Battle Monument

West end of Nassau Street, before it merges into Stockton Street, at intersection of Bayard Lane, Stockton Street, and Nassau Street, Princeton, NJ

This fifty-foot marble sculpture depicts Washington leading his troops and the mortally wounded Mercer. Thomas Hastings designed the sculpture, and Frederick MacMonnies sculpted it in 1922.

Nassau Hall

Nassau Street (Route 27) near the intersection with Witherspoon Street, Princeton University, Princeton, NJ (Arrange tours through the Orange Key Service located nearby in the President's House [see below])

Princeton is perhaps best known for Princeton University, which settled in the town in 1756. One of the best-known buildings of the university is old Nassau Hall, which saw some action during the Battle of Princeton.

Princeton was just one of the colleges (others were Brown University and Dartmouth) founded as a result of the Great Awakening, which began in the 1730s. This religious revival swept through the colonies, attracting those persons less economically well off with its emphasis on the more emotional, personal side of religion. During this revivalist period, the Presbyterians split between prorevivalists (referred to as New Lights) and antirevivalists (labeled Old Lights). The New Lights decided to establish their own college, called the College of New Jersey. It opened at Elizabeth Town (now Elizabeth) in 1747. In order to obtain a charter from the Anglican governor of New Jersey, the founders added a clause that promised equal education to young men of every denomination.

Less than five months after the founding of the college, its first president, Jonathan Dickinson, died. Another of the founders of the college, Aaron Burr, Sr. (father of Aaron Burr, who shot Alexander Hamilton in a duel, and son-in-law to the Great Awakening preacher Jonathan Edwards), was chosen president of the college. Since Burr was a pastor of the Newark Presbyterian Church, the college moved to Newark.

The new location did not seem central enough, and so another location was sought. Among others, John Stockton, one of six sons of Richard Stockton, signed a bond for a thousand pounds to make sure the college came to Princeton.

In the fall of 1756, college president Burr and seventy undergraduates moved into Nassau Hall. Robert Smith of Philadelphia built the hall around

1755. The building has been remodeled twice after fires: the first remodeling by Benjamin Latrobe and the second by John Notman, who added the towering cupola. New Jersey governor Jonathan Belcher named Nassau Hall in honor of "the immortal memory of the Glorious King William III" of the House of Nassau.

Nassau Hall has had a long and distinguished career. The year after its completion, President Burr died. His father-in-law, Jonathan Edwards, succeeded him, but a year later he too died. In 1776 the first legislature of the state of New Jersey convened here, and the first state governor (William Livingston) was inducted.

During the retreat from New York in the Revolutionary War, Washington left Lord Stirling and twelve hundred men in Princeton to guard against a sudden cavalry attack. Some of the American soldiers billeted in the hall. The students of the College of New Jersey, as well as the American troops, left as the British approached. The British occupied Princeton, and the regiment quartered in the hall stabled their horses in the basement and stripped the library of books.

As mentioned earlier, American cannon fire slightly damaged the building at the end of the Battle of Princeton. In the rear of the building, near the roofline, you can see where the cannonball hit.

Several years after the Battle of Princeton the British relinquished New Jersey. From June to November 1783, the Continental Congress sat in Nassau Hall. Elias Boudinot, president of the United States in Congress Assembled (i.e., president of Congress), moved the Congress here following several humiliations in Philadelphia when the state of Pennsylvania was unable to provide protection for Congress from American troops demanding their pay. (Visit Boudinot's home in Elizabeth, New Jersey.) During the Princeton session, Congress thanked Washington in person for his conduct of the war and received news that the Treaty of Peace had been signed.

The old prayer hall in the building is now used for meetings of the faculty and Board of Trustees, as well as other gatherings. It contains portraits of Princeton presidents, prominent graduates, and early trustees. One of the more interesting portraits, by Charles Wilson Peale, shows Washington at the Battle of Princeton with Nassau Hall in the background.

President's House

Next to Nassau Hall, Princeton University, Princeton, NJ (private)

Next to Nassau Hall is the home built for the university presidents. John Witherspoon was the first president to occupy it. Besides being college president, he was a member of the Continental Congress, signer of the Declaration of Independence, and leader in the move to oust New Jersey Tory governor William Franklin, son of Benjamin Franklin. The Orange Key Service gives campus tours that start from this house.

Morven

**55 Stockton Street, between Library Place and Bayard Lane, Princeton, NJ
(Open Sat 10–1, Wed 10–2, all year)**

In 1754 John Stockton gave his son, Richard (the younger) a piece of
land, which Richard's wife, Annis, called Morven. Annis was the sister of Elias
Boudinot. Richard built a Georgian mansion on the land around 1755, the
same year Nassau Hall was built. He was one of six students to graduate from
the first class of the College of New Jersey in 1748, while it was still located at
Newark. As one of the signers of the Declaration of Independence, he was
imprisoned and brutally treated. Forced to sign a loyalty oath—a deed that
brought him much criticism from American patriots—he was freed. The
poor man died of cancer before the war ended.

During the American Revolution, British General Cornwallis seized
Morven for his headquarters. As he withdrew, his troops looted, defaced,
and partially burned the mansion. In 1783, when the Continental Congress
met in Princeton, Boudinot made the mansion his headquarters. Here the
American leaders gathered to celebrate the signing of the treaty ending the
war. Washington, at nearby Rocky Hill, was a frequent visitor.

Jumping ahead in time, another famous resident of Morven was Robert
Field Stockton, the first president of the Delaware and Raritan Canal of New
Jersey. As commander of United States naval forces in the Pacific, he helped
"free" California from Mexico.

In January of 1954 Governor Walter E. and Mrs. Edge deeded the property to New Jersey. A committee appointed by Governor Robert Meyner
voted to make it the official governor's residence. It is not at present serving
in this capacity.

Princeton Cemetery

Corner of Witherspoon and Wiggins streets, Princeton, NJ

This cemetery contains the graves of Aaron Burr, Sr., Aaron Burr, Jr.,
President Grover Cleveland, Jonathan Edwards, and Paul Tulane (founder of
Tulane University). Across from the cemetery at 110 Witherspoon Street
(corner of Green and Witherspoon streets) is the childhood home of Paul
Robeson, African-American concert artist, actor, and political activist.

Bainbridge House

**158 Nassau Street, at the corner of Nassau and Vandeventer streets, Prince-
ton, NJ (Open Tues–Sun 12–4, all year)**

Commodore William Bainbridge, who in the War of 1812 commanded
the USS *Constitution* (known as "Old Ironsides"), was born in this house

built by the Stockton family. Bainbridge is considered the founder of the modern navy, and eight ships have been named for him. The house served as British General Howe's headquarters in the fall of 1776. Soon after the battle at Princeton, the Bainbridge family had to leave because of their Loyalist sympathies. In 1783 the building housed members of the Continental Congress.

It is now home to the Historical Society of Princeton. The Society has placed antiques, including a portrait of Commodore Bainbridge, in period rooms. Many of the furnishings are from the Boudinot collection of Princeton University. Pick up a walking-tour map of Princeton here.

Drumthwacket

344 Stockton Street (three blocks past Elm Road), Princeton, NJ (Open Wed 12–2; all year)

This house was built around 1835 for Governor Charles Smith Olden. The Scottish name means "wooded hill." One of the university's major benefactors, Moses Taylor Pyne, lived here. At that time it became a center for the social life of the university. The state of New Jersey recently acquired it as a residence for its governors.

Other Sites to Visit

See the section on Woodrow Wilson for other sites to see in Princeton. Nearby, in the town of Rocky Hill, is Rockingham. In 1783 this white clapboard farmhouse served as Washington's headquarters. At that time the Continental Congress was in Princeton deliberating the final peace treaty with England. The house contains authentic furnishings of the period, the majority of which date from before Washington's stay.

10

The British Take Philadelphia

The British high command wanted General William Howe's forces in New York City to support General John Burgoyne's invasion of the colonies from Canada. The overall plan was to sever New England from the rest of the colonies by gaining control of the entire Hudson River valley. The plan was a good one, but Howe did not receive his orders until it was too late. He had already put into effect his plan to capture Philadelphia. The British needed to concentrate their strength, but instead they spread it out—too thinly, as would ultimately be demonstrated. The foiled strategy resulted in a three-way split of their forces—in the Hudson River valley, New York City, and Philadelphia.

There were many battles connected with the British occupation of Philadelphia. This chapter traces the major actions from the Battle of Brandywine in September 1777 to the Valley Forge encampment during the winter of 1777–1778.

Battle of Brandywine

Brandywine Battlefield Park itself contains only fifty acres around Washington's and Lafayette's headquarters. The battle raged over a much larger area. To see this larger area you have to be willing to use a map and drive to the other battle landmarks. If combined with a visit to the nearby art museum, the visit should take an entire day.

Howe wanted to approach Philadelphia overland from New York City. However, a defeat in New Jersey at the Battle of Short Hills foiled this plan. So the general decided to proceed with the attack by sea. On July 23, 1777, British forces sailed from New York for Philadelphia. Howe, intending to sail up the Delaware River, changed his plan when he received erroneous information that this passage was well defended. The British instead sailed into Chesapeake Bay and landed at Head of Elk (fifty-five miles from Philadelphia) on August 25. Marching toward the city, they met the Americans at Chadds Ford.

To help you imagine the battlefield, draw a clock. Washington's and Lafayette's headquarters are at 6:00. The American defensive line at Chadds Ford, just west of the two headquarters, extended from 7:00 to 8:30. The John Chadd house is located around 8:05. The British flanking attack extended from 10:00 to 12:00. The Birmingham Friends Meeting House is at 11:00. Dilworthtown is at 2:00 and the American escape route at 5:00.

The British encountered the American defensive positions along Brandywine Creek from Chadds Ford north to Brinton's Ford. As Howe approached, he decided to try a maneuver that had brought him success at the Battle of Long Island. He sent Knyphausen to attack the main American lines at Chadds Ford in order to make Washington think this was the main attack. Meanwhile, the bulk of the British army under Cornwallis would sweep north, cross the Brandywine, and come in behind the American right flank. The actual battle began on September 11 at 9:00 A.M.

Visitors' Center

Brandywine Battlefield Park, U.S. 1 between Routes 100 and 202, Chadds Ford, PA (Open Tues–Sat 10–4:30, Sun 12–4:30, all year)

The center has dioramas depicting battle scenes, along with a gift shop that sells guides to the battlefield area.

Washington's Headquarters

Brandywine Battlefield Park, Chadds Ford, PA (Open Tues–Sat 10–4:30, Sun 12–4:30, all year)

This building is a restoration of the house of the Quaker Benjamin Ring. Inside are life-sized figures of Generals Washington and Sullivan listening to farmer Thomas Cheyney as he brought news that the main British force had marched around the right flank of the Americans. Sullivan did not believe the farmer and was discourteous to him. When he agreed to let the farmer tell the story to Washington, the commander in chief was courteous, but also disbelieving. The staff officers just smiled at their visitor. They did not believe the story because they had been assured (incorrectly, as it would turn out) that there was no ford for twelve miles above the one covered by American troops. A scout should have been sent out to check on the farmer's story, but apparently the American officers were just too confident of their information.

Lafayette House

Brandywine Battlefield Park, Chadds Ford, PA (Open Tues–Sat 10–4:30, Sun 12–4:30, all year)

This house of Quakers Gideon and Sarah Gilpin is another restoration. It is a two-story stone house, typical of the area. Life-size figures portray

Lafayette House, Brandywine Battlefield Park, Chadds Ford, Pennsylvania

Lafayette sitting at a table being attended by a servant. In the coachhouse is the coach in which Lafayette rode during his 1825 tour of the United States.

John Chadd House

PA 100, one-quarter mile north of U.S. 1, Chadds Ford, PA (Open Fri–Sun 12–5, June–Aug; Sept–May by appointment)

This is a restoration of the two-story bluestone house that was originally built here in 1726. The Americans placed their artillery on the ridgeline behind it. Brandywine Creek is just to the west of the house. It is very difficult to see the creek or the opposite side, where the Hessian troops were located, due to the dense foliage. But this is as it was during the battle. Indeed, the artillery duel here was largely ineffective because the trees blocked a clear view and deflected the cannonballs. The Chadd House suffered some damage during the battle. The south wall has obviously been patched. The house is now a living-history museum. It has been restored, but retains its original oak floors and paneling.

Birmingham Friends Meeting House (private)

1245 Birmingham Road off Route 926, Chadds Ford, PA

Washington had been completely fooled by the Hessian attack at Chadds Ford. The commander in chief had even decided to counterattack this force. However, he had been gradually receiving more intelligence indicating a British end run (flanking attack). It took two and a half hours of crucial time before he finally figured out what was happening. Then he quickly canceled the counterattack and rushed troops to meet the oncoming British forces.

Fortunately for Washington, Howe's end run was taking longer than it had at the Battle of Long Island. By the time Howe and Cornwallis completed their flanking movement, it was 3:30 P.M. This delay had given Washington enough time to divert the American right wing from their positions along the Brandywine to new positions in the path of the oncoming British flanking movement (just below what is now Route 926). Fighting raged around the Birmingham Friends Meeting House, which was used as a hospital by both sides as possession of the building changed hands. Just north of the meetinghouse are battle monuments in honor of Lafayette, Casimir Pulaski, and a Colonel Taylor (a relative of the man who erected the monuments).

During the battle, the British forced the Americans back five times, and the Americans persistently regained their ground. But on the sixth enemy attack, they fell back and took up new defensive positions a short distance east of the meetinghouse. George Weedon's brigade arrived about 6:00 P.M. to reinforce this line. (There is a monument along Birmingham Road that marks the position of the second American line. Lafayette was wounded in the calf of his left leg just west of this monument.) The enemy forced the Americans back to a third defensive position at Dilworthtown, just a little northwest of the Dilworth Inn (built in 1758 and now open as a restaurant).

Meanwhile at Chadds Ford, General Anthony Wayne (known as "Mad Anthony") had been pushed back by Knyphausen to just west of Washington's headquarters. Indeed, the two separate British forces, under the Hessian and Cornwallis, virtually met together east and northeast of Lafayette's headquarters. At 8:00 P.M. Howe halted the action along Harvey Road. Under the cover of darkness, the American army retreated to Chester, with Wayne fighting a holding action to prevent the closing of the retreat route.

In all, 200 Americans were killed and 750 wounded, while 90 British were killed and 480 wounded. This American defeat cleared the way for the British march into Philadelphia. Washington apparently felt very ashamed of his handling of the battle. He had fallen for the same flanking trick that Howe had previously used. After the war, the commander in chief enjoyed discussing the battles in which he had participated. However, he never talked about the Battle of Brandywine.

Other Sites to Visit

While in the Chadds Ford area, visit the Brandywine River Museum on Route 1, which contains the art works of the Wyeth family, and the 1714 Barns-Brinton House, a restoration of a tavern one and one-half miles west of the art museum. Also see the sections on the Swedish settlements and the

Du Ponts of Delaware. Visit the Nathaniel Drake House, 602 West Front Street, Plainfield, to learn more about the Battle of Short Hills.

Battle of Germantown

There are so many homes to see in Germantown that it would take several days to see them all. Some of these houses, such as Stenton, are outstanding examples of architecture that can be visited without reference to the Battle of Germantown. You may want to pick the sites you are most interested in seeing. Many of the homes will be mentioned in the following account of the battle.

Although my description approaches Germantown from the perspective of the Revolutionary War battle, please note that it was the first Pennsylvania Dutch town. Francis Daniel Pastorius, agent for a group of German investors, came to Philadelphia in 1683 and was soon joined by thirteen families from the Crefeld area in the Rhineland. Pastorius and most of the original settlers were Quakers (although originally they were Mennonites). William Penn granted them land in the Germantown area for settlement.

And now to a description of the battle. Following the Battle of Brandywine, Washington sent General Wayne to threaten the British rear. The Pennsylvanian camped in the woods near the town of Paoli with a force of about 1,500 men. Unfortunately, the Tory Joseph Galloway informed the British of his position and a surprise attack using the bayonet inflicted 150 American casualties. Although the British took prisoners, the Americans referred to the battle as a massacre because of the bloody appearance of the dead and wounded and because they considered the bayonet an uncivilized weapon.

Now the British could move into Philadelphia. They did so on September 26, 1777. However, due to serious supply problems, they found their hold on the city to be rather tenuous. Their ships coming up the Delaware River were blocked by two American forts, Mifflin and Mercer. Howe also needed a great number of troops to keep open his supply route to Head of Elk, where he had landed to begin the Philadelphia campaign.

The main body of around nine thousand British troops encamped in and around Germantown. Others stayed in downtown Philadelphia. With the British forces spread out, Washington decided to move against the enemy at Germantown. The American army was at the present village of Schwenksville, sixteen miles away. On October 2, the American commander made camp at Worcester. His headquarters was the large stone farmhouse of Peter Wentz.

Peter Wentz Farmhouse

Shultz Road (from Exit 31 of the Northeast Extension of the Pennsylvania Turnpike, head east onto Sumneytown Pike, turn right onto Route 363 heading south, go under the Turnpike, turn left by the Central Schwenfelder Church, and left onto Schultz Road), Worcester, PA (Open Tues–Sat 10–4, Sun 1–4, all year)

The town of Worcester is northwest of Philadelphia. Therefore, it might be hard to see this house and Germantown on the same day. In 1758 Peter Wentz built the fieldstone farmhouse in the English Georgian style (with German touches). It was here that Washington planned the attack on Germantown. The commander in chief also used the house as his headquarters following the battle, from October 16 to October 21. The house museum offers a slide tape on the history of the farm, followed by a house tour. One of the rooms has been set up as Washington's office. The furniture in the house is of the period. Don't miss the traditional German five-plate heating stove in the dining room.

The battlefield itself is relatively easy to describe because most of the fighting occurred along just one road, Germantown Avenue, which runs northwest to southeast. Instead of drawing a battle clock, just draw a large **X** on a piece of paper (be sure to label the compass directions for the four ends of the figure). The British and Hessian troops at Market Square aligned themselves along the cross-street known as School House Lane (now Church Lane), which ran northeast to southwest. Generals Anthony Wayne and John Sullivan, heading southeast straight down Germantown Avenue, were to attack this main line of defense head-on. Nathanael Greene was to attack northeast and Generals William Smallwood and David Forman east of the British right wing. General John Armstrong was to come from the southwest and hit the enemy's left wing.

The plan here was just like that at Trenton. Washington wanted to surround the enemy forces. Unfortunately, Germantown consisted of more than just two streets, as was the case with Trenton. The plan was really too complicated to be carried out by amateur soldiers and officers. It involved too many separated troop columns with little or no contact with one another. Indeed, the column under Armstrong and columns under Smallwood and Forman were able to contribute little to the battle, since the distances involved were too great. These complicated movements were made all the worse by the foggy weather of October 4.

To follow the battle, travel to Mount Airy, the town north of Germantown.

Lutheran Theological Seminary

Germantown Avenue and Allen's Lane, just south of Spring Garden College (take Norristown Interchange 25 of I-276 and head south on the Germantown Pike, which becomes Germantown Avenue)

The Americans forced the British outposts located here to withdraw. The British put up a hasty skirmish line, but Wayne's brigade (using the bayonet unmercifully in seeking revenge for the defeat at Paoli) pushed them back. The British retreated along Germantown Avenue. Proceed down the avenue to the Chew House.

Cliveden (The Chew House)

6401 Germantown Avenue, bounded by Cliveden and Johnson streets, Germantown, PA (Open Tues–Sat 10–4, Sun 1–4, Apr–Dec; other times by appointment)

While the British retreated down Germantown Avenue, British Lieutenant Colonel Robert Musgrave threw six companies of his regiment into the Chew House. Wayne took his troops around the mansion and pressed against the main British line at School House Lane and Germantown Avenue.

Quaker Benjamin Chew, chief justice of the provincial supreme court before the Revolution, owned the house. He had studied law under the famous Philadelphia lawyer Andrew Hamilton. Suspecting Chew of being a Loyalist, the Americans confined him at Union Forge (now High Bridge), New Jersey. He had to sell his mid-Georgian house, but was able to buy it back eighteen years later. The most notable room in the house is the front entrance hall. Its focal point is a screen of Tuscan columns leading into a smaller hall, where the stairs are located. Notice the painting of the Lafayette reception held in the mansion in 1825 when the French hero returned to America to celebrate the revolutionary victories. In the sitting room, guests inscribed their names on the windowpanes with a diamond-point stylus.

Bilmeyer House (private)

6505–6507 Germantown Avenue, Germantown, PA

Washington conferred with his officers here on what to do about the British forces holed up in the Chew House. Unfortunately, General Knox advised that the house be taken. The bookseller turned artilleryman argued that, according to classical principles of war, it would be unmilitary to leave a "castle in our rear." This action denied valuable support to the Americans attacking the main British line. Washington directed the assault from the Bilmeyer House. It is said he observed the attack through a telescope from the top of a horse-mounting block.

Knox bombarded the house with cannon, but the balls simply bounced off the thick stone walls. Meanwhile, the British were killing a great many Americans. A precious half-hour was wasted in trying to take the citadel. Getting desperate, the Americans tried to burn the house. Major John White attempted to apply the torch to straw gathered before the door and received a bayonet thrust in the mouth for his efforts. He later died of his wound.

Upsala

6430 Germantown Avenue, across the road from Cliveden, Germantown, PA (Open Tues & Thurs 1–4, Apr–Dec; or by appointment)

This house did not exist during the battle, but it was in this vicinity that General Knox set up his artillery to fire at the Chew House. The Federal mansion was built in 1798 for John Johnson, a trustee of the Germantown Academy, which became the town's leading nineteenth-century educational institution. The house contains many Philadelphia pieces.

Johnson House (private)

6306 Germantown Avenue, Germantown, PA (open by appointment through the Germantown Mennonite Information Center)

This 1768 "Germantown Georgian" house, noted for its fine interior woodwork, was in the thick of the fighting and was badly damaged. The Johnsons hid in the cellar for protection. Mr. Johnson was a tanner.

Germantown Mennonite Church and Mennonite Information Center

6117 Germantown Avenue, Germantown, PA (Open Tues–Sat 10–12, 1–4, all year)

This 1770 stone building is the first Mennonite church established in North America. The first minister was William Rittenhouse (whose house is located at 207 Lincoln Drive in Fairmount Park). Here a group of local citizens ambushed a British column marching to battle, an action contrary to then-existing rules of war. Shooting from behind the wall, they mortally wounded British General James Agnew. The general died in the Grumblethorpe mansion. Adjacent to the meetinghouse is a combination bookstore and museum, the latter dealing with the congregation's history.

Home of William Shippen (private)

6043 Germantown Avenue, Germantown, PA

This house was also in the thick of the battle. It was the home of Dr. William Shippen, director-general of military hospitals under Washington. He was also the cousin of Judge Edward Shippen, who was the father-in-law of Edmund Bird of Ormiston and the father of Peggy, whose husband was Benedict Arnold.

Wyck House

6026 Germantown Avenue, Germantown, PA (Open Tues & Thur, Sat 1–4, Apr–Dec; or by appointment)

This 1690 house built by Swiss Quaker Hans Millan is Philadelphia's oldest standing house, owned by nine generations of the same Quaker family. It is really two stone houses (the second one built by daughter Margaret and her husband, Dirk Jansen) joined together on the second floor in the early 1700s and remodeled in 1824 by architect William Strickland. The architect changed the cartway into a beautiful central conservatory. The pieces in the house are eclectic, reflecting the eight generations of Millans who have lived in the house. Be sure to visit the gardens, noted for their many varieties of roses. During the battle the mansion served as a field hospital.

Old Green Tree Tavern (private)

6023 Germantown Avenue, Germantown, PA

This building marks the farthest penetration by Wayne's brigade.

Under Wayne's assault, the British retreated down Germantown Avenue. Suddenly, disaster struck. A part of Greene's command, coming in to attack the British right wing, wandered away from the rest of the troops and got in behind American troops attacking the British center. Suddenly Americans were firing at Americans; panic spread, and the troops started running from the battlefield. Thus, from the jaws of victory, defeat was snatched. The commander of the wandering American soldiers had been inebriated. After the battle he found himself court-martialed and cashiered.

The advancing British relieved the Chew House garrison. Fifty-three American dead lay on the ground, with another four sprawled on the doorsteps. In all 152 Americans were killed, 521 wounded, and 400 captured. A total of 70 British were killed, 450 wounded, and only 14 captured.

When the fighting ended, Washington sent a squad of soldiers to British headquarters. They brought with them a small dog whose collar was inscribed with the name of General Howe. The dog had accidently fallen into American hands.

Battle Monument

Vernon Park, Germantown Avenue, Germantown, PA

Standing in this park is the monument to the Battle of Germantown. The mansion in the park's center was built in 1803 and later purchased by John Wister. The owner named the park in honor of Washington's home at Mount Vernon.

Market Square

Intersection of Germantown Avenue and Church Lane, Germantown, PA

This square was early Germantown's marketplace. The location marks the center of the British line, which stretched along School House Lane, northeast and southwest of Market Square.

Deshler-Morris House

5442 Germantown Avenue, Germantown, PA (Open Tues–Sun 1–4, Apr–Dec; or by appointment)

Built by the wealthy India merchant David Deshler in 1772, this house was the headquarters of General Howe during the battle. In November 1793, during the yellow fever epidemic that hit Philadelphia when it was the nation's capital, Washington rented the house to escape the city. This makes the house the only "White House" still standing in which the president actually lived. Four cabinet meetings took place here. One of the discussions concerned the establishment of a military academy.

When Deshler died in 1792, Isaac Franks bought the property. In 1803 he sold it to John and Elliston Perot. Their eldest child and her husband, Samuel B. Morris, then purchased it. The estate remained in their family until 1949, when the National Park Service bought it. On the second floor is a room set up as an office. In the room is a map showing the western part of Pennsylvania. This was the time of the Whisky Rebellion of western farmers, upset over taxation of their product. The mahogany dining table is set with China-trade porcelain. This seems appropriate, since the Washingtons were known for having sumptuous formal dinners starting promptly at 4:00 P.M.

Grumblethorpe

5267 Germantown Avenue, Germantown, PA (Open Sat 1–4, all year)

This 1744 house built for merchant John Wister was the first summer home in Germantown. It is simpler in its exterior and interior than most of the Germantown mansions. It became the headquarters of British General

James Agnew, mortally wounded near the Mennonite Meeting House. He was brought here to die. Blood stains from the general can be seen on the floorboards of the northwest parlor.

Sally Wister, a young girl at the time, described in her diary the people and events associated with the house during the British occupation. Among other things, she mentions the British Grenadier, a life-size figure (now in the Germantown Museum) painted on a wooden panel, supposedly by Major John Andre, for the Meschianza—the pageant held by British officers in May 1778 as a farewell to Sir William Howe. Sally's father and a number of visiting American officers used the Grenadier to scare one Major Tilly, who had mentioned his anxiety about meeting the British in battle. The pranksters placed the figure near the front door, dimly lit by a lantern. They called Tilly to the door, while a hidden officer demanded to know if there were any rebels in the house. The poor major became so frightened that he ran out the rear door. While making his escape, he fell into a mill pond. His laughing comrades caught up with him, finally explaining the joke.

Stenton

Eighteenth Street and Windrim Avenue, Germantown, PA (Open Tues–Sat 1–4, Feb–Dec)

General Howe made his headquarters in this mansion. Its former owner was none other than James Logan, who in the first half of the 1700s was the dominant figure in Philadelphia. He was secretary to William Penn and one of the leaders of the proprietary party that opposed the Quaker party.

Logan had been a clergyman until he converted to Quakerism in 1671. He also tried his hand at teaching. Penn recognized the young man's talents. When the great Quaker leader left Pennsylvania for good, he appointed his secretary to be his legal agent in the colony, which meant that the young man would be secretary of the council, mayor of Philadelphia, chief justice, and acting governor. In this position he was able to mass a considerable fortune, mainly from the fur trade with the Indians.

Stenton was named after the birthplace of Logan's father. Workers completed this first Georgian-style building erected in the Delaware Valley in 1730. The mansion once sat on six hundred acres of land. The approach to the house was through a graceful corridor of hemlocks that made a lasting impression on visitors.

Logan was also a man of science and sponsored many scientific pursuits. It is said his collection of three thousand books was the finest scientific library in the colonies. He was devoted to botany and in 1737 published a botanical essay in Latin on his experiments with Indian corn. Ten years later it was translated and republished with an introduction by Dr. John Fothergill of London (who financed one of William Bartram's botanical expeditions). Logan also encouraged such men as John Bartram, the plant collector.

The rooms in the mansion reflect the three generations of Logans who lived at Stenton. One room, set up as Logan's office, contains his Pennsylvania walnut gateleg table of 1690–1730, as well as a terrestrial globe and a celestial globe (although the latter is not original to the house). Outside the room, notice the unusual brick floor in the entrance hall. The brick served to handle the great number of visitors. Among these were many Delaware Indians, who camped at the house on their way to Philadelphia. The master bedroom was downstairs because of the owner's bad hip. Upstairs are three bidets, the only ones I have seen in the region.

James Logan's son, William, added the kitchen and piazza. The son became an attorney for the Penn family and, starting in 1747, served for almost thirty years on the Provincial Council.

William's son, George, inherited the mansion upon the death of his parents. At the time, he was studying medicine in Edinburgh, Scotland. The young physician did not return to Stenton until the fall of 1780, at which time the mansion was in great decay. Unable to restore it because of his limited funds at the time, he lived in Philadelphia, where he practiced medicine. Three members of the Pinckney family, aristocrats from South Carolina, lived in the house while awaiting exchange as prisoners of war.

The physician decided in 1781 to abandon medicine for life at Stenton as a farmer. He gradually turned the estate into a model farm, adding a stone barn to the property. Fellow agriculturalists thought of him as the best farmer in Pennsylvania. Even Napoleon's brother, Joseph Bonaparte, living in exile in Bordentown, came to him for agricultural advice.

In addition to his interest in farming, George was intensely involved in politics. He served in the state legislature starting in 1786. The gentleman farmer became such an avid Republican (now the Democrats, but at that time the spokesmen for the agriculturalists), that he called for a revolution to control the growing power of the Federalists. For this, in 1791 the Society of Friends disowned him. Nevertheless, he was a man of peace who tried by private diplomacy to avert war, first with France in 1789 and later with England in 1810. The peace advocate served as a United States senator during Jefferson's administration. His wife, Deborah Logan, was the first woman member of the Pennsylvania Historical Society and published the Logan/Penn correspondence.

Other Sites to Visit

Visit the Paoli Memorial Grounds at Monument Avenue in Malvern. Ironically, General Wayne's home is just about four miles from the battlefield (visit Waynesborough at 2049 Waynesborough Road, Paoli vicinity).

The Germantown Historical Society Museum complex located at 5214 Germantown Avenue has a number of interesting exhibits, including ones on quilts and costumes. It also has the life-size figure of Andre's British Grenadier. Another mansion in the area to visit is Loudoun (4650 Germantown Avenue), the home of Philadelphia merchant Thomas Armat. At times, members of the Logan family occupied the house, since they were related to the Armat family by marriage. Also see the Victorian Ebenezer Maxwell house (at Tulpehocken and Green streets). In addition, pay a visit to Fort Mifflin (Fort Mifflin Road, near the Philadelphia Airport) and the earthwork remains of Fort Mercer (west end of Hessian Avenue off US 130, Red Bank, New Jersey).

Valley Forge

A tour of Washington's winter encampment following the Philadelphia campaign should take about half a day. The huge open area sits on a plateau. The visitor drives around the park stopping at various pull-offs.

Washington tried to end the British occupation of Philadelphia through actions at Brandywine, Paoli, Germantown, and Forts Mifflin and Mercer. Failing to stop the enemy, he decided to set up winter quarters at White-marsh, not far from Germantown. The position proved too close to the British, however, for the enemy sent forces against the Americans. Fortunately, the Continentals were forewarned and prepared themselves. They stopped the British at the Battle of Whitemarsh, but the actions proved that the area was just too close to Philadelphia.

With winter approaching, Washington had to find shelter for his men. About twenty miles northwest of Philadelphia is a hilly, wooded area on high ground. Here a town of a dozen or so buildings had grown up around a small charcoal furnace that produced iron. Around ten thousand American troops, many with only rags to cover their feet, marched eight days from Whitemarsh to Valley Forge, arriving on December 19, 1777. Washington later remarked that one could have traced the army's trek by the blood from the men's feet.

There was so much disease among the troops that hospitals had to be established in the surrounding towns of Yellow Springs, Bethlehem, Ephrata, and Lititz. Fully twenty-five hundred, or 25 percent, of the men were lost to disease, either through death or serious illness. In addition, there was the ever-present problem of desertion. Of the nine or ten thousand men who reached Valley Forge, around three thousand deserted.

The men built nine hundred huts laid out in orderly streets and sections by military unit. The sixteen-feet-long-by-fourteen-feet-wide structures could house as many as twelve men apiece. In most of the cabins the floor was sunk a couple of feet into the ground. While this made the huts warmer, it also made them damp. There were no boards for the roofs, so the men used straw, earth, and clay for caulking. This, however, did not stop the constant leaks during rain or thaw.

The winter of 1777–1778 was a comparatively mild one for the times. The first couple of months were the worst, with conditions rapidly improving with warmer weather. In the first months the men often had to eat *fire cake,* made by grilling a mixture of flour and water.

Valley Forge National Historical Park

Located three miles west of the Pennsylvania Turnpike (from the Valley Forge Interchange 24 of I-276, drive north on Route 363 to its junction with Route 23), Valley Forge, PA (Open daily 8:30–5, all year)

All of the sites listed below are located within Valley Forge National Historical Park.

General Washington's Headquarters

Valley Forge National Historical Park, Valley Forge, PA

This house was built for John Potts. At the beginning of the winter encampment period, Mrs. Deborah Hewes lived in the house. Washington lived in a large tent until she had time to move into a neighbor's house. The commander in chief used the house as his headquarters, staying here for six months. His wife visited him for a while. The park service has provided period furniture that reflects the minimal comforts available in the house at that time.

One of the biggest causes of worry for Washington while stationed here was what came to be known as the Conway Cabal. A number of political leaders, exasperated by the many defeats suffered by the commander on the battlefield, plotted to replace him with General Gates. Gates had been the winning commander at the Battle of Saratoga (although Benedict Arnold and others deserved more of the credit). Many felt he could do a better job than Washington. However, when the intrigue became public knowledge, the scheme blew up in the faces of the conspirators. Support rushed in for the embattled veteran from all sides. Ironically, the affair actually solidified Washington's position. He was now seen as indispensable.

As if Washington did not have enough problems, Major General Lee rejoined the army after his release in a prisoner exchange. On his first night back, he stayed in the Potts house in a small room behind Mrs. Washington's sitting room. A shocked Elias Boudinot discovered that the ingrate had brought "a miserable dirty hussy" (a British sergeant's wife) with him from Philadelphia and had slept with her that very night. As thanks for the hospitality shown him, Lee remarked that his host was not fit for command.

One piece of good news was that France had signed a treaty of alliance with the Americans in February. Cheers of "Long live the King of France!" went up from the troops.

Parade Ground

Valley Forge National Historical Park, Valley Forge, PA

One of the most important developments at Valley Forge was that the American troops received some excellent instruction in conventional military skills. Washington had long wished his troops to be trained and disciplined enough to fight in the conventional European style. His wish was delayed by the infighting of the Conway Cabal and until the arrival of Lieutenant General Baron von Steuben. The German was not really a baron and had not really held high military rank before. The commander in chief knew this, but also knew the man to be an excellent drillmaster. Von Steuben and some American officers worked out a simplified manual of arms. The troops also learned how to use the bayonet and how to maneuver in ranks. The importance of this training proved itself at the Battle of Monmouth in June 1778.

Washington Memorial Chapel

Valley Forge National Historical Park, Valley Forge, PA

The church has thirteen stained-glass windows that tell the story of the founding of the country.

Valley Forge Historical Society Museum

Valley Forge National Historical Park, Valley Forge, PA

Located on private property within the park, this museum has a collection of Revolutionary War memorabilia.

Other Sites to Visit

In Fort Washington, there are a number of places connected with the battle to visit: Fort Washington State Park at 500 Bethlehem Pike; the Clifton House near the intersection of Bethlehem Pike and Morris Road; and Hope Lodge at 553 Bethlehem Pike.

Very close to Valley Forge is Mill Grove, the first home in America of the famous ornithologist John James Audubon (1785–1851). To get to Mill Grove, take 363 north and turn left onto Audubon Road. Also visit Whitemarsh or nearby Philadelphia.

Last Activity in the North

Once the French had entered the war on the side of the Americans, the British decided that their troops in Philadelphia, under the command of General Howe, should be consolidated in New York under General Henry Clinton. Clinton proceeded to Philadelphia to lead the troops to New York, while Howe sailed for England.

The British troops stationed in Philadelphia marched across New Jersey headed for their troop ships at Sandy Hook. Learning of the move, General Washington with his troops at Valley Forge vowed to hinder it. In June 1778 the American army proceeded across New Jersey, eventually catching up with the British at the town of Freehold.

Battle of Monmouth

Washington gave the command of an advance force of four thousand men to General Lee, who had recently been released by the British from a very pleasant captivity. At first the great egotist was reluctant, feeling that American troops were no match for the highly trained British. He took command only after it had been offered to his junior officer, Lafayette.

Before starting the tour, stop at the Visitors' Center at Combs Hill for background information and a battlefield map. (From the Hightstown Exit 8 of the New Jersey Turnpike, travel east on Route 33, which goes directly to the battlefield, sandwiched between Route 527 and U.S. 9.) The visit could take more than half a day because the sites are separated from one another by substantial distances. If visiting all the sites, the trip will take an entire day. If time is limited, be sure to see the battle museum.

This is the most complicated Revolutionary War battlefield in the region because there were two main battle areas. The fighting began the morning of June 28, 1778, in the town of Freehold itself, which is considerably east of the Visitors' Center. The second battle area, where the afternoon's actions took place, is west of town along the former causeway (bridge) across Weamaconk Creek. The road over the creek (now County Route 522) connects the early, eastern part of the battlefield with the later, western part.

To better understand the action, draw a battle clock of the eastern area. Make the clock slightly oblong rather than round. At 12:00 is the western edge of Lake Topanemus (due north), at 2:00 is Weamaconk Creek, at 3:00 is Battle Monument, at 4:00 is St. Peter's Church and the Courthouse, at 5:30 is

General Clinton's headquarters (Covenhoven House), at 8:00 is Carr's House, and at 10:00 is Craig's House. Start your tour of the battlefield in the town of Freehold.

Site of the Old Courthouse

Northwest corner of Main and Court streets (from the Combs Hill Visitors' Center, turn left onto Route 33, left/north onto U.S. 9, right/east onto Route 522, and left/north onto Main), Freehold, NJ

This is the site of the old Monmouth County Courthouse. On June 28, 1778, Lee arrived at this location. From this position he could see in the distance the enemy rearguard of about five hundred men marching out of town. He ordered Wayne to attack. As the Pennsylvanian did so, a large part of the British army turned around to join the fight. Seeing the gathering enemy forces, the American commander ordered a retreat back to Freehold.

The American forces spread out north to south, with Scott in the north at Lake Topanemus, Wayne in the south next to Weamaconk Creek, and Lee in the middle. British forces under General Cornwallis succeeded in routing Scott.

Monmouth Battle Monument

Across the street from the Monmouth County Historical Association Museum at 70 Court Street, Freehold, NJ

Scott retreated south and took up position near this present-day ninety-four-foot shaft depicting scenes from the battle. Wayne soon joined him. Fearing they would be surrounded, they retreated. Wayne made his way to the Carr house, while Scott escaped past Craig's house.

Monmouth County Historical Association

70 Court Street, Freehold, NJ (Open Tues–Sat 10–4, Sun 1–4, all year)

Located across from Battle Monument, this museum contains some battle relics. It also has collections of furniture, paintings, and decorative arts of all periods. Don't miss seeing the court-martial papers of General Lee and the Leutze painting of the battle (German artist Emanuel Leutze also painted *Washington Crossing the Delaware*).

St. Peter's Church

33 Throckmorton Street, Freehold, NJ

Lee retreated even farther south than Scott and Wayne to St. Peter's Church near the center of town. As British troops descended on the town, he decided to retreat west to the area around Carr's House. St. Peter's Church used to be a Quaker meetinghouse. The congregation converted to Episcopalianism under the influence of the Quaker-turned-Episcopalian George Keith.

Now turn to the action in the area to the west. Imagine the western battlefield as a clock with the causeway in the center. Craig House is at 2:00, Carr's House at 4:00, General Greene's cannon at 7:00, and General Stirling's cannon at 10:00.

Site of Carr's House (private)

U.S. 9, south of state highway #33 (now owned by Bell Laboratories), Freehold, NJ

From the center of town, Lee retreated to Carr's House. General Wayne joined him there. Meanwhile, a third of the American forces under Scott, who had been with Wayne on Monument Hill, retreated north of Weamaconk Creek past Craig House (see below) and thus took themselves out of the picture. With a third of his forces absent, Lee decided to retreat farther to the northwest across the causeway.

As Lee reached the end of the causeway, he was met by General Washington coming up with the main American army. In a rage, Washington demanded to know the reason for such disorder. Stunned, the retreating general blurted out a series of lame excuses, ending with the accusation that the whole plan had been flawed and against his better judgment. Reaching the end of his patience, the commander in chief shouted that if the major general had felt that way he never should have undertaken the assignment. The mortified Lee did as his superior officer commanded, taking his troops back toward the British. He and Wayne delayed the enemy long enough for Washington to get the rest of the troops into position. There is a plaque on a boulder on the side of Country Road 522 marking the approximate spot of this action.

Combs Hill Visitors' Center

Route 33, three miles from Freehold, NJ (Open Daily 9–4:30, all year)

Here on Combs Hill, American General Greene fired his cannon at the British off to the northeast (by the causeway). At the same time, General Stirling also fired on the British from his position overlooking the causeway.

Molly Pitcher Well

Southeast corner of Wemrock Road and County Route 522, Freehold, NJ

Near this well the ten pieces of cannon under General Stirling were fired at the British across the causeway in a two-hour artillery duel. The day was so hot that many men and horses dropped dead of dehydration.

During the duel, Molly Hays, whose husband manned one of the cannons, carried water to the crews. In the heat of the battle her wounded husband fell to the ground. The officer in charge ordered the cannon to be removed. Molly shouted to let the cannon stay, that she would take her husband's place. She pitched in to fire the weapon. After the battle, Washington personally commended this brave woman, who has come to be known at Molly Pitcher. Actually, there were many Mollys who carried water to the cannoneers. The origin of the well-known name came from the cries of hot, exhausted, thirsty men: "Molly! Pitcher!"

Following the cannon duel, the Americans under Wayne attacked across the causeway, only to be repulsed. The enemy then counterattacked. After two failures to cross the bridge, the British retreated to Carr's House as darkness fell. The following day, June 29, they left around midnight and marched to Sandy Hook, where they boarded ships for New York.

The Battle of Monmouth was a draw. The Americans lost around 70 dead, the British about 220. The most important aspect of the battle is that it showed how the training at Valley Forge had helped make better troops of the Americans. In this battle they met the enemy in traditional combat style and held their own.

Lee, still smarting from his public humiliation during the battle, charged Washington with incompetence and personal abusiveness. He demanded an army judgment of his conduct of the battle. He got it in a court-martial that found him guilty of disobeying orders and disrespect to the commander in chief. Suspended from command for a period of twelve months without pay, he never again saw service with the army. Washington must have breathed a sigh of relief at being rid of the man he felt had cheated him of a major victory.

Other sites to visit in connection with the battle are listed below.

Covenhoven House (General Clinton's Headquarters)

150 West Main Street, Freehold, NJ (Open Tues, Thur & Sun 1–4, Sat 10–4, June–Oct)

Located southwest of St. Peter's Church is the Covenhoven House. In 1752–1753 William Covenhoven built the large Georgian section of this oldest house in Freehold. British General Henry Clinton occupied it as his headquarters just prior to the battle. Following the war, sea captain William

Forman, along with his brothers and sisters, lived here. They welcomed Captain James Lawrence (of "Don't give up the ship" fame) of Burlington by strewing roses in his path.

The Tennent Church
Main Street, Tennent, NJ

The church is named for one of the preachers of the Great Awakening, Reverend William Tennent. He served the church for forty-three years and is buried beneath the center aisle. The graves of some of the men who fought in the Battle of Monmouth are in the cemetery. Lee's forces traveled by this church on their way to Freehold.

Craig House
Intersection of U.S. 9 and Schibanoff Road, Freehold, NJ (Tours available on summer weekends by reservation)

The American troops under General Scott retreated past this house.

Other Sites to Visit

Also located in Monmouth County is the Deserted Village of Allaire, an old iron village. At Long Branch, visit the Church of the Seven Presidents (1260 Ocean Avenue). You can also visit Sandy Hook and the Twin Lights in Highlands.

Winter Quarters at Morristown

Morristown, New Jersey, was home to Washington's army for many a winter, and there are several sites available for touring. Seeing all the sites requires an entire day. To make the outing even more enjoyable, there is a walking trail around the grounds at Jockey Hollow. Combining a leisurely stroll with stops at historic structures makes for a nice change of pace.

Washington's choice of Morristown was an excellent one. To the east, the Watchung Mountains provided a great defensive barrier against the British quartered in New York City. From Morristown the Americans could proceed in many different directions—north to protect the Hudson Highlands or south to protect Philadelphia. The enemy periodically tried to entice Washington to battle on flat ground east of the mountains or to break through the mountains, but they never succeeded.

The first time the Americans used Morristown was during the winter of

1776–1777, following Washington's victories at the Battles of Trenton and Princeton. Three thousand soldiers found lodging in the town and in the surrounding villages and farms scattered across northern New Jersey. Washington himself took up lodging at the Arnold Tavern on the north side of the Morristown Green.

The next two winter seasons the army quartered elsewhere. The winter of 1777–1778, following the Philadelphia campaign, found American troops quartered at Valley Forge. And, following the Battle of Monmouth, the problems of supply scarcities and inflation made it impossible for Washington to quarter his army in one camp for the winter of 1778–1779. Instead, the army hutted on both sides of the Hudson River, in a line stretching for some seventy miles through New York and New Jersey.

The main action in the north in 1779 consisted of the storming of Stony Point by men under the command of General Anthony Wayne. For the 1779–1780 winter quarters the army again returned to Morristown. This season's winter was the severest of the century. There were some twenty-eight snow falls between November 1779 and April 1780. At times the snow lay four feet deep. In this situation, transportation broke down and the army faced starvation. The troops here probably suffered more than those at Valley Forge. However, Morristown is not as well known, because the fighting season preceding the Valley Forge encampment was much more critical.

In the 1780–1781 winter season, only Pennsylvania Line troops wintered at Morristown. Most of the forces were at New Windsor, New York, just north of West Point. For the next two winter seasons the troops were mostly at New Windsor.

Morristown National Historical Park Visitors' Center

From I-80 Exit 43, travel south on I-287 to exit 32, left/south onto Ridgedale Avenue, left/north onto Morris Avenue driving past the center, circle around by turning left/south onto Lafayette Place, and left onto Washington Place (Open daily 9–5, all year)

Start the tour of the Morristown National Historical Park at the Visitors' Center. At the center they show a film on the hardships faced by the troops quartered in the vicinity. There are also displays of Revolutionary War items and dioramas of some of the key events of the winter encampments.

Ford Mansion

230 Morris Street at Washington Place, Morristown, NJ (Open daily 9–5, all year)

Next to the Visitors' Center is the Ford Mansion. Although Washington did not live lavishly, he had a definite preference for the better things in life. Therefore, wherever he went, he always chose the best available house in an area for his headquarters. The grandest house in Morristown was this Georgian house, built in the years 1772–1774. The original owner, Colonel Jacob Ford, Jr., died while serving his country in January 1777. Two years later, his widow offered the use of the mansion to George and Martha Washington. The commander in chief stayed here for almost seven months.

Be sure to see Washington's conference and dining room, which has a Chippendale mirror belonging to the Ford family, as well as a Chippendale desk. In General and Mrs. Washington's bedroom there is a carved Chinese Chippendale dressing table, a mahogany highboy, and a Queen Anne mirror.

Alexander Hamilton, one of Washington's aides, occupied a room in the mansion in 1781. The young man wanted to see action and felt, despite his repeated entreaties, that the commander in chief blocked him. Washington was known for both his personal reserve and his temper, and this behavior helped to further disillusion the idealistic Hamilton with his commander. The resentment boiled over on February 14. Washington, at the top of the stairs, requested an audience with his aide. Hamilton replied that he would be right back. His return was delayed about two minutes, according to his calculations, but his commander thought it more like ten. According to Thomas Flexner in his book *(Washington: The Indispensable Man)* on Washington, the enraged Virginian blurted out: "Colonel Hamilton. . . . You have kept me waiting at the head of these stairs ten minutes. . . . You treat me with disrespect." To which Hamilton responded: "I am not conscious of it, Sir, but since you have thought it necessary to tell me so, we part."

Washington tried to make up, but the determined young man would have none of it. He wanted out. He got his wish to lead troops—at the Battle of Yorktown, the final battle of the war. The two men never fully reconciled, but the younger one always asked for special favors and Washington tried to oblige.

Schuyler-Hamilton House

5 Olyphant Place, off Morris Avenue, Morristown, NJ (Open Tues–Sun 1–5, all year)

In 1780 in this house, Alexander Hamilton fell in love with Elizabeth Schuyler, daughter of General Philip Schuyler of Albany. Betsy Schuyler had come to visit an aunt and uncle who were temporarily stationed in the house of Dr. Jabez Campfield, senior surgeon for the American army. The uncle was Dr. John Cochran, chief physician and surgeon of the Continental army.

Hamilton proposed and Ms. Schuyler accepted. The couple were married in the great hall of her Albany house. Marriage into this patrician family was quite the accomplishment for the groom, who was very sensitive about his illegitimate birth.

Burnham Park

Located at the southwest edge of town, on Washington Street (travel south on Morris Avenue to South Park Place bordering the town square, turn left/west onto West Park Place, which becomes Washington Street/Route 24, turn left into the park), Morristown, NJ

In this city park is a reproduction of one of the log hospital huts used here. Nearby is a statue of Thomas Paine. This park was also the site of General Knox's Park of Artillery, 1779–1780.

Fort Nonsense

Located off Route 24 on Ann Street (from Burnham Park, travel north on Washington Street and turn left onto Court Street, which runs into the park), Morristown, NJ

In the winter the town of Morristown is visible from here, but trees partially block the view in the summer. The site supposedly got its name from the soldiers' resentment at having to build a fort here for reasons not apparent to them. The hills were used for beacon fires and observation. Look for the large boulder with a bronze dedication plaque on it.

Jockey Hollow Visitor Center

Jockey Hollow Road (take exit 29 off I-287, Harter Road west, south on Mt. Kemble Avenue/Route 202, then west on Tempe Wick Road, which runs into Jockey Hollow Road), Morristown, NJ (Open daily 9–5, all year)

Here one sees a film on the sufferings of the soldiers. At one time the main army of thirteen thousand men constructed twelve hundred winter huts.

Pennsylvania Line Troops

Jockey Hollow northern part of the park on the Grand Parade grounds along Jockey Hollow Road, Morristown, NJ (Open daily 9–5, all year)

Here are examples of the huts in which the Pennsylvania troops lived. In January 1781 these troops, dissatisfied with not being paid and by the lack of supplies, mutinied. They prepared to march on Congress. Meeting with representatives of both the Congress and the state of Pennsylvania at Princeton, they got some satisfaction and returned to their winter quarters. Anthony Wayne played a key role in defusing the anger of the rebellious troops.

Wick House

Jockey Hollow (just east of Pennsylvania Line troops huts), Morristown, NJ (Open daily 9–5, all year)

This Cape Cod house is somewhat out of place here in New Jersey, but its builders previously had been residents of an area of Long Island dominated by English influence. In the 1777–1778 encampment, several invalid army officers quartered here. In the 1779–1780 season, Major General Arthur St. Clair, commander of two Pennsylvania brigades, used the house as his headquarters.

In the house is the room of Tempe Wick, the only Wick offspring (her father was a farmer who owned 1,400 acres) living in the house at the time. A charming, but undocumented, story involves the twenty-one-year-old woman. During the 1781 mutiny of Pennsylvania Line troops, she rode to ask her brother-in-law, Dr. William Leddell, to come to the house to attend to her sick and recently widowed mother. On her return, some of the mutinous soldiers stopped her, saying they wanted to use her horse. When they momentarily let go of the bridle, the intrepid young lady quickly rode off. It is said she concealed her horse in her bedroom until the soldiers had gone.

Other Sites to Visit

There are numerous sites to visit in Morristown itself. See the sections dealing with Thomas Nast, the Morris Canal, and Samuel F. B. Morse. Also see the

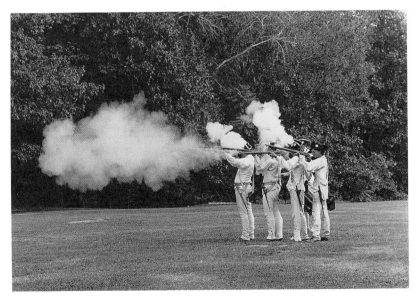

Firing demonstration, New Windsor Cantonment, Vails Gate, New York

Morris Museum of Arts and Sciences (6 Normandy Heights Road). Just north of the Ford Mansion is the Frelinghuysen Arboretum (on Whippany Road—Route 511). Just east of Jockey Hollow is the Great Swamp National Wildlife Refuge.

American troops also wintered at the New Windsor Cantonment, located at Temple Hill Road, one mile north of Vails Gate in the Newburgh area. Also visit Stony Point Battlefield Reservation, located off U.S. 9W, Stony Point, New York, not far south of West Point.

PART

FIVE

The Federal Period

During the Revolution, the colonies had to cooperate with each other to meet wartime emergencies. However, once independence had been obtained, the states went back to their old ways of promoting their own interests, rather than those of the nation as a whole. Ultimately, this situation could not continue, because building a new nation involves problems different from those arising from war. And frankly, the government created by the Continental Congress was just too weak to solve these new problems.

That the new democracy was not at all firmly established is shown by what happened at New Windsor Cantonment in the winter of 1782–1783. The troops stationed there following the final victory at Yorktown plotted to coerce Congress to take more power for itself. Congress could then force the states to provide enough revenue to ensure that all the soldiers would be paid. Had Washington been a different man, he might have taken advantage of this unrest to increase his personal standing. However, it was the commander in chief himself who nipped the revolt in the bud.

What little government there was arose from the Articles of Confederation, adopted by Congress November 15, 1777, but not ratified until March 1, 1781. These articles primarily protected the rights of the states. Congress had no power to tax and therefore had to rely on state revenues paid in proportion to the value of their land. Nor could Congress regulate domestic or foreign commerce, establish a federal judiciary, or enforce the restricted powers it did have. These limited powers included such things as conducting war, establishing post offices, coining money, and regulating the Indians.

This was all to change in the Federal period, 1787–1828. The desire to create a more powerful federal government increased in reaction to Shays's Rebellion. Massachusetts farmers revolted against the many foreclosures of properties for nonpayment of war-related debts. The federal government was powerless to help Massachusetts put down the rebellion. This scared many states into pushing for a stronger centralized government.

The tours in this section cover four places connected with the Federal period. The first visit is to Philadelphia, where the actual formation of the more powerful government took place. Following a brief period in which New York City was the nation's capital, the City of Brotherly Love held this honor. The need for a stronger American army brought about the establishment of the United States Military Academy, better known as West Point. The next chapter tours the academy in search of its origins. The War of 1812 reinforced the belief that the country needed a strong military. We visit Burlington, New Jersey, to tour the home of one of the great naval heroes of that war, Captain James Lawrence of "Don't give up the ship!" fame. Following this, we look at life in the Federal period by touring the exquisite mansions of Fairmount Park, Philadelphia.

In architecture, the Federal period is not very different from that of the late Georgian. One of the more notable differences is the presence of a fanlight—a window shaped like an open fan—over the front door, often accompanied by sidelights (narrow, door-length windows by the sides of a door).

The Adam brothers greatly influenced interior decoration in this period. The brothers, Robert and James, sons of a Scottish architect, were influenced by classicism as revealed in the excavations at Herculaneum and later Pompeii. Practitioners of the style designed furniture to look like Roman temples. The characteristics included thin, square-tapered legs; inlays of pale satinwood; decorative motifs of garlands, ovals, and eagles (the symbol of the new nation) and sometimes hand-painted portraits.

The Hepplewhite style (1785–1800) of furniture derives from the London cabinetmaker George Hepplewhite. He collaborated with the Adam brothers, adding modifications based on the French style of Louis XVI. Chairs in this style often have delicate backs shaped like shields, ovals, hearts, or wheels and slender tapering legs, sometimes with spade feet (looking something like whiskey glasses with very straight sides). Decoration is often of drapery festoons, medallions of eagles, or classical figures and feathers.

The Sheraton style (1800–1820) derives from another Londoner, Thomas Sheraton. This style modifies the Hepplewhite use of straight lines. The legs are still thin and tapering, but are now also round and reeded. Arms and legs are also more curved. The shield back is replaced by the square back of the French Empire style (which is explained in the next section). The decoration consists of low-relief carvings of drapery festoons, bowknotted wheat ears, and rosettes. To avoid possible confusion, please note that in England the Regency style (1793–1820) dominated. Regency style is an increased Frenchification of the Sheraton style.

An American making outstanding furniture at this time was Duncan Phyfe, a cabinetmaker from Albany. He bridged the gap between the two styles of Sheraton and Empire, often using the lyre motif in chair backs and tables bases.

Before the American Revolution, most American-designed furniture followed English styles. Once the Revolution began, American designers adopted French designs. In the late Federal period, Philadelphia was extraordinarily influenced by French styles. This is in part due to the many French aristocrats, merchants, and craftsmen who immigrated to the area to escape the aftermath of the French Revolution and, later, the overthrow of the Napoleonic empire. Among the immigrants were Du Pont and his family, former French minister Talleyrand, and the exiled brother of Napoleon, Joseph Bonaparte.

An interesting example of French influence is the use of French wallpaper. An entire room can be covered with the most elaborate scenes, such as the voyages of Captain Cook. Wallpaper at Eleutherian Mansion (Hagley Museum, Wilmington, Delaware) depicts the view from Trophy Point at the U.S. Military Academy, looking north up the Hudson River. Another French influence was the increased use of iron railings.

12

Federal Philadelphia

It will take at least two days to see all the sites listed below. If your time is limited, tour only the houses in which you are most interested.

The creation of the United States Constitution culminated in Philadelphia, but the process began in various states of the Union—largely in response to Shays's Rebellion (1786). Another force working toward greater government centralization was the need for greater economic cooperation between the colonies so that business could prosper. An economic recession, starting shortly after the end of the American Revolution and lasting until 1787, helped strengthen this force.

George Washington was president of the Potomac Company, which considered building a canal connecting the headwaters of the Ohio and Potomac rivers. To accomplish this, interstate cooperation was necessary. So, in March 1785, commissioners from Virginia and Maryland met. At the conference, James Madison suggested that a convention of all states meet to consider commercial conditions and amend the Articles of Confederation.

The representatives of six states gathered at the Annapolis Convention in September 1786. None of the New England states sent representatives. The poor turnout led Hamilton to draft a report suggesting that all states send delegates to Philadelphia in 1787. Congress consented, and the Constitutional Convention opened on May 25, 1787.

Most of the antifederalists did not attend, which made the convention's job much easier. In fact, the biggest problem was working out the dispute between large and small states. The Connecticut Plan, presented by Roger Sherman, provided the basis for a compromise between the big-state plan, introduced by Virginia's Edmund Randolph, and the small-state counterplan, presented by New Jersey's William Paterson. Under the compromise plan the states would have equal representation in the Senate, but there would be proportional representation in the lower house.

The delegates wrote the Constitution and presented it for approval on September 12. The Constitution was signed and submitted to Congress on September 17, and the convention adjourned to City Tavern.

New Hampshire became the ninth state to ratify the document in June 1788. This enabled the first Congress under the new federal constitution to meet in March 1789 in New York City. Coming as a surprise to no one, on April 6 Congress chose the myth-in-his-own-time, George Washington, as president and John Adams as vice-president. Washington took the inaugural oath on the steps of Wall Street's Federal Hall.

New York did not remain the capital for long. The industrially oriented Alexander Hamilton, of the developing Federalist party, wanted votes for federal assumption of state war debts. The agriculturally oriented Jefferson, of the developing Republican party (the forerunner of the modern Democratic party), wanted the capital to be located on the Potomac near his native Virginia. The two arranged a deal: Hamilton got what he wanted, and Jefferson got the Potomac location. While construction proceeded on the new capital city, Philadelphia served as capital (1790–1800).

Epidemics of yellow fever marred the ten years in Philadelphia. The doctors were of little assistance because at that time medical science did not know that mosquitoes transmit the disease. The epidemic killed thousands of Philadelphia residents. Many of the more wealthy were able to escape the center city to places like Fairmount Park and Germantown.

Independence Hall

Chestnut Street between Fifth and Sixth streets, Philadelphia, PA (Open daily 9–5, all year)

From 1775 to 1783 the Second Continental Congress met here, except for those times when British occupation of the city forced Congress to evacuate. In 1781 delegates in the Assembly Room adopted the Articles of Confederation. Here also, delegates wrote the Constitution. Independence Hall was also used to house the executive branch during the government's early years.

Interior, upstairs, Independence Hall, Philadelphia, Pennsylvania

Congress Hall

Southeast corner, Sixth and Chestnut streets, Philadelphia, PA (Open daily 9–5, all year)

Constructed in 1787–1789, this building served as the Philadelphia County Court House before it became the meeting place of the United States Congress, starting in December 1790. The house of Representatives met on the main floor. The members sat in studded leather chairs behind rows of long semicircular mahogany desks. The color combination in the room is very pleasing, with dark green valances (a valance is a short ornamental piece of drapery across a window top) set against creamy green walls. The Senate met upstairs. Looking down the hall, one sees the impressive meeting room. Chairs covered in red leather sit behind mahogany desks facing a chair and desk behind a low railing on a raised platform. The chair is almost thronelike because of the red canopy above it and the matching red valances across the windows located on either side. The impressive rug has an eagle in the center circle surrounded by circles representing the seals of the then-fourteen states constituting the nation.

In Congress Hall, President Washington took his second oath of office and John Adams his first and only; Congress ratified the Bill of Rights in December 1791; delegates established the First Bank of the United States, the Federal Mint, and the Department of the Navy; and Congress ratified John Jay's highly controversial treaty with England. Federal and local courts took over the building after Congress moved to Washington, D.C.

Old City Hall

Southwest corner, Fifth and Chestnut streets, Philadelphia, PA (Open daily 9–5, all year)

The United States Supreme Court used this building from 1791 (when the building was constructed) until 1800. Sitting at a long table behind a low railing on a raised platform were one chief justice and five associate justices. The first chief justice was John Jay, followed by John Rutledge (who took the oath of office and sat on the bench, but whose appointment was never confirmed by Congress) and Connecticut's Oliver Ellsworth. The building was later used by municipal government and courts.

The first floor now contains exhibits dealing with the early court. The second floor has displays on late eighteenth-century Philadelphia.

First Bank of the United States

Across from the Visitors' Center, 120 South Third Street, between Chestnut and Walnut streets, Philadelphia, PA (Not open to the public except for special exhibits)

This bank was built between 1795 and 1797 at the urging of Secretary of the Treasury Alexander Hamilton. It served its function until 1811 when its charter expired.

The very idea of a bank was controversial. Congress passed Hamilton's bank bill over the opposition of James Madison. When interpreting the Constitution, the Virginian argued for strict constructionism, as opposed to the New Yorker's loose constructionism. A furor arose in Washington's cabinet because Madison's two fellow Virginians, Thomas Jefferson (secretary of state) and Edmund Randolph (attorney general), opposed the bill. Despite this, Washington signed. This dispute foreshadowed the growing disharmony in Washington's cabinet and the growth of political parties: Federalists and Republicans. Washington was perplexed by this whole affair because he could not foresee, nor did he believe in, the importance of political parties. Completely misunderstanding the social class basis of politics, he stressed the value of everyone working for the common good of the nation as a whole. The dispute also foreshadowed the Civil War: the South opposed, and the North supported, the bill.

The Treasury Department became the largest government agency in the city. Hamilton formulated financial policy in an office near the southwest corner of Third and Chestnut streets.

Bishop White House

309 Walnut Street, between Third and Fourth streets, Philadelphia, PA (Open daily 9–5, all year; make reservations at the Visitors' Center of Independence Park)

This Federal brick town house built in 1786–1787 represents the lifestyle of an upper-middle-class Philadelphian. It was home to William White, the first Episcopal bishop of Pennsylvania (1787) and a signer of the Declaration of Independence. When the British occupied Philadelphia, the good bishop traveled to York, Pennsylvania, to serve as chaplain to the United States Congress. White was rector of Christ Church and was also responsible for changing this Anglican church into the Protestant Episcopal Church. He was a personal friend of John Adams and John Marshall, third chief justice of the Supreme Court. Washington dined at the bishop's home.

Bishop White lived in the house from 1787 until his death in 1836. The house is strategically located between the two churches he served so faithfully, Christ Church and St. Peter's.

Directly behind the house is a depression in the open ground. This was where Dock Creek ran, flowing beneath the cobblestoned Dock Street, which is located next to the Visitors' Center. This stagnant body of water became a breeding ground for mosquitoes. Bishop White had netting around his bed, which no doubt increased his chances of survival. He, of course, did not know that mosquitoes carry yellow fever; he just did not want to get bit.

The house has a long entrance hall with terrible yellowed wallpaper (a painted oilcloth). The stairs are located at the very rear of the hall. In the dining room are Heppelwhite chairs with shield backs.

Todd House

Fourth and Walnut streets, Philadelphia, PA (Open daily 9–5, all year; pick up the tickets at the Independence Park Visitors' Center)

This house represents a middle-class home. It is small and feels a little cramped, especially considering that a family of four lived here. John Todd, Jr., a lawyer, and his wife, Dolley Payne Todd, both Quakers, lived in the house from 1791 to 1793. Here they entertained many of the leaders of the new nation. Mr. Todd died in 1793 in the yellow fever epidemic. Their son William also died of the fever. Little wonder, since the house is only a block away from Dock Creek.

Aaron Burr formally introduced the widowed Mrs. Todd to James Madison. The Virginian, who was small (five feet four inches, one hundred pounds), shy, and reserved, had seen the young widow and asked to be introduced. You can see the parlor where they first met. About a year after the death of her husband, Dolley married James, who later became the fourth president of the United States. The Friends expelled her for marrying a non-Quaker. She is remembered as an outstanding first lady because, during the War of 1812, she saved many valuable items from the White House when the British attacked and burned Washington, D.C.

Hill-Physick-Keith House

321 South Fourth Street, between Cypress and Delancey streets, Philadelphia, PA (Open Tues–Sat 10–4, Sun 1–4, all year)

This is the last of the large Federal-era houses in downtown Philadelphia. It represents the house of an upper-class person. Henry Hill, a Philadelphia legislator in the 1780s and also a wine merchant who imported Washington's favorite (Madeira), made this his home. He died of yellow fever. Abigail Physick purchased the house for her brother, Dr. Philip Syng Physick, the "Father of American surgery." He lived in the house from 1790 to 1837. (You can tour his grandson's house in Cape May, New Jersey.)

The Hill-Physick-Keith House is the only Federal house in Philadelphia that has been restored with Federal-style furniture. The fanlight above the door was one of the first large ones in the city. Joseph Bonaparte gave Dr.

Hill-Physick-Keith House, Philadelphia, Pennsylvania

Physick the painting of the Roman ruins hanging in the drawing room.

The doctor married Elizabeth Emlen in 1800. In the dining room hangs a Thomas Sully portrait of this attractive woman. When the couple separated in 1815, the doctor got custody of the children. We laughed when the guide told us that Mrs. Physick took up residence in a nearby house as "Mrs. Physick, widow." Another interesting tidbit is that the famous surgeon was addicted to laudanum (a tincture of opium). You might also be interested in the flocked wallpaper with its raised designs.

On the second floor is a display of medical instruments. The good doctor used instruments like these to remove one thousand kidney stones—without benefit of anesthesia—from Chief Justice John Marshall. In gratitude, the chief justice gave him the silver wine cooler on display in the house. Also on display is the silver bowl the city presented to him in appreciation of his staying in town in August 1793 to help fight the yellow fever epidemic. Be sure to see the garden before leaving this site.

Powel House

244 South Third Street, between Locust Street and St. James Place, Philadelphia, PA (Open Tues–Sat 10–4, Sun 1–4, all year)

This 1765 Georgian town house is best known as the home of Samuel Powel, mayor of Philadelphia in 1776. When the British occupied the city, the lord high commissioner took over the mansion, 1777–1778. The Powels lived in a rear wing. After the Revolution, Philadelphia again elected him mayor.

The Powels were very influential people: Mrs. Eliza Powel's father, Thomas Willing, had been the financial mentor of Robert Morris, financier of the Revolution; her brother, Charles, was Morris's business partner; her mother, Anne Shippen, was a cousin to Peggy Shippen, who married Benedict Arnold; and the Powels were personal friends of George and Martha Washington. In fact, Eliza Powel was the president's favorite female friend. She urged him to seek a second term as president. Samuel Powel died of yellow fever.

In the house is Eliza Powel's portrait, painted after the original by Matthew Pratt. Also here are two goblets that belonged to Robert Morris. Most of the present furniture did not belong to the Powels. On the second floor is the ornate ballroom where Eliza Powel frequently held dances. Benjamin Franklin's daughter attended a ball here in honor of the twentieth wedding anniversary of George and Martha Washington. Leave enough time to sit in the garden. On several occasions Washington walked here, conferring with Mrs. Powel.

Thaddeus Kosciuszko National Memorial

301 Pine Street, corner of Third and Pine streets, Philadelphia, PA (Open daily 9–5, all year)

The Polish Revolutionary War officer and engineer Thaddeus Kosciuszko built the fortifications at West Point and Saratoga. After the war he returned to Poland to help in that country's unsuccessful attempt to win its independence from Russia.

In 1794 Kosciuszko was wounded, captured, and taken as a prisoner to Russia. The authorities released him after two years of captivity on condition that he never return. He traveled to England accompanied by Julian Niemcewicz, a Polish author and statesman who had served with him in the Polish Insurrection and who himself had been a prisoner of the Russians. A servant also came with the two men. One of his duties was to carry the crippled Kosciuszko, who had been seriously wounded at the Battle of Maciejowice in the Polish Insurrection against Russia (October 10, 1794).

The trio arrived in Philadelphia in 1797. The Polish engineer left for three months to avoid a second yellow fever epidemic threatening the city. Upon his return, he and his two companions moved into the second-floor back bedroom of Mrs. Ann Relf's three-and-a-half-story brick rooming-house, constructed in 1775.

A stream of visitors came to talk with the Polish officer. A frequent guest was Thomas Jefferson, who helped the patriot obtain from Congress nineteen thousand dollars in back pay. Jefferson also helped him return to Europe. In May 1798 Kosciuszko sailed for France, where he unsuccessfully tried to get that nation's support for Polish independence. He died in Switzerland in 1817.

At the small house there is a slide presentation on the Polish freedom fighter. The house itself is virtually empty, except for a display bedroom on the second floor where the famed soldier stayed.

Other Sites to Visit

See the Geographic Cross-Reference for a list of other Philadelphia sites.

13

West Point

West Point is one of the most beautiful campuses in the United States. The view from Trophy Point north along the Hudson River has been painted and photographed many times. For a great day trip, have brunch on campus at the Thayer Hotel and then tour the grounds. You might want to pack a lunch and eat in the picnic area by the river. Then walk around the magnificent grounds.

The dominant architectural style at the academy is English Tudor. Richard Delafield, superintendent from 1838 to 1845 and from 1856 to 1861, adopted this style with its crenellated towers as best suited to inspire martial virtues. Under Delafield, workers constructed the library in 1841, the oldest academic building still used by cadets.

East of the plain stand three buildings overlooking the Hudson River. They were built around the time of the academy's centennial. From south to north are the Officers' Club, Cullum Memorial Hall (erected with money left to the academy by former superintendent George Washington Cullum), and the Bachelors' Building for bachelor officers. Built between 1898 and 1903, these buildings were designed by the famous architectural firm of McKim, Mead, and White. The neoclassical style chosen by the firm contrasts strongly with Delafield's Tudor Gothic.

An even greater rebuilding took place between 1903 and 1913. Ralph Adams Cram, the senior partner of Cram, Goodhue, and Ferguson, was largely responsible for the Gothic style (more in harmony with Delafield's Tudor style) that characterizes many of the academy buildings: the Administration Building (1909); the Cadet Chapel (1910); and Thayer Hall (1911).

Added to the physical beauty of West Point is its long and distinguished history. During the American Revolution (in 1777), Burgoyne attacked the colonies from Canada. Sir Henry Clinton, stationed in New York City, made a feeble attempt to aid the northern invasion by mounting a campaign up the Hudson River. The ease with which the British advanced awoke the Americans to the need to better fortify the Hudson Highlands. This is when West Point (at that time little more than wilderness) came to be selected as the center for these fortifications.

West Point was such a valuable position that Benedict Arnold saw it as the ideal fortification to hand over to the British in exchange for the promise of money. Arnold tricked Washington into giving him command, which was below the man's talents. The traitor assumed the position in August 1780.

The new commander turned over a map of the fortifications to British Major John Andre. Andre attempted to make his way through Westchester County back to British-held New York City. At that time, Westchester was neutral ground between the Americans and the British. Roving bands of men, some sympathetic to the British and others to the Americans, patrolled the area, stopping travelers and at times robbing them. When stopped by three of these men at Tarrytown, Andre virtually revealed his identity through careless requests for their assistance to take him to the British lines. Foolishly, he had assumed that the men were pro-British. Suspicious now, the men searched him and found a map in a boot heel. They then turned him over to the American army. There is a statue dedicated to Andre's captors on Broadway in Tarrytown.

During the war, West Point's commandant would stay in the confiscated home of Tory Beverley Robinson in Garrison, on the east bank of the Hudson River. While at this house, Arnold learned of Andre's capture. He escaped by having himself rowed to a British ship anchored in the Hudson River, and he rewarded his unwitting assistants by turning them over to the British for imprisonment.

Although the traitor got away, his compatriot was not so fortunate. The Americans executed the major in Tappan, New York, in October 1780 for his part in the espionage. (You can visit the George Washington Masonic Shrine, the De Wint House, in Tappan, New York, where Washington signed the order for Andre's execution.) The condemned man accepted his fate like a gentleman, engendering great sympathy in the Americans who were with him during his final days. His only qualm was the shock he received when he saw the method of execution. The British subject thought he would be honorably executed by firing squad. He blanched at the sight of the hangman's noose, but quickly recovered his composure and died with dignity.

Visitors' Center

Located just outside the gates of the Military Academy in High Falls, New York (off U.S. 9W) (Open daily, 8–4:15)

The first stop on your tour of West Point should be the Visitors' Center. The center has a wide variety of souvenirs and also shows a film on life at West Point.

West Point Museum of Military Arms

Located in Olmsted Hall, West Point, New York (Open daily 10–4:15, all year) The museum is now behind the Visitors' Center

Be sure to see this museum, one of the world's outstanding collections of military weaponry.

Fort Putnam

North of Lusk Reservoir atop Mount Independence, West Point, NY (Open daily 10:30–4, May–Nov)

Thaddeus Kosciuszko, the Polish engineering officer who had constructed the Bemis Heights defensive barriers at Saratoga for General Gates, also built the fortifications at West Point. Fort Putnam was one of these.

This is a great place for an overview of the campus. The fort is located on Mount Independence and was built in 1778 (restored 1907–1910). The fort protected the rear of Fort Clinton, located on the field below. Fort Putnam was named for Colonel Rufus Putnam, who commanded the Massachusetts regiment that built it. A relief map in the fort's museum shows the locations of all the surrounding redoubts. Following his capture, Major Andre was held in the fort for a short period.

Kosciuszko's Monument

Cullum Road, West Point, NY

This monument to the Polish officer stands atop the bluffs on the site of Fort Clinton. There is a marker with information about the fort just south of the statue. Previously known as Fort Arnold, the name was changed following Benedict Arnold's treachery.

Walk along Cullum Road and you will see the statue of General John Sedgwick (of the famous literary Sedgwick family of the Berkshire area of Massachusetts), who was killed at the Battle of Spottsylvania in 1864. Now walk toward the Hudson River and you will see one of the most beautiful views anywhere of the river. From left to right are Storm King Mountain, the city of Newburgh, Bannerman's Castle on Pollepel Island, and Constitution Island. Everyone asks about the castle on Pollepel Island. It was built by an arms dealer to house his wares. It is presently not much more than a shell of crumbling walls.

Walking west along Cullum Road the next stop is Battle Monument, located at Trophy Point. This monument was erected in 1897 to the memory of the 2,230 officers and enlisted men of the regular United States Army killed in action during the Civil War. The famous architect Stanford White designed it. The winged statue of *Fame* atop the column is by Frederick MacMonnies.

Great Iron Chain

Near Trophy Point, West Point, NY

A giant iron chain was stretched across the Hudson River from Constitution Island to just above Gee's Point in 1778 to prevent enemy ships from sailing farther upriver. The chain was forged at the Sterling Iron Works about twenty-five miles west of the academy. The links weighed from 98 to 130 pounds each. The chains were attached with staples to heavy logs floating in the river. This prevented them from sinking too far below the water's surface. The chain never had to be tested in actual battle.

Sylvanus Thayer Monument

On the plain near the intersection of Jefferson and Washington roads, West Point, NY

This is a monument to the Father of the Military Academy. Don't be misled by the title, however, for Thayer did not create the Military Academy. It took more than one man to get this accomplished in the United States—a nation distrustful of standing armies.

In 1790 General Henry Knox, secretary of war, recommended the establishment of a military academy. Washington, as well as others, pushed for such a military school, but got nowhere until 1798, when war with France loomed on the horizon.

The United States may have won its independence, but that did not mean automatic respect for the new nation's status. Both France and England began to test the mettle of the new country. This situation arose from the European conflicts over the French Revolution and the resultant Napoleonic empire. The United States wanted to remain neutral, but both European countries pushed it to take sides. In the United States itself, the Federalists were pro-England, while the Republicans were pro-France. The new nation actually engaged in armed conflict with both European nations, but eventually declared war only against England.

In 1799 Alexander Hamilton, who wanted war with France, drafted a plan for a system of military education. When a call went out for recruitment of an army, only about three thousand men enlisted—a meager showing indeed. This was the final argument that tipped the scales in favor of a more permanent school for military education. On his last day in office, President Adams appointed the first faculty for a school for gunners and sappers at West Point. In 1802 President Jefferson and Congress enlarged the school to create the United States Military Academy. At the same time, they reduced the navy by about two-thirds.

The academy suffered because its early superintendents were also chief engineers and had to be away for long periods performing their specialties. The military school also suffered during the War of 1812 due to the mobilization of the faculty.

In 1817 John C. Calhoun, secretary of war, appointed Major Sylvanus Thayer superintendent of the academy. Thayer served in this position until 1833. He restored confidence in the school, in part by hiring an outstanding faculty. This is what earned him the title Father of the Military Academy.

Superintendent's Quarters (private)

Across Jefferson Road from the Thayer Monument, West Point, NY

Dating from around 1820, this building was constructed under the superintendency of Sylvanus Thayer. It is the oldest building at the Point still in active use. Perhaps the most famous of the superintendents who occupied this house was Robert E. Lee (1852–1855). Here a young cadet by the name of J.E.B. Stuart would often visit fellow cadet Custis Lee (Robert E. Lee's son).

Commandant's Quarters (private)

Just north of the Superintendent's Quarters on Jefferson Road, West Point, NY

This is the quarters of the commandant of cadets. The cadets were organized into a battalion in 1817. The temporary commander of this battalion was G. W. Gardiner. The regulations of 1825 legally recognized this position as commandant of cadets. In 1858 Congress legally designated the Department of Tactics and the position of commandant of cadets and instructor of artillery, cavalry, and infantry tactics.

Old Cadet Chapel

North side of Washington Road near the West Point Cemetery, West Point, NY (Open daily 8–4:15, all year)

The buildings at West Point have changed considerably over the years. A survivor from the early days of the academy is the Old Cadet Chapel, dating from 1837. Originally located on the site of Jefferson Hall, it was moved to its present site in 1911. It is in the Classical Revival style, popular at that time in history, but regarded as not martial enough to suit the Point.

In the chapel the inquisitive can look up the locations of the graves of such famous people as Sylvanus Thayer, General Winfield Scott, General George Armstrong Custer, Margaret Corbin (Revolutionary war hero honored by Congress), Susan and Anna Warner (who owned Constitution Island before giving it to the government), and Major Robert Anderson (defender of Fort Sumter against the Confederate attack that opened the Civil War).

Other Sites to Visit

After visiting West Point, drive north on Route 218 along the west bank of the river and make a stop at the very small pull-off area on Storm King Mountain. The stop provides great views of the river. Looking south with binoculars, you can see Battle Monument at West Point.

South of West Point is Bear Mountain, where people picnic in the summer, ice skate and ski in the winter, and eat year-round at Bear Mountain Inn. There is a great view of the Hudson River from atop Bear Mountain (reached via Perkin's Drive). From here one can look south to the town of Peekskill. Great views of the military academy are available from pull-offs along Route 9W.

Across the river from West Point is the town of Cold Spring. Many people come here to shop in the quaint stores. From the village dock there is a nice view of Storm King Mountain and the river. The Foundry School Museum of the Putnam Historical Society at 63 Chestnut Street (open Wed 9:30–4 and Sun 2–5, Mar–Dec) features displays of both military and household artifacts made at the village's West Point Foundry.

Visit Boscobel, which has absolutely stunning interior decoration. This museum of the decorative arts is a showcase of Federal design and is highly recommended. The mansion, which once belonged to Tory States Dyckman, is located on Route 9D in Garrison (open Wed–Mon 10–4:30, Apr–Oct; Wed–Mon special program at 3:30, Nov–Dec, Mar). Dyckman was a Loyalist who fled to England, where he became a clerk in the Quartermaster Department of the British army. He siphoned off money, as did others, came back to the United States with his fortune, and had Boscobel built. The house itself is built after the style of Robert Adam. Among the many items here, notice the furniture by Duncan Phyfe.

14

James Lawrence's Burlington

The War of 1812 has been called America's Second War of Independence because the country felt it had to assert itself against the European nations whose bullying showed disrespect for American military possibilities. The immediate causes of the war were many, but a few stand out. There was a great deal of resentment against England, which had been stopping American ships and impressing American sailors. In addition, many Americans wanted to end any British claims to the American Northwest Territory.

In the war itself the Americans took the offensive with attacks against Canada. The campaign went badly. The United States did have some success in the west, where the Battle of the Thames reestablished the northwest military frontier. When the British and Canadians went on the offensive, they did no better than the Americans had done.

The final conflict of the war was the Battle of New Orleans, which made Andrew Jackson a national hero. The battle was actually fought Christmas Eve 1814, after peace had been declared. The war itself was inconclusive, but it did establish the United States as at least a Western Hemisphere power.

Although the war yielded mixed battle results on both land and sea, it did produce a bumper crop of naval heroes. A visit to Burlington to see the house of one such hero, combined with a walking tour of the town, should take an entire day. (Burlington is reachable via Exit 5 of the New Jersey Turnpike; travel north on Route 541, which becomes High Street.)

James Lawrence House
459 High Street, Burlington, NJ (Open Wed 1–4, Sun 2–4, all year)

This house is the birthplace and boyhood home (up to age seventeen) of Captain James Lawrence. He was born in Burlington in 1781. His father was a mayor and a Tory—even entertaining the Hessian commander in his house. Given his father's sympathies, it is somewhat ironic that James became a great American naval hero with six American ships named for him.

His father wanted him to be a lawyer like himself, but James, who for many an hour had watched the sailboats on the nearby Delaware River, wanted to go to sea. When his father died, his uncle helped him obtain the necessary foundation for a naval career.

At the age of eighteen the young man became a midshipman. Promoted to lieutenant, he took part in the Tripoli campaign against the Barbary pirates, distinguishing himself in battle. Returning home, the naval hero commanded a number of ships. He settled in New York City and there married a local woman.

In 1813 he commanded the *Hornet* in the squadron of a fellow New Jerseyan, Captain William Bainbridge of Princeton. Lawrence's ship sank the British ship *Peacock* with only one American killed and two wounded. As a result of his successes, the Navy gave Lawrence command of the Boston-harbored *Chesapeake*, with thirty-eight guns, following the deterioration in health of the ship's captain. Unfortunately, superstitious sailors had declared that there was a jinx on the ship. Morale was further lowered following a dispute among the crew over the division of prize money.

In May 1813 the HMS *Shannon*, a frigate with thirty-eight guns, blockaded Boston harbor. The captain issued a challenge to Lawrence to come out and fight. It was an offer the proud American could not refuse. On June 1 the two ships lay side by side for twelve minutes and poured shot into each other. Lawrence was wounded and had to be carried below. As the battle raged, he gave his last order: "Don't give up the ship!" It was already too late; the enemy had boarded his vessel. The American captain died on the British vessel during its voyage to Halifax.

The house contains a lithograph of the battle between the two ships and articles from the period, such as an Eagle Hilt saber sword, a document signed by Lawrence, some Lawrence family furniture, and other memorabilia.

The United States Navy is very proud of this man from Burlington. One of the guides at the house mentioned the occasion when the navy band marched up High Street to the house. It must have been a thrilling sight. Next door to the Lawrence house is the Cooper House.

James Fenimore Cooper House

457 High Street, Burlington, NJ (Open Wed 1–4, Sun 2–4, all year)

The early romantic American writer James Fenimore Cooper was born in this house in 1789. He stayed here for only a year because the family moved to New York to found Cooperstown. Inside the house, the Burlington County Historical Society displays a portion of the manuscript of *The Spy*. There is also a copy of a Cooper portrait by Delaware artist Bass Otis and a chair used in the father's High Street general store.

Upstairs is a room devoted to Frenchman Joseph Bonaparte, who lived in exile in nearby Bordentown. The introduction to this section mentioned the importance of French influence on Philadelphia. Therefore, a brief synopsis of the French exile's story is in order.

The former king of Naples and Spain arrived in Philadelphia after Napoleon's defeat at Waterloo. He lived at 260 South Ninth Street until he moved to his Point Breeze estate in Bordentown. Known as open-hearted and generous, he played a significant role in the development of the arts in

Philadelphia. He joined the Pennsylvania Academy of Fine Arts and, through his neighbor, the poet Joseph Hopkinson, lent many of his European paintings to the institute.

While living in Philadelphia, he purchased from Stephen Sayre (Benjamin Franklin's private secretary) a dwelling and lands at Bordentown. He had Philadelphia craftsmen expand the house into a mansion. Here he refused the crown of Mexico, saying that he had "worn two crowns, and would not lift a finger to secure a third."

His two daughters, Zenaide and Charlotte, visited him in Bordentown, while his wife stayed in Europe. Zenaide and her husband, Prince Charles Lucien Bonaparte, lived in a nearby house that was connected to Joseph's mansion by an underground tunnel. Zenaide had a buoyant personality and soon became a favorite of Philadelphia society. She painted Bordentown landscapes and translated dramas by Schiller. Her husband studied American birds, eventually publishing his studies. His book was an important forerunner of Audubon's later work. Charlotte was hostess for her father at Point Breeze. She was considered an artist in her own right, having several exhibits of her work at the Pennsylvania Academy.

In the United States, Joseph Bonaparte fell in love with a young Quaker woman, named Annette Savage, who sold him suspenders from her mother's small dry-goods shop in Philadelphia. The heavyset, genial exile lived with her in the city, but they later moved to a villa south of the city. This situation shocked the good people of Philadelphia, and they ostracized Annette Savage. Suddenly, many friends stopped visiting the prince. Outraged, in the early 1820s he rented a red-brick house, known as Bow Hill, three-quarters of a mile outside Trenton. Here he installed his mistress in a room that he could enter through a secret door. Bonaparte had a child by his mistress. Besides her daughter, the mother's only company was Bonaparte's Hungarian bodyguard.

In 1822 Bonaparte invited her to stay at his villa in the town of Diana in Jefferson County, New York. After Bonaparte returned to Europe, Annette Savage married a young Frenchman. Ironically, she eventually returned to being a small shopkeeper.

The former king lived in the United States for seventeen years, returning to Europe in 1832. He then lived in England for three years. The wandering exile returned to New Jersey for two lengthy visits. In 1844 he died in Florence, having rejoined his wife.

In 1820 the original Point Breeze mansion, overlooking the Delaware River in what is now Bonaparte Park in Bordentown, burned down. Bonaparte then converted his stables into a mansion. Unfortunately, a fire also destroyed this structure.

Among the items in the collection at the Cooper House are a picture of Joseph as king of Spain; his bed, with a coverlet bedecked with the Bonaparte bee symbol; a French dressing table owned by one of his daughters; and two fancy Sheraton chairs from the Bordentown estate. The house also has many

Revolutionary War and Civil War items. Pick up a walking-tour map of Burlington here. Next door to the Cooper House is the Pearson-How House.

Pearson-How House
453 High Street, Burlington, NJ (Open Wed 1–4, Sun 2–4, all year)

Burlington was at one time known for its clocks, and Isaac Pearson was one of the best of the clockmakers. He was also an ironmaster and politician. Pearson never actually lived in the house, but there is a Pearson clock on display. The house was built by Judge Samuel How in 1705.

Take a walking tour of Burlington, which was founded by Quakers. Quaker John Fenwick's hurried pace of colonizing activities in south Jersey worried other Friends, and they quickened settlement of their own landholdings. Two companies of Friends, one from London and one from Yorkshire, came together to found Burlington in 1677. High Street became the dividing line between the two groups, with Yorkshiremen to the east and Londoners to the west.

In 1681 Burlington became the capital of West Jersey, as well as a port of entry. When West Jersey and East Jersey reunited into the present New Jersey in 1702, the capital of New Jersey alternated between Burlington and Perth Amboy, the former capital of East Jersey. In 1792 Trenton became the permanent capital.

Friends Meeting House
Corner of High and West Broad streets, Burlington, NJ

This 1785 building replaced a 1685 meetinghouse. It contains the original seats and tables from the 1780s.

Surveyor General's Office
West Broad Street near High Street, Burlington, NJ

When the Friends and George Carteret officially divided New Jersey into West and East Jersey in 1676, the proprietors of West Jersey met in this tiny, one-room, red-brick building to dispose of lands. Each year the General Council of Proprietors meets here, but there is not that much land left to dispose of these days.

Old St. Mary's Church

West Broad between Talbot and Wood streets, Burlington, NJ

This 1703 Georgian Colonial church is the oldest Episcopal church in New Jersey.

New St. Mary's Church

West Broad between Talbot and Wood streets, Burlington, NJ

The designer of Trinity Church in New York City, Richard Upjohn, also designed this 1854 church, one of the best Gothic Revival churches in the United States. In the cemetery are the graves of Elias Boudinot, at one time president of the United States in Congress Assembled, and his son-in-law, William Bradford, attorney general in Washington's administration.

Boudinot House (private)

207 and 209 West Broad Street, Burlington, NJ

Boudinot built this house in 1804 and lived here with his daughter and her husband. The attorney general died in 1795. Mrs. Bradford lived in the house until her death. The house is now divided into two apartments.

Thomas Revell House

Adjacent to 217 Wood Street, between East Union and Pearl streets, Burlington, NJ (Open by appointment)

This 1685 house (the oldest in the county) once stood at 8 East Pearl Street. The house was the office of Thomas Revell, registrar of the Proprietors of West Jersey and clerk of the Provincial Assembly from 1696 to 1699. The house is sometimes called the Gingerbread House. The story is that Ben Franklin, on his way to Philadelphia in 1723, was given a piece of gingerbread here by an old woman.

General Grant House (private)

309 Wood Street, Burlington, NJ

General Ulysses Grant sent his family here during the Civil War. John Wilkes Booth planned to assassinate Lincoln and, at the same time, have co-conspirator Lewis Paine kill the general. However, on the terrible day of the assassination, Grant left for Burlington following a cabinet meeting. Booth

Thomas Revell House, Burlington, New Jersey

found this out and in the early evening told Paine to change his target to Secretary of State Seward. Paine attacked Seward with a knife, but the secretary survived thanks to the assassin's incompetence and to Seward's heavy neck collar—worn as a result of a recent carriage accident.

Other Sites to Visit

Near Burlington is another Quaker settlement, Mount Holly, which has several interesting attractions, including the Burlington County Prison Museum, Friends Meeting House, and John Woolman Memorial House. Quaker John Woolman was an early worker for the abolition of slavery.

15

Fairmount Park

In order to get a better idea of life in the Federal period, or at least of the lives of the affluent, tour Fairmount Park, Philadelphia. The park is an architectural feast and a festival of interior decoration. Quite a few of the mansions are open, and you can see many furniture styles. To increase your enjoyment, read about the different types of furniture. There are so many mansions that to see them all would require three or four days. If time permits only viewing two of them, visit Strawberry Mansion, which is very popular with the public, and Mount Pleasant, because its exterior is so beautiful. The visit to the latter mansion will be enhanced by a walk in its gardens. Also available is a ninety-minute trolley-bus tour, covering seventeen miles and twelve major sites in the park. The tour starts from the Center City Convention and Visitors Bureau at Sixteenth Street and J.F.K. Boulevard. Or the houses can be visited individually. (From the Independence Park area in downtown Philadelphia, the park is easily reached by traveling west on Vine Street and then heading north on the Benjamin Franklin Parkway, which itself is in the park.)

Fairmount Park was an outgrowth of the romantic movement for naturally landscaped public parks that also produced New York City's Central Park (built 1859–1876) and the Mall in Washington, D.C. This movement was, in part, a reaction against the ugliness of ever-spreading industrialization and urbanization. In 1855 the Lemon Hill area of Philadelphia was set aside to serve as a common for city residents. The tract was enlarged by various additions on both sides of the Schuylkill River until it reached some nine thousand acres, making it the largest city park in the United States.

Some of the houses were built prior to the Federal period and some during the period. In this section all the mansions are discussed because they were all used during the later period. You may visit the mansions in any order you like, but here the houses are discussed in a more chronological order. Some of them were first built as summer cottages in order to escape the yellow fever epidemic that swept Philadelphia and killed ten thousand residents between 1793 and 1800.

Cedar Grove

Lansdowne Drive off North Concourse Drive, West Fairmount Park, Philadelphia, PA (Open Wed–Sun 10–4, all year)

This is the only house that was not actually built on park ground. It is also different from the other houses in that it does not look like a mansion.

Cedar Grove is a larger version of what a Quaker home of the 1700s might look like. Indeed, the roof is similar to those found on Quaker meeting-houses. In 1748 Elizabeth Coates Paschall built the oldest part of the house as a country retreat. She enlarged the gray fieldstone farmhouse in 1752 and 1795. The piazza was added in the 1840s. Federal-style elements can be found in the lunette (moon-shaped) attic window and the interior wood-work. A relative of the family was Captain Samuel Morris, "the Fighting Quaker," whose portrait is in the dining room.

In the house are nearly five generations of antique furnishings used by the family. Some of the styles included are William and Mary, Queen Anne, Chippendale, Sheraton, and Hepplewhite. There is also a collection of Canton and Nanking china. Because different parts of the house were built at different times, the rooms are at various levels (but this just adds to the over-all charm of the place).

Woodford

Woodford Drive near the intersection of Dauphin and Thirty-third streets (next-door to Strawberry Mansion), East Fairmount Park, Philadelphia, PA (Open Wed–Sun 10–4, all year)

In 1756 the original part of this mansion was remodeled from a 1735 smaller house for Judge William Coleman of the colonial Pennsylvania Su-preme Court. At that time the builders added the Palladian window on the second floor. Benjamin Franklin often visited here. While Washington was at Valley Forge, the then-Tory owner, David Franks, entertained General Howe. Franks and his daughter Rebecca added a second story to the mansion in 1772 before their Loyalist activities forced them into exile in 1780. Rebecca was one of the belles of a famous ball (referred to as the Meschianza) held in the city in 1778 to honor General Howe upon his replacement by Sir Henry Clinton. On display is a page from a Loyalist newspaper, dated May 18, 1778, giving an account of the ball, including a reference to Rebecca.

The mansion houses the furniture collection of Ms. Naomi Wood, one of the owners of the house. The collection represents various time periods. One of the unusual pieces on display is an *inner-and-outer man*, that is, a combination bed warmer for the outer man and hot-toddy warmer for the inner man. Also here is a large Delftware collection.

Laurel Hill

Randolph and East Edgely drives, off East River Drive, East Fairmount Park, Philadelphia, PA (Open Wed–Sun 10–4, all year)

In 1760 Francis and Rebecca Rawle ordered the construction of the Georgian center section of this mansion. Francis died in a hunting accident,

Laurel Hill, Fairmount Park, Philadelphia, Pennsylvania

and Rebecca later married Samuel Shoemaker. Officials confiscated the house and property when the Tory Shoemaker was convicted of treason. Dr. Philip Syng Physick, discussed in the Federal tour of the downtown area, bought the house in the early 1800s as a wedding gift for his daughter.

Mount Pleasant

Mt. Pleasant Drive off Reservoir Drive, East Fairmount Park, Philadelphia, PA (Open Wed–Sun, 10–4, all year)

This Georgian stone mansion with projecting central pavilion was built in 1761 for Scottish sea captain and privateer John Macpherson. Benedict Arnold bought the mansion for his wife, but the couple never lived in it. Jonathan Williams, a great-nephew of Benjamin Franklin and first superintendent of West Point, was one of the last owners. Some noteworthy features of the mansion are the fine woodwork and Palladian windows (one of the first homes in America to have them). Notice the portrait of Macpherson's son, Major John Macpherson. In 1775 he was an aide-de-camp to General Montgomery at Quebec, where both were killed. There is a garden in the back that extends around the west side and part of the front.

The above houses are of Georgian or earlier designs. The Federal-style mansions are discussed below.

Mount Pleasant, Fairmount Park, Philadelphia, Pennsylvania

Solitude (zoo office—private)

Located in the Philadelphia Zoo, which is between Thirty-fourth Street and Zoological Avenue, West Fairmount Park, PA (Open daily 9:30–5, all year)

This home, built in 1785, was once the home of John Penn (1760–1834), a grandson of William Penn. Penn named the house for a lodge that belonged to the duke of Württemberg.

Following the American Revolution, the Penns feared that the new American government would not recognize their proprietary rights to Pennsylvania quitrents and lands not yet purchased or allocated. The young landlord, faced with losing most of his inheritance, left London for Philadelphia in 1783. He bought fifteen acres of land and drew up designs for a bachelor's villa. Unfortunately for the gentleman, the Pennsylvania legislature turned down his petition in 1787. He returned to England two years later. Solitude is the simplest of the Fairmount Park houses, but those who have seen it say the interior is elegant.

Strawberry Mansion

In the middle of the circle made by the intersections of Strawberry Mansion and Woodford Drives (next-door to the Woodford Mansion), East Fairmount Park, Philadelphia, PA (Open Wed–Sun 10–4, all year)

This is the largest house in the park and most visited. The house is white, with white shutters on the first floor and black shutters on the second. The central section is early Federal in style and was built in 1789 for Judge

William Lewis. The judge is best known for his defense of Quaker pacifists accused of treason for not fighting in the Revolutionary War.

In the 1820s Judge Joseph Hemphill took over the house. His wife was Margaret, daughter of Robert Coleman of Lancaster. Margaret's sister was the fiancée of James Buchanan, who some say died of a broken heart over the breakup of the engagement (see the section on Buchanan).

In today's world there are cases where, when parents go away on a trip, the children hold parties that end in the virtual destruction of the houses. In the case of Strawberry Mansion, when the parents were abroad, son Alexander added an entire ballroom to the south end of the house. He wanted to join the First City Troop, a volunteer cavalry group, and thought entertaining them in a new ballroom would gain him admission. The gregarious and very tolerant judge added the two Greek Revival wings to correct the imbalance created by his son's impetuosity.

Judge Hemphill went bankrupt in the bank failure of 1833. His sister-in-law purchased the place and then sold it. At this time it became a dairy farm, featuring strawberries and cream (hence the name Strawberry Mansion). In 1867 the city purchased it.

Federal, Regency, and Empire furnishings are represented in the house. Note the circular "chatting couch" and the French Empire upholstered furniture in the ballroom and the use of punch-and-gouge styling (Philadelphia carpenters used the punch-and-gouge tools to design elaborate fireplace surrounds). Also here are two Chippendale chairs from President Washington's residence (the Robert Morris house, which no longer stands).

Sweetbriar

Off Lansdowne Drive, West Fairmount Park, Philadelphia, PA (Open Wed–Sun 10–4, all year)

This home was built in 1797 for Samuel and Jean Breck, who wanted to escape the yellow fever epidemic raging in Philadelphia. Breck was a wealthy merchant and a member of the Pennsylvania legislature, where he introduced legislation to emancipate those slaves still remaining in the state. He was also a patron of John James Audubon, the naturalist painter. The mansion displays bird prints by the artist. The owner of Sweetbriar knew a great many important Frenchmen who had fled to Philadelphia during the Reign of Terror. Among others, he entertained Lafayette here on his return tour of the United States.

The couple had only one child, a daughter named Lucy, on whom the parents doted. When she was twelve, they gave her a party attended by eighty people. In 1828, shortly after her twenty-first birthday, she died, perhaps of typhus. Her father never recovered from the blow. He closed Sweetbriar following her death and sold it ten years later.

The house epitomizes the Adam style in America. Note the floor-to-ceiling windows, punch-and-gouge mantle over the fireplace, the sketch by Breck of family friend Talleyrand, and the ten prints by the artist William Birch, known for his landscapes and city views.

Ormiston

Reservoir Drive near the East Park Reservoir, East Fairmount Park, Philadelphia, PA (Open Wed–Sun 10–4, all year)

On this site Joseph Galloway, lawyer and Speaker of the Assembly, built a house, which he later forfeited when convicted of treason. General Joseph Reed then acquired the house. Lawyer Edmund Burd, son-in-law of Chief Justice Edward Shippen, purchased the estate and tore down the mansion. In 1798 he built the present mansion on the site and named it Prospect after his ancestral seat in Scotland. It is a red-brick Georgian house with wide porches and a Scottish bake oven and open fireplace. Changing exhibits treat the British heritage in the Delaware River valley.

Lemon Hill

Poplar Drive near the intersection with Sedgely Drive, East Fairmount Park, Philadelphia, PA (Open Wed–Sun 10–4, all year)

The land on which Lemon Hill sits was once owned by Robert Morris, one of the financiers of the American Revolution. Morris went bankrupt, and the property was sold to Henry Pratt, son of portrait painter Matthew Pratt.

In 1799 Pratt built this Federal mansion of stucco over stone, complete with fanlight and sidelights at the raised first-floor entrance door and a Palladian window on the second floor. On both sides of the house are open porches. The mansion is named for the lemon trees that once grew in the estate's greenhouses. Henry Pratt probably never lived in the mansion, but he did open the gardens to the public, even selling tickets. In 1844 the city purchased the estate. At one time the mansion served as a restaurant. You can see the Philadelphia Museum of Fine Arts from the upstairs oval room. The dining room contains several Thomas Sully portraits, as well as Empire sofa and chairs.

Fairmount Water Works

Between Boathouse Row and the Philadelphia Museum of Fine Arts, East Fairmount Park, Philadelphia, PA (Open Wed–Sun 11–7, Apr–Nov)

This early municipal waterworks illustrates the Greek Revival style (discussed in part 6). The works were designed by Frederick Graff and built between 1819 and 1822. From the dammed part of the river, pumps forced water up to a reservoir located on the site of the present art museum.

The complex includes Frederick Graff's house, a bust of the engineer, and a small Greek Revival temple and pavilion. Also here are several sculptures by America's first sculptor, William Rush (1756–1833). Nearby are the falls of the Schuylkill. If you stand by the falls alongside the many fishing enthusiasts, you can see the boathouses of some of the many scullers on the river.

Other Sites to Visit

Other Fairmount Park mansions are open. The Belmont Mansion (West Fairmount Park; open Tues–Fri 11–4 and weekends by appointment) is Georgian in design. The Chamounix Mansion (north end of West Fairmount Park; open daily 9:30–4:30 all year or by appointment) was the first city-owned permanent hostel in the country (still operating today as such). See the Geographic Cross-Reference for the many other sites to see in Philadelphia.

When in Westchester County, New York, stop in the village of Katonah to see John Jay's retirement house, located on Route 22. Jay promoted reconciliation with the Crown rather than separation, but once independence was a fact he became a devoted public servant. During the Federal period, he wrote many articles promoting a stronger central government. He was also the first Supreme Court justice of the United States. Very close to the Jay house is the Caramoor Center for Music and the Arts (NY 137, Girdle Ridge Road). Mansion tours show rooms filled with eclectic collections of Oriental and European antiques. The mansion grounds contain a formal sunken garden.

PART

SIX

The Jacksonian Revolution

Andrew Jackson was elected president of the United States in 1828. This event marks the beginning of the age of Jacksonian democracy, which extended through the presidencies of Martin Van Buren, John Tyler, James K. Polk, Franklin Pierce, and James Buchanan.

The phrase Jacksonian democracy refers to the extension of democracy (and its consequent social impact) to a new group of voters as states gradually eliminated property qualifications for voting.

To get a better feel for the Jacksonian age, in this section we visit a number of regional sites from the period. I have divided these sites into two categories. The sites in the first category relate to political developments, including the homes of prominent people of the era: Nicholas Biddle, the president of the Second Bank of the United States, and Martin Van Buren, president of the United States after Jackson.

As the Jacksonian revolution extended political democracy, in the realm of literature and art the nation sought a truly American style, not one merely imitative of the English. The American people found this style in their own distinctive interpretation of the romantic movement. Therefore, the age of Jackson can also be seen as America's first great creative period in the arts. In the second part of the section I discuss painting and literature in the romantic age, focusing on two painters, Thomas Cole and Frederic Edwin Church, and three writers, Washington Irving, Edgar Allan Poe, and Walt Whitman.

During the period, important changes took place in exterior and interior design. The major styles of architecture during this period were Greek Revival (1825–1860), Gothic Revival (1840–1880), and Italianate (1840–1885). The principal identifying feature of the Greek Revival style is the use of porches supported by prominent columns. Gothic Revival is one of the easiest styles to spot because of the prominent use of pointed arches for the windows and gables. The gables often have decorated verge-boards (boards carved with fancy shapes and placed at right angles to the eaves). The use of these highly decorative features reminded people of icing on a cake, hence the name "Gingerbread" style. The Italianate, also easily recognizable, uses rounded window shapes (from the Romanesque style). In many cases, the two- or three-story houses are topped with a square cupola.

An outstanding architect of the period was Alexander Jackson Davis. In the 1830s, with his partner Ithiel Town of New Haven, he worked in the Greek Revival style. During the next decade, with Andrew Jackson Downing, he designed in the Gothic Revival style (Lyndhurst castle is the best known). Later, Downing and Davis worked in the Italianate style. Davis designed the Samuel F. B. Morse house in Poughkeepsie partly in this style.

Interior decoration followed patterns similar to those of architecture. Paralleling the Greek Revival period, the Empire style (1820–1840) dominated the early Jacksonian period. The style takes its name from neoclassical architecture and decoration created under Napoleon's reign. This second phase of the classical revival period was a continuation of late Sheraton, with French design details inspired by classical forms.

The romantic period fostered numerous revivals of styles and mixtures of styles, truly justifying the label "eclectic" as applied to the Victorian period. Among the revivals are Gothic Revival (1840–1870) and Rococo Revival (1830–1865). Furniture designed in the Gothic Revival style is characterized by arched points and undulating curves with carvings of leaves, flowers, and fruits in high relief. Davis designed Gothic Revival furniture with pointed arches for Lyndhurst castle. The Rococo Revival style was concurrent with the Italianate style in architecture. The emphasis was less on design and more on decoration with naturalistic carvings of roses, grapes, vines, and birds. The style supposedly borrows from the Italian Renaissance, but greatly resembles the French baroque.

16

Political Developments

More than four times as many men would vote in 1836 as in 1824. The westward movement of population led to the destruction of voting restrictions. When the western states applied for statehood, their constitutions guaranteed universal white male suffrage. This movement in turn affected the eastern states, which also began to liberalize their voting laws.

The fight for the extension of democracy was partly a sectional dispute, the West against the rich East, and partly a class dispute, the less versus the more fortunate. But the basic dispute was over what type of society the United States was going to be. Would the country be run by the large landowners and their allies, similar to the domination of the early executive branch by the Virginia dynasty of Presidents Washington, Jefferson, Madison, and Monroe? Or would the country open up to the other social classes and actualize its ideals of a nonaristocratic society?

In this chapter, we visit sites connected with Andrew Jackson and his handpicked successor Martin Van Buren.

Nicholas Biddle of Andalusia

One of the first acts of the United States Congress was to charter the Bank of the United States under a bill drawn up by Secretary of the Treasury Alexander Hamilton. The bank was first located in Philadelphia's Carpenters' Hall, then moved to a new building on South Third Street. The charter of the First Bank expired in 1811. Five years later it was succeeded by the Second Bank of the United States.

Western voters did not like the bank, seeing it as an example of a special monopoly working to favor the rich over the newly enfranchised. Jackson shared their dislike. The bank charter was to expire in 1836 unless renewed by Congress. A great controversy ensued over the renewal of the charter, and this, of course, brought Jackson into direct conflict with the president of the Second Bank, Nicholas Biddle.

Nicholas Biddle (1786–1844) was a very talented and accomplished man. He was the son of a vice-president of Pennsylvania under the constitution of 1776. He entered the University of Pennsylvania at the unprecedented age of ten and would have graduated at the age of thirteen, but the university would not allow him to receive the degree at such a young age. Biddle switched to Princeton, from which he graduated in 1801 at the age of fifteen.

He went to France in 1804 to be secretary to the American minister. While abroad, he traveled extensively in Europe. Minister James Monroe chose him to be secretary of legation at London. In 1807 Biddle finally returned to the United States. Two years later he was admitted to the bar, but he concentrated on writing rather than the law. He wrote a narrative of the Lewis and Clark expedition into Louisiana country (published in 1814). In 1811 he married Jane Craig, daughter of John Craig, owner of the Andalusia mansion.

The future bank president served in the Pennsylvania legislature, an activity that curtailed some of his writing. His friendship with James Monroe, then secretary of war, further forced him from his beloved lifestyle. The country lacked funds to carry on the War of 1812, and he helped the secretary obtain the necessary monies. The frustrated writer reluctantly accepted President Monroe's appointment as one of five government directors of the bank. In 1822 he became the bank's president.

Jackson became president of the United States in 1829. In that year he began his attack on the bank. Biddle fought back with the pen, starting a writing campaign against Jackson and all other bank enemies. As part of this campaign, he decided to apply to congress for a new charter in 1832, four years before the expiration of the old one. Given Jackson's popularity, this was a political mistake. The president vetoed the bank recharter, and this became the central issue of the election of 1832, actually serving to help reelect the president.

After the loss of its federal charter, the bank operated under a Pennsylvania charter. Old Hickory removed federal deposits and placed them in state banks, referred to as "pet banks." It became difficult to extend credit, which led to a financial crisis. Biddle worked tirelessly against Jackson. One measure he took was to ease credit restrictions to lessen the country's economic problems.

In 1839 Biddle resigned from the bank. Not long afterward, the bank failed, largely because of the overextension of credit to states in the South and West. Although Jackson won the battle, the result was the panic of 1837 with which his successor, Martin Van Buren, had to deal.

In 1841 the bank again failed, and Biddle was held to blame. He was even accused of snatching four hundred thousand dollars in bank funds. Although he was never brought to trial, he was financially ruined, hated, and discredited.

Andalusia (Nicholas Biddle Estate)

Biddles Lane off State Road (14 miles north of Philadelphia on PA 32), Andalusia, PA (Open by appointment only)

Andalusia is a beautiful mansion with especially lovely grounds by the Delaware River. In front of the mansion are the gardens, which have been

Andalusia, Andalusia, Pennsylvania

maintained as an English park, a popular landscaping fad of the times. A tour of the mansion takes a couple of hours but visitors are free to roam among the flowers, shrubs, and trees.

The original farmhouse here was altered in 1806 by architect Benjamin Latrobe. The Biddles acquired Andalusia on the death of Mrs. Craig, Mrs. Biddle's mother. The new owners hired architect Thomas U. Walter to enlarge the house. The architect designed the classical additions, and today the mansion is known as one of the nation's finest examples of Greek Revival architecture.

The mansion is one of the last great country estates once lining the Delaware River between Philadelphia and Bristol. Residing at the estate, Biddle could pursue his interest in farming, even becoming the president of the Philadelphia Society for the Promotion of Agriculture. Life at the mansion was intellectually exciting, with many visits from European exiles. Among the notable guests was Joseph Bonaparte. (Notice the absence of distinguished American visitors.)

In the dining room is a collection of French china brought home by Biddle's brother, Commodore James Biddle, who tried to open Japan to American trade ten years before Perry accomplished this goal. Opening into the Red Parlor is an unusual feature: a half-door/half-window. Biddle's favorite room was the library, and it is most representative of the man. Don't miss the beautiful bookcase.

Mrs. Biddle was very shy and modest. Her chief delight was music. She loved to sing, but had great difficulty in performing before groups. Her nervousness was so great that her voice quavered.

The grounds of the estate slope down to the Delaware River. Close to the river are two small buildings. In the billiards room, the host entertained guests with billiards on the first floor and card games on the second. The other building is the Grotto, stylishly built to simulate a ruin.

Be sure to tour the wonderful gardens. In the spring, visitors can see azaleas, dogwoods, Scotch broom, cherry laurel, fragrant viburnum, lilacs, wisteria, horse chestnut, and empress tree.

Second Bank of the United States

Facing Chestnut Street between Fourth and Fifth streets, Philadelphia, PA (Open daily 9–5, all year; free guided tours on request)

William Strickland designed this bank building between 1819 and 1824 in the Greek temple style for Nicholas Biddle, who had fallen in love with Greek architecture on a visit to Greece in 1806. Today the former bank houses a portrait gallery.

Nicholas Biddle Home (private)

715 Spruce Street, between Seventh and Eighth streets, Philadelphia, PA

Biddle lived here during the fight over the Second Bank of the United States.

Other Sites to Visit

Andalusia is just a short distance north of the Philadelphia city line, so a trip here can be combined with a visit to that city. Burlington, New Jersey, is also very close. Tour the boyhood home of naval war hero Captain James Lawrence. Not far from Andalusia is Glen Foerd, a twenty-five-room, nineteenth-century mansion on the Delaware, located at 5001 Grant Avenue (by appointment only).

Martin Van Buren

The man designated to carry on the Jacksonian tradition was Martin Van Buren. His retirement home, known as Lindenwald, is in Kinderhook, New York. To see the mansion does not take long, but there are many other places in the area to visit.

Van Buren was born just three miles from Lindenwald in the town of Kinderhook. When he became a lawyer, his first office was in nearby Hudson. In 1807 he married his cousin on his mother's side, Hannah Hoes. Tragically, she died just twelve years later, leaving four boys motherless.

The future president served in the New York State Senate for eight years. During this period, he is given credit for starting the development of the Democratic party (which is the continuation of the old Republican party). He stressed the importance of the states in opposition to the growing concentration of power in the hands of the federal government.

In 1821 he was elected United States senator, and in 1828 governor of New York. He only served in the latter post for seventy-one days, resigning in order to become Jackson's secretary of state. As an advisor to the president, he helped plan and execute the war against the Bank of the United States.

The New Yorker had to engage in some infighting in the cabinet against the supporters of Vice-President John C. Calhoun, who thought he should be Jackson's successor. Three Calhoun supporters on the cabinet and their wives shunned the wife of Secretary of War John H. Eaton. Gossip had it that she had committed adultery when married to her first husband. The president, remembering the death of his wife (brought about in part by political harassment), came to the poor woman's defense. The secretary of state endeared himself to the president and enraged the Calhounites when he declared that he would treat all cabinet wives equally. He was not called the Red Fox simply because of the color of his hair.

Calhoun tried to trim Van Buren's sails and get back into the president's good graces by blaming him for the break that had occurred between himself and Jackson. (The breach arose when the president found out that it was Calhoun who had proposed to Monroe's cabinet that commander Jackson be disciplined for entering Spanish Florida during the Seminole War). The Red Fox outmaneuvered Calhoun again when he and Eaton resigned their cabinet positions. This gave the president the chance to reform his entire cabinet by asking for everyone's resignation. As a reward, Jackson appointed his ally minister to Great Britain.

The future president became vice-president upon Jackson's reelection in 1832. Jackson handpicked him as his heir apparent, and he was subsequently elected president in 1836. The only campaigning he did was in Albany and Saratoga Springs.

Soon after entering the White House, the depression of 1837 began. The new president spent the rest of his term preoccupied by this economic downturn. He got Congress to establish an independent treasury, which remained the government's basic fiscal-financial institution until the establishment of the Federal Reserve System in 1913. Largely because of the depression, Van Buren was not reelected. William Henry Harrison won that post in the election of 1840.

Martin Van Buren National Historic Site

South of Kinderhook on NY 9H, Kinderhook, NY (Open daily 9–4:30, mid Apr–early Dec)

Lindenwald was the ex-president's retirement home. It was named for the many linden trees on the property (*wald* means "forest" in Dutch). In

Martin Van Buren House, Kinderhook, New York

1797 Judge Peter Van Ness built the house. Washington Irving frequently vis-
ited here and for a short period was even tutor to the children of the house.
In 1839 Van Buren purchased it, and ten years later he had architect Richard
Upjohn make additions in the Italianate tradition.

The ex-president lived at Lindenwald from 1841 until his death in 1862.
Although supposedly retired, he remained very active in politics. He nearly
became the Democratic presidential candidate in 1844, but was squeezed
out by dark horse James K. Polk. Polk emerged to the forefront because he
favored the annexation of Texas. In 1848 Van Buren was the Free Soil party's
presidential candidate. This antislavery party tried to pass the Wilmot
Proviso, which would have prevented slavery from spreading to the new
territories.

That the man from old Kinderhook was still active is shown by a romantic episode. He asked Margaret Sylvester, daughter of his old legal mentor, to
marry him. She turned him down, telling him she had remained single all
these years and intended to continue so.

His sons would often visit Lindenwald. On the house tour, you will see
John and his wife Elizabeth's bedroom and the bedroom of Abraham and
his wife Angelica. Abraham, a West Point graduate and later a lieutenant
colonel, served as his father's secretary, while Angelica served as White
House host. Another son, Martin, Jr., had a mysterious malady that no one
could cure, and so he was often at Lindenwald. And finally, Smith, along with
his wife, Ellen James, and their children, was a frequent visitor. Upon his
wife's death, Smith married Washington Irving's niece Henrietta.

The Van Burens entertained in the main hallway of the house with its
French mural wallpaper, *Landscape of the Hunt*. They used the sideboards

to hold refreshments. An especially interesting room is the library, an 1849 addition built by Richard Upjohn. The walls contain many political cartoons. Also here is a sketch of Henry Clay, a political opponent but also a friend. On display is the ex-president's curling iron, which was used to curl the frills on some of his shirts. The president was an impeccable dresser, and the press often derided him for his natty appearance.

The retiree ran a farm at Lindenwald, directing the work himself. In 1853 he took an extended trip to Europe with his son Martin, Jr. Tragically, in 1855 the young man died while abroad. The ex-president himself died of bronchial asthma in his Lindenwald bedroom in 1862, four months short of his eightieth birthday.

Other Sites to Visit

The Luykas Van Alen House is a Dutch house located on Route 9H just north of Lindenwald. Local legend says that Washington Irving used the house as the model for the home of character Katrina Van Tassel. Next to the house is a small white building, supposedly the schoolhouse where the model for Irving's Ichabod Crane taught. The James Vanderpoel House, also known as the House of History, is a Federal house (ca. 1819) located at 16 Broad Street, Kinderhook. The owner, along with Van Buren, studied law under Francis Sylvester, and later became a judge. The house has a collection of excellent furniture. Other sites in the area include Olana, the home of Frederick Church; the Shaker Museum in Old Chatham; and the Clermont Mansion in Clermont State Park.

17

American Romanticism

In its very early history, religious concerns dominated American art and literature. During the Revolutionary period, political concerns prevailed. As political and economic stability grew in the new nation, attention could be paid to more purely artistic concerns. And when Americans turned to the world of art, they found it dominated by the romantic movement. Romanticism, in part a reaction against the restraints and rules of classicism, stressed such ideas as sensibility, primitivism, love of nature, mysticism, and individualism. (Not exactly a list of Puritan values! Indeed, American romanticism can be seen as a revolt against Puritanism.)

For an American romantic movement to develop, the harsh religious spirit in the country had to be softened. This was accomplished to some extent with the rise of Unitarianism, which became very successful among more literate classes, especially in and around Boston.

The freer religious climate allowed the spread of the philosophy of transcendentalism in literary circles. This belief system stressed that knowledge could be obtained by individuals intuitively—knowledge that transcended the reach of human senses and the narrow confines of puritanical ministers. Ralph Waldo Emerson declared that one should even write one's own Bible.

Transcendentalism's emphasis on the human ability to find God in nature provided American romantics with a defense against the charge of the Europeans that America had no real history about which to be romantic. The stress on finding God and truth in nature allowed the Americans to emphasize the pristine nature of the nation's forests and mountains as a source of romantic inspiration. The Hudson River school cultivated this love of nature in landscape paintings. The Hudson River school began in 1825 with Thomas Cole's early landscapes and lasted for over fifty years. Other artists in this tradition were Albert Bierstadt, Jasper Cropsey, and Asher B. Durand.

The houses of two famous painters, Thomas Cole and Frederic Edwin Church, are close to one another, so you can visit them both in the same day. While the Cole house is relatively plain and being restored, the Church house is a mansion out of the *Arabian Nights*. Combined with a trip to the Catskill Mountains to hike or sightsee, this can be a memorable visit.

Thomas Cole

Thomas Cole was born in England in 1801 and at age seventeen immigrated with his family to America. They first settled in Philadelphia, but later moved to Ohio, where he became an itinerant portrait painter. He eventually returned to Philadelphia to pursue his interest in art. There he noticed the landscapes of a local artist, Thomas Doughty. The landscapes were a breath of fresh air to the young painter, because most American painting consisted of portraits or paintings of historical scenes in the classical vein.

The Cole family moved to New York City after a business failure. Thomas, to help out, joined them after still another bankruptcy. While living there, he traveled to the Catskills to explore and paint landscapes.

In 1825 he convinced the manager of a frame shop on Broadway to place some of his art work in the shop window. When Colonel John Trumbull, president of the American Academy of Fine Arts, saw the paintings, he thought he had discovered a genius. He quickly purchased *Kaaterskill Falls*. The young painter's fame spread just as quickly.

The innovative painter became a member of writer James Fenimore Cooper's Bread and Cheese Club (also called the Lunch), which included artists, authors, professors, and leaders of the business world. Here he met poet William Cullen Bryant, and a lifelong friendship began.

In 1829 he traveled to Europe to study painting. Before his departure, he had begun to paint biblical scenes. Upon his return, he drew further away from American landscapes. Luman Reed became a patron, agreeing to commission five paintings in the moralistic *The Course of Empire* series. Reed's influence proved somewhat restraining because Cole felt that, in order to satisfy his benefactor, he had to turn out rather pedestrian American views.

Thomas Cole House (Cedar Grove)

218 Spring Street (make a left turn soon after passing over the Rip Van Winkle bridge), Catskill, NY (Open Wed–Sat 11–4, Sun 1–5, July–Labor Day)

Each summer the landscape painter visited the village of Catskill, where he stayed in the home of John Alexander Thomson. In this home also stayed Thomson's sister and her four daughters, among them the future Mrs. Cole, Maria Bartow. The couple married in 1836 and made Cedar Grove their home. The painter's first studio was a carriage barn and stable close to the house. Here he created such works as *The Course of Empire* (1834–1836) and *Voyage of Life* (completed in 1839). Luman Reed died in 1836 before the artist exhibited *The Course of Empire* in the fall of that year. Critics praised the painting, but preferred his landscapes.

After finishing the *Voyage of Life* series, the painter made another trip to Europe, establishing a studio in Rome. On his return he had a showing of his work, but the show was not financially successful. His moralistic paintings were just not popular. In the same year, he took Frederic Edwin Church from Hartford, Connecticut, as a pupil. After two years of apprenticeship, Church went out on his own.

Thomas Cole House, Catskill, New York

Toward the end of his life, the great landscape painter became increasingly bitter that his fellow artists and the American public did not care for his attempts to use art to uplift them. He became increasingly isolated and depressed.

It was in the Cedar Grove house that all five Cole children were born and where, in 1848, their father died of inflammation of the lungs at age forty-seven. The house is being improved and has exhibits dealing with some of the artist's paintings and a few of his possessions.

Kaaterskill Falls

There is a parking space off Route 23A, just after going around the big horseshoe bend before reaching Haines Falls, NY

You can reach this place of beauty by driving through Kaaterskill Clove. This is a visual treat, with mountains on both sides of the road. Pick up the Escarpment Trail by the smaller falls along the highway, at the apex of the big horseshoe turn. There are many different ways to get to the falls. This particular one is extremely rough at first. The first obstacle is the climb up a steep hill.

It takes about forty-five minutes to walk to the falls. But what a gorgeous sight awaits the hiker! These are the highest falls in New York State. Actually there are two falls, because the water hits a large rocky area below and then falls again. Sit at the base of the falls and let the water lightly spray you.

Walking farther, you come to a place with excellent views of Kaaterskill Clove. In the distance is Hunter Mountain with its ski trails.

North-South Lake Public Campground

Take Route 23A to Haines Falls and then Mountain House Road, Haines Falls, NY

American romanticism drew great inspiration from the Catskill Mountains. Writers Cooper, Bryant, and Irving described them, while artists Cole, Durand, and Church painted them. The artistic discovery of the Catskills did much to make the mountains America's first popular summer resort area. To meet the demand for accommodation, great hotels (known as mountain houses) were built. These hotels catered to the upper classes of the East Coast, both North and South.

Starting in 1824 Charles Beach gradually built the first mountain house, known simply as Catskill Mountain House, in the vicinity of North and South lakes near Haines Falls. This hotel became as popular a site as Niagara Falls. It was followed some years later by various copycats.

The Catskill Mountain House no longer exists, but you can reach the site of the famous resort via a trail east from the day-use parking area at South Lake. To see the site from the vantage point of the painters, hike the trails. Follow the Blue Trail all the way to North Point and back. A ten-minute walk brings the hiker to a gorgeous view of the Hudson Valley. At this point you are at the edge of the plateau looking down at the flat area extending into the distance. Gazing toward the horizon, Albany can just be seen in the distance. Also visible are the town of Catskill and Church's Olana mansion atop a hill on the east side of the Hudson River. The views of North and South lakes are also stupendous from Bear's Den and North Point.

Frederic Edwin Church

Frederic Edwin Church (1826–1900) was a native of Hartford, Connecticut. As a youth he had seen many Cole paintings hanging on the walls of the home of Daniel Wadsworth (of Hartford's Wadsworth Atheneum fame). The young man persuaded his father to use his influence with Wadsworth to get the master to take him as a pupil.

Starting in 1844 the young painter studied under Cole for two years in the town of Catskill. While exploring the Hudson River in the vicinity of Cedar Grove, he fell in love with a plot of land on the east bank of the river. He vowed to purchase it one day and build a house there.

After his apprenticeship the Connecticut artist moved back to Hartford, where he painted *Hooker's Party Journeying through the Wilderness*. His ancestors had participated in the founding of that city, so this painting had special significance for him.

In 1848 Church moved to New York City. His painting *West Rock, New Haven* won him membership in the National Academy. Cyrus Field, later famous as the promoter of the first transatlantic telegraph cable, purchased the painting. The two men became great friends and in 1851 traveled together through the southern states. They also traveled to South America to view and sketch the beautiful landscapes of the Andes. Back in New York, the traveling artist painted South American landscapes, which brought him widespread recognition and made him the most prominent artist of the time. He later painted Niagara Falls after two visits there.

In 1859, soon after Church returned from another trip to South America, he exhibited the painting *The Heart of the Andes*. The painting became an immediate sensation, attracting many visitors. The artist wound up marrying one visitor, Isabella Carnes, a cousin of his friend Lockwood de Forrest.

Olana: The Home of Frederic Church

Route 9G, five miles south of Hudson, NY (Open Wed–Sat 10–5, Sun 1–5, late May–Labor Day; Wed–Sat 12–5, Sun 1–5, Labor Day–late Oct)

You won't see another mansion like this one in the entire travel area, so don't miss it. Also available are spectacular views of the Hudson River, five hundred feet below it.

In 1867 the now-famous man bought the Catskill property he had fallen in love with when working with Cole. After a trip to Europe and the Middle East, he decided to build a house on the property that would catch some of the spirit of the Near East. He worked with architect Calvert Vaux of Central Park fame on the design of Olana (a Latin corruption of the Arabic Al'ana, or "Our Place on High"). The house was completed in 1874. It is an Italian-style villa with "Islamic" (Moorish, Persian, and other Middle Eastern styles) influences. Church wanted minarets and different rooflines, but Vaux had great difficulty in translating this into reality. He did succeed in adding the open tower, Islamic arches, balconies, and polychrome stonework.

Church loved the house and painted here in a studio room. He said Olana was his greatest work of art. To increase the balance in the landscape, the artist created a lake on the property. In the mansion's interior, the rooms lead into a central hall (in the shape of a Greek cross) in the Persian manner. The doors are stenciled, also in Islamic patterns. Originally, the inner courtyard was to be left open. The owner had planned a skylight, but moved to the second floor and roofed over the courtyard. The family used the yard's middle ground as a stage for plays and charades. Samuel Clemens (Mark Twain) would read from his works here. The diminutive Mrs. Church was a concert pianist, whose favorite place in the house was the sitting room. Her desk is so small, one assumes it belonged to one of the children.

Nine of the mansion's thirty-seven rooms are decorated, while the others are almost as austere as a monk's cell. There are several reminders that Church's family was one of the seven that founded Hartford, including a picture of Hartford's Charter Oak Tree and a charter oak chair made from the wood of the great tree. Also here are the many paintings the artist collected over the years.

Jasper Cropsey House, Hastings-on-Hudson, New York

Other Sites to Visit

There are a few Cole possessions to be seen at the Bronck House Museum, Route 9W, Coxsackie, New York. In addition, the museum has a few remnants from the Catskill Mountain House. Also nearby is the Clermont Mansion near the town of Germantown. The Jasper Cropsey house is located at 25 Washington Avenue in Hastings-on-Hudson. The private house is only open periodically, so call the town's historical society for information. On Long Island, the home of William Sidney Mount, a romantic genre painter, is in the town of Stony Brook on Long Hill Road. It is presently being restored, so call the local historical society before traveling to the house.

Washington Irving

Washington Irving was a romantic writer who today is best known for his folklore stories. Many of these are retellings of Dutch folk tales from New Netherland days. The author's house reminds some observers of the witch house in the Hansel and Gretel story. The house is a terrific mixture of styles, and of all the houses in the region, it best embodies the romantic movement. Everyone should be grateful that the house has kept the great Dutch gabled entrance, one of only a few left in the region.

Washington Irving was born in New York City in 1783. He was a sickly child and spent most of his time enjoying such pursuits as the theater, music, art, travel, and conversation. As a possible future vocation he studied law. He traveled in Europe between the years 1804 and 1806. Upon returning to New York, he continued his law studies and gained admittance to the bar. He did not care for this profession, saying that it was not that he knew only a little law, but that he knew damn little.

He wrote a series of humorous stories for the periodical *Salmagundi*, and this success led him to write what came to be known as the *Knicker-bocker History*. Published in 1809, this work poked fun at the old Dutch families.

The romantic writer was deeply in love with Matilda Hoffman, the daughter of the man with whom he had studied law. In the same year that he published the *Knickerbocker History*, Matilda died of tuberculosis. Haunted by her memory, he remained a bachelor for the rest of his life. This did not prevent him from having a roving eye, but he simply was never serious about any other woman.

In 1815 he and his brother Peter traveled to Liverpool, England, to try to put the family import firm in order. Their efforts were in vain, but the trip was not. During his stay, Irving met Sir Walter Scott, the great English author who influenced an entire generation of romantic writers. (Matilda had been a friend of Rebecca Gratz, who is buried in Philadelphia's Mikveh Israel Cemetery. Irving mentioned the beautiful and kind Rebecca to Scott as a possible model for the heroine in *Ivanhoe*, and the English author did, in fact, use her.)

About this time Irving made a commitment to make his living by writing. This was not an easy decision in an age when there were no American authors of repute. Indeed, many thought America incapable of producing literary talent.

While living in Europe, a mountain of literary works poured from his pen. In the years 1819 and 1820 he published serially in the United States *The Sketch Book of Geoffrey Crayon, Gent.* This work contains some of his most famous characters, including Rip Van Winkle, Ichabod Crane, and the Headless Horseman.

In 1826 the writer moved to Madrid and served as an attaché at the United States legation in that city. This was followed by a position as secretary to the legation in London (1829–1832). It was not until 1832, after an absence of seventeen years, that he returned to the United States. Not quite over the travel bug, he wandered in the Midwest, especially through Missouri.

Sunnyside

West Sunnyside Lane, off Route 9, Tarrytown, NY (Open daily 10–5, all year; closed Tues, Dec–Mar)

Irving first saw the farmhouse and property that came to be known as Sunnyside in 1798 on a visit to a friend living near Tarrytown. The country farmhouse had been built in the late seventeenth century for tenants of the Philipsburg Manor, Upper Mills. In 1835 he purchased the house and soon

Sunnyside (Washington Irving House), Tarrytown, New York

transformed it into the romantic dwelling it is today. He planted the wisteria that now grows around the entrance to the house. Even the grounds became romanticized. The European traveler named the large pond the Little Mediterranean.

Working on the house did not slow down this prodigious writer. He used his study as a one-room apartment for both writing and sleeping. In 1836 he published *Astoria*, which deals with the great fur empire of John Jacob Astor. In the following year he published *Adventures of Captain Bonneville*. And between 1839 and 1841 he wrote some thirty essays and stories for the *Knickerbocker Magazine*.

Irving returned to Europe in 1842 when he accepted President Tyler's appointment to be envoy extraordinary and minister plenipotentiary to the court of Spain. He stayed in Spain until 1846.

Upon returning to Sunnyside, he added a three-story tower to the house to accommodate his nieces and the increasing number of visitors to the house. He enjoyed having young people in the house, saying it kept him from the profligate life led by so many bachelors. The nieces, Catherine and Sarah, acted as hosts. They often played the square rosewood piano their uncle purchased for them.

The author moved from the study to an upstairs bedroom. There he worked on the *Life of George Washington*. Some say he worked too hard and ruined his health. He finished the five volumes just before dying of an enlarged heart at Sunnyside in 1859. He is buried in the churchyard of the Dutch Reformed Church on U.S. 9 in North Tarrytown.

The house is filled with the author's belongings. His study is exactly as it was during his lifetime, including the sofa that doubled as a bed. The guest room has a sleigh bed in the alcove and cottage furniture made of painted pine. At the entrance to Sunnyside Lane off U.S. 9 is the Washington Irving Memorial, sculpted by Daniel Chester French, who modeled the Lincoln Memorial in Washington, D.C.

Other Sites to Visit

Visit the other sites associated with Sleepy Hollow territory. Lyndhurst, another spectacularly "romantic" building, is just a short drive up Route 9.

Edgar Allan Poe

Another early American writer in the romantic tradition is Edgar Allan Poe. A multitalented man, he not only wrote hauntingly beautiful poetry, but contributed to the development of the horror and detective stories. In this tour we visit two of the author's many places of residence, one in Philadelphia and the other in the Bronx. Both sites are modest ones and are widely separated. Unless you are a real Poe admirer, you should save them for when you are in these areas seeing other places.

A great many myths have existed concerning this popular writer. He was not an alcoholic or a drug addict, nor was he mad. His horror stories, seen by some as a sign of mental illness, fit in with the romantic emphasis on the macabre. However, his phobia of death and his dysfunctional family life made it doubly difficult for him to stay employed. Therefore, he was always fending off poverty. This poverty kept him in a state of anxiety, which in turn led him to alcohol. This does not mean he was an alcoholic, for he never became physically addicted. Indeed, his body rejected alcohol. From his college days it was noted that the young man never could drink much. The drinking he did do, however, was of serious concern given his probable diabetes.

His fear of death stemmed in part from a sensitive nature reacting to the deaths of important women in his life. His actor father abandoned the family, and in 1811 his actress mother died when he was only three years old.

The future poet was taken in by the wealthy Allan family of Richmond, Virginia. He loved his new mother, but he and his father were temperamental opposites. Mr. Allan, a businessman, regarded his son's interest in literature as a reflection of sheer laziness.

The differences between the poet and his father turned to animosity sometime after the father began a series of extramarital affairs. Mr. Allan was afraid that his son might reveal his transgressions to Mrs. Allan. This, combined with his dislike of the young man, led him to hatch a scheme to discredit the youth. His method of destruction was to send him to the University of Virginia at Charlottesville in 1826 without adequate financial support. At the university, Poe was soon in debt and fell in with the wrong crowd, drinking and gambling. He soon returned to Richmond in disgrace, whereupon he came in for such virulent abuse from his father that he ran off and joined the army.

Poe kept writing to his father, literally begging him for money and assistance in obtaining an appointment to West Point. He felt he belonged to the Southern aristocracy and wanted to become an officer as a route to acceptance as a gentleman. Failing in this, in 1829 he obtained a discharge from the army following the death of Mrs. Allan.

His father finally agreed to help him, but in a virtual repeat of the University of Virginia story, inadequately supported him at the academy. The new cadet had thought he could whiz through the whole course in six months. Inadequate funds, combined with his discovery that one could not speed graduation, caused him deliberately to gain enough demerits to force the academy to drop him from its rolls.

From West Point he made his way to Baltimore, where he had relatives, including his brother, Henry; his widowed aunt, Mrs. Clemm; and his cousin, Virginia Clemm. He lodged in the small attic of Mrs. Clemm's brick row house, which is now a museum. In 1833 he won a prize from the Baltimore *Saturday Visitor* for "MS. Found in a Bottle." The following year, his father died without mentioning his son in his will.

In 1835 Poe moved to Richmond to help edit the *Southern Literary Messenger*. Often persons who have been reared in dysfunctional families find it hard to delineate what is proper and improper conduct. When the young editor began to write book reviews in a blistering vein, it brought him so much notoriety that he got himself banned from New York literary circles.

While in Richmond, Poe married his fourteen-year-old cousin. His early marital life was made more difficult when he was fired from the *Messenger*. His attempt to make the magazine into a literary giant brought him into open conflict with the owner, who wanted the magazine to remain small.

Discouraged, the writer and his wife moved to New York in early 1837. That city's closed doors soon forced them to journey to Philadelphia. There in 1839 he became editor of *Burton's Gentleman's Magazine*, in which he published "The Fall of the House of Usher." He became embittered over not receiving payment for his literary contributions to the magazine and in 1840 left with plans to publish his own. The budding publisher had to abandon his dream because he could not raise the needed capital.

In 1841 he became editor of *Graham's Magazine* and published "The Murders in the Rue Morgue." With the success of the magazine, he became one of Philadelphia's major literary personalities.

Then his slow decline began. Virginia exhibited signs of spreading tuberculosis. In May 1842 he left *Graham's Magazine*. He moved his family into the center of Philadelphia to Spring Garden, near the journalists' quarter, in an attempt to save on rent.

Edgar Allan Poe National Historic Site

532 North Seventh Street between Green and Spring Garden streets, Philadelphia, PA (Open daily 9–5, all year)

This is the only surviving home of the writer in Philadelphia. He lived in the small brick house behind 530 North Seventh Street beginning sometime between the fall of 1842 and June of 1843 and ending in April 1844. The house marks the decline of the relative fortunes of the Poes. While living here, he wrote "The Gold Bug" and "The Black Cat."

Since none of the furniture that was in the house belonged to the Poes, the Park Service removed it. You can see a video at the museum, talk to a museum guide, and see several displays on the life of the writer.

Edgar Allan Poe Cottage

Corner of the Grand Concourse and East Kingsbridge Road, Bronx, NY (take the Fordham Road exit of I-87, travel east on Fordham Road, and turn left onto the Grand Concourse) (Open Wed–Fri 1–5, Sat 10–4, Sun 1–5, all year)

In order to earn more money, the poet decided to try New York again. He set out with no more than ten dollars to his name. In January 1845 he published his best-known poem, *The Raven*, which made him a minor literary sensation. He also became editor of *The Broadway Journal*. Tragically, he threw away his chance for more permanent acceptance by returning to his bitter critical reviews, this time taking on Longfellow.

In the spring of 1846 he rented a cottage surrounded by farmland at Fordham. He felt this was a healthier place for his tubercular wife. But these were not to be happy days. Virginia died in the small cottage bedroom in January 1847. His mother-in-law and Mrs. Shew, a friend, would sit with the widower at night as he could not bear to be alone in the dark.

He did pull himself together long enough to write "Annabel Lee," "Ulalume," "The Bells," and "Eureka." In addition, he had several romances with women he met in amateur literary circles.

In June 1849 he and his mother-in-law left Fordham for Brooklyn. Mrs. Clemm stayed at the home of a friend while her son-in-law went on a subscription-raising trip for a new literary magazine. While in Philadelphia, he had a paranoid delusional attack worsened by drinking. The doctors warned him that another such attack would kill him. He made it to Richmond, but on his way back to New York, he may have had another delusional attack and, with no one to help him, drank himself into a coma. He was found on a street in Baltimore and taken to a hospital, where he died in October 1849.

The Poe Cottage itself is now set in a little park amid the hustle and bustle of Fordham Road and the Grand Concourse. The simple white frame dwelling was built around 1812. Here you can see a slide show on the poet's life and poetry. It is said that the great author liked to visit the library at St. John's College (now Fordham University) then walk to the Bronx River, where the botanical gardens and zoo now stand. Or he would walk in the other direction, over to the Hudson River. You can also see a few pieces of furniture belonging to the Poes and the eight-feet-by-eight-feet room where Virginia died. Her mother may also have used the room.

Other Sites to Visit

If journeying to Philadelphia to see the Poe House, combine the trip with other Philadelphia tours. If visiting the Bronx, continue north into Sleepy Hollow territory.

Walt Whitman

Walt Whitman, the great poet of American democracy, celebrated the simple life, common people, and everyday things. He was a romantic, because his philosophy shares the pantheism of transcendentalism and because he was less concerned with the problems of life than with celebrating what we find around us.

The Walt Whitman house on Long Island was the poet's childhood home, so the tour here is relatively brief. Combine it with other sites on Long Island to make it a day trip. The Whitman house in Camden, New Jersey, has more of the poet's belongings and takes longer to see, but still is not a day trip in and of itself. On the other hand, Camden is just across the Delaware River from Philadelphia with its multitude of historical sites.

The poet was very much a product of his times. Like the New England writers, he was searching for a purely American literature. Like his father, who was a friend of the deist Thomas Paine, he fought for greater freedom from the overly strict aspects of religion.

There were, however, key differences between Whitman and his New England colleagues. The Long Islander proved too much for many of his contemporaries, with the exceptions of Emerson, Thoreau, and Alcott (and even Emerson asked him to tone down his writings). In a nation where puritanical values dominated, readers were shocked by the frank discussions of physiological subjects, especially those relating to sex. As a consequence, in his lifetime he was more fully appreciated in the more lenient atmosphere of Europe.

The great poet was not only an innovator in subject matter, but in style as well, blending poetry and prose. He kept improving and adding poems to his book *Leaves of Grass*, publishing nine editions during his lifetime.

Walt Whitman House, Camden, New Jersey

Walt Whitman House

246 Old Walt Whitman Road, sandwiched between Old Walt Whitman and Walt Whitman roads (take exit 40 of the Northern State Parkway, travel north on Route 110 and then north on Walt Whitman Road), Huntington Station, Long Island, NY (Open Wed–Fri 1–4, Sat–Sun 10–4, all year)

The author was born in 1819 in this shinglesided farmhouse built by his father about three years before his birth. The house is in the town of West

Hills, near Huntington, Long Island. His father was a carpenter and often moved the family from town to town. They left the West Hills home when Walt was only four years old.

Upstairs are two rooms that contain Whitman memorabilia. The first room contains pictures and sculptures of the great poet. The second room has a small library, bookstand, and postcards.

At the age of twelve, Walt worked as an office boy. He was a printer for a short period in New York City and then taught school on Long Island. He tried his hand at running his own newspaper, went back to teaching, returned to printing again, and then edited several newspapers.

In 1845 he settled in Brooklyn, and the following year became the editor of the *Brooklyn Eagle*. Some two years later, he was discharged from this job for writing editorials supporting the Wilmot Proviso, which proposed a ban on slavery in annexed territories. Whitman edited other newspapers, but did not last long in these jobs due to shifting political winds. Becoming disgusted with politics, he turned his back on writing editorials. He became the main support of the family (his father was ill), running a combination bookstore and printing shop on the first floor of his home.

By 1855, at the age of thirty-six, he was ready to devote himself fully to poetry. This is the year he came out with his first edition of *Leaves of Grass*. Some friends of his printed the work, since he could not get a publisher. The only writer of eminence to praise the book was Emerson. Whitman shocked the literary world in his second edition because, without asking permission, he put Emerson's comment on the binding: "I greet you at the beginning of a great career." In the spirit of Emerson's remark that each man should write his own Bible, the second edition physically looks like the Holy Book. The new poems in this 1856 edition were quickly condemned for being frank about sexual matters. Not deterred by the negative reactions, in the 1860 edition his growing emotional attachment to men came to the fore.

George Whitman, Walt's brother, was slightly wounded in the Civil War, and the poet rushed to Fredericksburg, Virginia, to be with him. This visit inspired him to take a more active role in tending to the wounded in Washington, D.C. His friends got him a job as a clerk in the Department of the Interior. Here he met John Burroughs, who became one of the early champions of his poetry. Burroughs later became famous as a nature writer. (One can think of him as the Whitman of nature.)

While in Washington, Whitman suffered a series of crises. He lost his government job because of his poetry. Fortunately, a friend got him another government position. Then he suffered an emotional crisis in 1870 over the breakup of his relationship with a young streetcar conductor, Peter Doyle, with whom the poet had fallen in love four years earlier.

His health was failing, and in January 1873, while at his work desk, he fell ill. He went home and, that night, woke up paralyzed on his left side (his leg was especially affected). He never completely recovered from the stroke.

Whitman, still feeling weak, accepted his brother George's offer to stay with his family in their house (which still stands) at the corner of Fifth and Stevens in Camden, New Jersey. However, relations between the two were not good, as businessman George never appreciated his brother's talents. To lessen the chances of interaction, Walt took the small third-floor room. His health improved enough for a trip out West in 1879.

Controversy continued to follow the poet. In 1882 irate readers threatened his Boston publisher with prosecution if two objectionable poems were not withdrawn from the book. In addition, the Boston post office banned the book from the mails. Fortunately, the controversy actually increased sales, enabling the author to buy a modest little house on Mickle Street in Camden.

Mickle Street House

320 Mickle Street, not far south of the Benjamin Franklin Bridge (take exit 4 of the New Jersey Turnpike, drive north on Route 73, then west on Route 38, north on Route 30, take the Federal Road exit and travel west, turn left on Fourth Street and right onto Mickle Street), Camden, NJ (Open Wed–Fri 9–12, 1–6, Sat 10–12, 1–6, all year)

Here in this 1840 Greek Revival town house the Quaker poet spent the remainder of his life, from 1884 to 1892. The widow of a sea captain, Mrs. Mary Davis, took care of him in his old age in return for her rent.

The house is filled with memorabilia. Besides the many photographs, the collection includes his Quaker hat (a symbol of equality worn indoors as well as outdoors), the rocking chair in which Thomas Eakins painted him, his collection of seashells (he stayed at Cape May many times), and the knapsack he used while going door-to-door to sell his book. What would the house owners have thought had they known that their salesman was one of the country's greatest poets?

The guide told us that many children stop at the door to ask, "Is this Santa Claus's house?" Apparently, the poet's white beard causes the confusion. In the house is a small library with many books by and about Whitman.

Harleigh Cemetery

Entering the cemetery from Haddon Avenue, turn left past the cemetery office and follow the semicircle around to the tomb, which is on your left just before the first of a series of ponds.

Whitman died in 1892. He is buried in this cemetery in a gray granite tomb, which he constructed after a design borrowed from William Blake. The mausoleum cost more than the house on Mickle Street, forcing the poet to borrow the money. Brother George lies on top of Walt, weighing him down in death as he did in life.

Other Sites to Visit

When in Camden, cross the Benjamin Franklin Bridge into Philadelphia. See the Geographic Cross-Reference for sites in both Philadelphia and Long Island.

P A R T

SEVEN

Industry and Transportation

In this section we follow trends in several industries, including transportation, in order to show the development of the Industrial Revolution in the United States. In the first part of the section, tours cover places that more generally deal with industrial development: the Du Pont gunpowder factory in Wilmington, Delaware; a museum devoted to the development of the steam engine in Exton, Pennsylvania; the industrial section of Paterson, New Jersey; and sites connected with the development of the telegraph in Poughkeepsie, New York, and Morristown, New Jersey. Other parts of the section cover developments in several major industries, including iron, coal, canals, railroads, and shipping.

18

The Industrial Revolution

Before the Industrial Revolution, goods were produced by four major sources of power: human, horse, wind, and water. Restriction to these relatively meager sources limited people's ability to increase their productivity and, thereby, their wealth. However, toward the end of the eighteenth century, inventors improved the steam engine to the point where dramatic increases occurred in industrial production.

New and better power sources made possible the building of large factories. Into these factories employers could crowd hundreds of workers to run the new machines. The implementation of a system of interchangeable parts further aided factory development. The social, political, and economic changes produced by the new system became known as the Industrial Revolution. Samuel Slater, working in Rhode Island, is often credited with starting this revolution in the United States. In 1790 he built the first American steam-powered cotton-processing machine.

Wilmington Area

It will take more than a day to see both the Hagley Museum and the Newcomen Library and Museum. In fact, it takes a whole day just to see Hagley Museum. The museum is highly recommended. It should only take a couple of hours to see the exhibits at Newcomen.

Hagley Museum

Three miles north of Wilmington on Route 141 between Route 100 and Rockland Road, Wilmington, DE (Open daily 9:30–4:30, Apr 1–Dec 31; Sat–Sun 9:30–4:30, Jan 2–Mar 31)

It is possible to trace the Industrial Revolution as it occurred in the Brandywine area in general, and in the Du Pont gunpowder factory in particular, by visiting the Hagley Museum. The museum's main exhibit building traces the development of increasingly sophisticated uses of power sources from the earliest Norse mills used by Swedish settlers, through various types of waterwheels, to the water turbine.

Exhibits also tell the history of the Du Pont family. Pierre Du Pont, son of a French watchmaker, worked his way into the French nobility through his

Demonstration at Hagley Museum, Wilmington, Delaware

talent for economic writing. He became an advisor to French kings, even administering the French Department of Finance. Because of his writings and governmental work, he met such Americans as Benjamin Franklin and Thomas Jefferson.

Pierre Du Pont had two sons, Victor and Eleuthère Irénée. Victor trained to be an ambassador/businessmen, while Eleuthère became a bookkeeper for the French chemist Antoine Laurent Lavoisier. Working with the chemist, Eleuthère received training in the making of gunpowder.

The Du Ponts had to leave the country following the French Revolution because of their close ties to the royal family. In 1799 they sailed for the United States on the ship the *American Eagle,* first settling in New Jersey.

Eleuthère chose a site along the Brandywine River for a gunpowder factory because a key investor lived nearby and because the Brandywine was a swift stream that provided bountiful water power. There was also a large supply of black willow trees, useful in making the charcoal necessary for gunpowder production.

Victor tried to run a house of commerce in New York City, but by 1805 the business went bankrupt. At first the gunpowder factory also had a hard time, but demand for gunpowder during the War of 1812 gave the struggling factory a helpful boost. Eleuthère eventually brought his brother to the Brandywine area. Victor lived on the east side of the creek and ran a woolen business.

Victor died in 1827 and Eleuthère in 1834. Eleuthère's son, Alfred, took over the company. Alfred, a chemist, developed a dye called iron liquor and the preservative creosote. He ran the firm until an explosion in the factory shattered what remained of his nerves. Henry, Alfred's brother, then took over and ran the company from 1850 to 1889.

The exhibits at Hagley Museum show how gunpowder is made from a combination of saltpeter, sulfur, and charcoal. The giant roll mills ground the powder finer and finer. This was very dangerous work, for there were more than 250 explosions (one killed 40 of the 140 workers). There are many other buildings on the property, including the foreman's cottage, the machine shop, and the millwright shop. A stationary steam engine, which powered the sifting machinery in the pack house, is demonstrated in one of the buildings.

While visiting the museum, take the bus ride to see Eleuthère Du Pont's 1803 Georgian-style mansion, Eleutherian Mills. In the dining room one finds French wallpaper showing the view north up the Hudson River from Trophy Point, West Point. Proceeding to the back terrace, visitors can look over the millyard below.

The house was dangerously close to the gunpowder mills. Eleuthère's wife, Sophie, was hit by a rock that flew through a window. She never fully recovered. The house, damaged in an 1848 powder explosion, was remodeled by Henry, who more than doubled the available space. In 1890 another severe blast drove Mrs. Henry Du Pont from the residence. The house remained empty for three years before becoming the clubhouse for company workmen. In 1921 powdermaking ceased along the Brandywine.

The rooms on the first floor of the house have been left as they were when Eleuthère's great-granddaughter, Louise Du Pont Crowninshield, lived here (1923–1958). On the second floor there are rooms in various styles, reflecting the different Du Pont generations. On the tour, visitors are also shown the building that once housed the company's business offices (built in 1837).

One other feature of Eleutherian Mills should be mentioned because it is seen in all the Du Pont homes (see the section on the Du Ponts of Delaware). In front of the house is the restored French garden planted by Eleuthère Du Pont. The founder of the family, an amateur botanist, had passed on this avocation to succeeding generations. Both Eleuthère and Victor took an interest in promoting French exploration for American plants and fought against the closing of the French gardens in New Jersey and South Carolina. Moreover, they knew many of the early plant hunters in the United States. They also bought plants from the Bartram nurseries in Philadelphia.

Newcomen Library and Museum

412 Newcomen Road, just east of the junction of Routes 100 and 30 (from Wilmington, travel north on Route 202, then north on Route 100, and east on Route 30), Exton, PA (which is north of West Chester) (Open Mon–Fri 9–5, weekends by appointment, all year)

The Newcomen Society is devoted to the promotion of the free-enterprise system. It takes its name from Thomas Newcomen, who in 1712 invented the steam engine. In pictures and models, the society's exhibit for the bicentennial of the United States traces the history of steam power from the early Greeks to the atomic age. In addition, the library has a number of models of famous railroad locomotives.

A third exhibit area traces the growing sophistication in the development of the steam engine. Note the improvement made by James Watt in 1782 when he patented the double-acting engine (in which steam acts alternately on both sides of the piston, doubling the power). Notice also the model showing how steam engines were used in textile mills.

Here also are models and actual examples of table engines (the first one patented in 1807). Small enough to sit on a tabletop, these engines were used in small factories for at least forty years. Further improvement in the steam engine was made by George Henry Corliss, who in 1849 patented an engine with rocking cylindrical valves. These engines were used for over fifty years in textile mills. The Corliss engine became virtually obsolete with the introduction of superheating using drop valves.

Other Sites to Visit

Brandywine Village, now a part of downtown Wilmington, became an early center of the flour industry. Farmers from the surrounding countryside would bring their grain to the mills to be ground. Some of the historic houses of Brandywine Village can be seen on Market Street. Number 1803 was the home of Joseph Tatnall, an important early miller whose house was used as headquarters by General Wayne during the Revolutionary War. Also read the sections on the Du Ponts of Delaware, the Battle of Brandywine, and the Swedish settlements.

Paterson

Paterson, New Jersey, is an excellent place to get an idea of the industrial development of the United States. Paterson, the nation's first planned industrial city, was home to industries producing such items as locomotives and textiles. To see all the sites will take a full day.

The Great Falls of Paterson

Haines Overlook Park, located along the Passaic River on McBride Avenue near its intersection with Spruce Street (from New York City, take exit 57 off I-80, turn left onto Grand Street, and right onto Spruce Street), Paterson, NJ

From the parking lot of Haines Overlook Park, walk over to the statue of Alexander Hamilton at the Overlook. Ponder the importance of this location, for it was the focus of the debate between the two great forces of agriculture and industrialism and of their representatives, Thomas Jefferson and Alexander Hamilton, respectively. Jefferson idealized agricultural society and the common man and thought both were essential for a healthy democracy. Hamilton was more insightful, at least on this point of demography, seeing that industrialization was inevitable. Both men believed that an educated elite would guide the country, but Hamilton made aristocratic statements that got him into trouble in the young democracy.

In certain respects, Hamilton was ahead of his time. He wanted Congress to allocate one million dollars to build a national manufactory. (In the rejection of his plan can be seen signs of the coming Civil War. The North favored Hamilton's arguments, while the South opposed them.) Failing in his endeavor to get congressional backing, he turned to other sources. In 1791 the New Jersey legislature incorporated the Society for Establishing Useful Manufactures (SUM), which actually built Hamilton's industrial complex. The facilities included cotton, printing, and bleaching mills. The town was named Paterson after William Paterson, then governor of New Jersey and a stockholder in SUM.

Unfortunately, the Paterson endeavor hit a major setback. William Deur, president of the SUM board of directors, started a stock-manipulation scheme using the organization's money. He created such a frenzy of speculation that it led to the nation's first depression, the panic of 1792. SUM did not dissolve, but in 1796 it had to abandon the Paterson factories. The population of the city fell from five hundred to forty-three.

Be sure to take a look at the falls themselves—no Niagara Falls, but still

The Great Falls, Paterson, New Jersey

impressive. Actually, much of the water is diverted by a dam for power. The steep gorge has been modified over the years because companies have used the brownstone for building blocks for such structures as Manhattan's Trinity Church. On the other side of the falls is Great Falls Park. You can walk along the bank of the Passaic River in an area called Valley of the Rocks.

Raceway Park

Along Spruce Street, across the street from the Great Falls, Paterson, NJ

The early industrial buildings are all gone, but if you walk across the street from Haines Overlook Park you can tour Raceway Park. The park signs explain how a system of canals, or "raceways," was built to channel river water to the mills. Walk along the upper raceway, completed in 1828, the last of three tiers (an upper, a middle, and a lower raceway) to be built. Along the McBride Avenue Extension are the remains of the middle raceway built between 1792 and 1802.

Paterson Museum

Rogers Locomotive Works building, 2 Market Street, between Spruce and Main Streets, Paterson, NJ (Open Mon–Fri 10–4:30, all year)

From the Great Falls area, walk or drive to the Paterson Museum. The museum has exhibits on some of the industries that made the city hum. For instance, the visitor learns how silk was processed and woven.

Paterson was also famous for its locomotives. The story begins in 1835 with the import of the McNeill from England. This locomotive was the first engine for the Paterson and Hudson Railroad. The engine arrived in parts, and no one knew how to put it together. Local carpenter Thomas Rogers decided he could build his own. Two years later the Sandusky rolled out of his factory. Until the end of the nineteenth century, the city produced 80 percent of the locomotives manufactured in the United States.

The museum itself is located in one of the buildings of the Rogers Locomotive Works. Outside is Locomotive 299 (built in 1906 by Paterson's Cooke Locomotive Works), the last of one hundred engines made to build the Panama Canal.

The city experienced a rebirth under the leadership of Roswell Colt (the governor of SUM in 1809 and a son of the man hired to replace architect Pierre L'Enfant, fired for being too extravagant). He encouraged the development of the cotton mills, and the city boomed with the coming of the War of 1812.

Walk to the corner of Mill and Van Houten streets to view the Colt Gun Mill. Samuel Colt, inventor of the revolver, started making his weapons here in 1835. The business failed after a few years due to lack of governmental need for arms and the failure of one of Colt's partners to pay his fair share of the royalties on the weapons produced. It was in a portion of this mill that Christopher Colt, Samuel's cousin, attempted to weave silk in 1840. This endeavor proved unsuccessful, and, within a year, George Murray bought the machinery. Murray hired John Ryle, an immigrant from England. Ryle became known as the Father of the Silk Industry. Walk up Mill Street to its intersection with Ellison Street. At this location is the John Ryle House (built in 1832), a two-story Greek Revival brick house (1840) that is slated for restoration.

The silk industry boomed when entrepreneurs abandoned hand looms for power looms and spinning machines. Increased tariffs on goods manufactured abroad made American silk manufacturing competitive with foreign manufacturing.

Walking further up Mill Street to its intersection with Market Street, one can see the Hamil Mill, built in 1857. Robert Hamil, along with George Murray and James Booth, was a pioneer in the city's early silk industry.

Continue to Elm Street and turn left. Here are examples of nineteenth-century workmen's homes and the Old German Church (1841).

Other Sites to Visit

For more information on Paterson, see the section on the 1913 labor strike.

Locust Grove and Speedwell Village

This section covers two sites, one in Poughkeepsie, New York, and the other in Morristown, New Jersey. Samuel Morse's home in Poughkeepsie should take about two hours to see; Speedwell Village in Morristown will take longer. Both visits are very enjoyable. The Italianate house in Poughkeepsie is very beautiful, and its Hudson River location adds to the charm of the estate. Speedwell Village is also interesting and can be easily combined with other sites in Morristown.

Samuel Finley Breese Morse was born in 1791 in Charlestown, Massachusetts. His father was a Congregational minister and a vocal opponent of Unitarianism. He fought to keep Harvard safe for orthodox Calvinism; failing in this, he sent his son to Yale.

In college, Samuel Morse showed an interest in two main areas: painting and science. After graduation he traveled to London to study with the American painter Washington Allston. Upon his return, he was able to eke out a meager income from portrait painting. In 1818 he married Lucretia Pickering Walker. After the birth of three children, in 1825 her early death cut the marriage short.

The widower settled in New York City and became a member of James Fenimore Cooper's literary club, the Lunch. He helped found the National Academy of the Arts of Design, formed by a group of students and artists dissatisfied with the conservatism and stuffiness of the Academy of Arts led by the elderly Colonel John Trumbull. Morse became president of the new organization, of which Thomas Cole was a member.

In 1829 Morse sailed from New York for a grand tour of Europe, where he painted his colossal work the *Gallery of the Louvre*. He thought that since few Americans could actually visit Paris, they would be willing to pay to see some fifty of the best works of the Louvre faithfully copied onto one large canvas.

In 1832, on his return voyage to New York, the talented painter talked with some of his fellow passengers about recent developments in electricity. He became convinced he could make a workable electric telegraph and drew several designs in his notebook.

Gallery of the Louvre was not a success with the public. Now desperately poor, he supplemented his income from painting with his nativist writings. He was extremely anti-Catholic and, sponsored by nativist forces, twice ran for mayor of New York.

In 1835 he became an unpaid professor of the literature of fine arts at New York University. When the new main building, located on Washington Square, opened, Morse moved into the tower section. Here he taught private students.

As soon as he moved into the tower, he began perfecting the telegraph. Alfred Vail, a former student at NYU, happened to be visiting when Morse was demonstrating his telegraph to some of his colleagues. The young man was so inspired that he vowed to help the professor. Vail's father, Stephen Vail, was the richest man in Morristown. The son got his father to agree that the Vails would provide the inventor with assistance, mechanical advice, a workshop, and money in order to perfect the telegraph. The father agreed to this because he wanted to bring his alienated son back home. They signed the contract in September 1837.

Stephen Vail became very impatient with the slow progress on the new invention, but the two inventors successfully demonstrated their handiwork in January 1838 by transmitting a message intended for the father: "A patient waiter is no loser." They gave other demonstrations in New York, at Philadelphia's Franklin Institute, and in Washington, D.C., to President Martin Van Buren.

It was Alfred Vail who made the telegraph practical. In addition, he helped develop the Morse code. Morse had used an unworkable system whereby complete words were given unique numerical codes. The user had to have a dictionary to translate the numbers into words. The New Jerseyan proposed that letters of the alphabet, instead of words, be given unique codes composed of dots and dashes. He also improved the telegraph receiver so that it embossed dents and lines, corresponding to dots and dashes, on paper.

Vail continued to improve the telegraph until 1849, but he never got any credit for his improvements because he mistakenly believed that the 1837 contract barred him from patenting any new inventions connected with the telegraph. In addition, Morse did not want to share any of the credit. To make a long story short, the invaluable assistant died a poor man.

Speedwell Village

From the northwest corner of the town green, drive to 333 Speedwell Avenue (Route 202), Morristown, NJ (Open Thur–Fri 12–4, Sat–Sun 1–5, May 1–Oct 31)

Jacob Arnold established ironworks here during the American Revolution. In the early 1800s, Stephen Vail took them over and created the

The first successful demonstration of the telegraph took place in the building on the left, originally designed for cotton weaving, Speedwell Village, Morristown, New Jersey

Speedwell Iron Works. The remains of the iron furnaces are not far from Speedwell Village in a park just off of Route 202 (Speedwell Avenue).

There are a number of buildings available for touring. One of these is the Vail House. Here are the portraits of Stephen Vail and his wife, Bethiah, commissioned from Morse, in order to assist the financially strapped inventor. Don't miss the painted Hitchcock chairs made in Riverton, Connecticut. The daughters of the house were sent to school at the Moravian Academy in Bethlehem, Pennsylvania.

In the factory, originally designed for cotton weaving, is the room in which the telegraph was first successfully demonstrated. Its walls still contain the nails used to string two miles of wire. Exhibits trace the development of the telegraph over time. For instance, Theodore N. Vail (1845–1920), a nephew of Stephen's, started and was president of the American Telegraph and Telephone Company (AT & T). On the second floor, a slide program on Morse and the telegraph is available. Children will enjoy playing with the telegraph model.

The Speedwell foundry was best known for its early steam engines. The company made the main drive shaft for the SS *Savannah,* the first steamship to cross the Atlantic. Don't miss the exhibit on this ship. Here is a spyglass belonging to Steven Rogers, the sailing master. Also here are a quadrant, a portable desk, and English spode China given to Mrs. Vail by Captain Moses Rogers, brother of Steven Rogers, on the return of the ship from its maiden voyage.

Young-Morse Historic Site (Locust Grove)

Approximately two miles south of the Mid-Hudson Bridge on Route 9, Poughkeepsie, NY (Open Wed–Sun 10–4, Memorial Day weekend–Sept)

Morse had hoped that the success of the telegraph would make possible a return to painting. He did not realize how tough it would be to actually establish a telegraph line. He worked hard to get Congress to pass a bill to construct a line between Baltimore and Washington for an actual demonstration. He wanted the government to have control of the telegraph so the country could have a united system. (This attitude is very different from those displayed by the men to come after the inventor—the robber barons.) Not until 1843 did Congress grant funds to build the line. In 1844 Morse sent the message "What hath God wrought"? over the wire.

The inventor of the telegraph had to be involved in many court and business battles before he secured a good income from his invention. After it proved successful, in 1847, he bought a house and a 200-acre parcel of land just south of Poughkeepsie. He named it Locust Grove because of the many locust trees on the property. For the first time in twenty years he was able to have his three children with him. The inventor bought a second home in New York City and used Locust Grove primarily as a summer retreat. Not long afterward, he married Sarah Griswold, a second cousin who was thirty-one years his junior. Sarah was deaf, but her husband was able to converse with her.

According to the tour guide, the house was built originally in 1830 as a

Locust Grove (Home of Samuel F. B. Morse), Poughkeepsie, New York

Georgian mansion (the centerpiece of the present house) by John and Isabel Montgomery. Alexander Jackson Davis, architect of Lyndhurst, significantly expanded the house, giving it its octagonal shape. He also added the Italianate tower and the veranda. The architect was an admirer and co-worker of the first American landscape architect, Andrew Jackson Downing, who lived in Newburgh. Davis applied Downing's landscape theories to the decoration of the outside of the house with iron urns containing fuschia and with boxwood shrubs planted along the driveway.

Another admirer and friend of Downing was banker Henry Winthrop Sargent, the son of Massachusetts painter Henry Sargent. Locust Grove contains some Sargent furniture. The banker's estate, Wodenethe (German for "wooden promontory"), was located in Beacon, not far south of Morse's home. He designed his own grounds and developed a species of hemlock that is now known as Sargent's hemlock. The grounds were said to be the most beautiful twenty acres in the United States, and their design influenced Downing.

Morse thought the telegraph would help unite the nation and was deeply upset by the outbreak of the Civil War. He believed in the enslavement of blacks and called Lincoln a weak and vacillating man. He was also a leading Copperhead, urging the North to sue for peace with the South. During the war, the old painter helped start Vassar College for women, which opened in 1865 in nearby Poughkeepsie. He was chosen a member of the Art Gallery Committee. The great man died in 1872 in his New York City home at the age of eighty-one.

Locust Grove is presently set up as it would have been when it was owned by the Young family. Mrs. Young liked to collect things, and you can see a number of her collections in the house. In the basement is a replica of the early telegraph.

Most children love animals, and they will be very interested in the dog cemetery behind the house. Nineteen headstones mark the graves of Mrs. Young's dogs, with names such as Penny, Lady, Tray, Rusty, Pinky Winky, Beauty, and Biz. There is also a walking trail that goes down to the river, around in a loop, and back to the house. Picnic tables are available.

Other Sites to Visit

See the section on Revolutionary War winter quarters at Morristown and the one on political cartoonist Thomas Nast. For the Poughkeepsie area, see the section on the Hudson River valley mansions and the homes of Franklin and Eleanor Roosevelt.

Iron Villages

Ironmaking was one of America's first large-scale industries. The earliest working iron furnace was erected at Braintree, Massachusetts, in 1644. The industry proceeded apace, and by 1775 there were actually more furnaces and forges in the thirteen colonies than in all of England and Wales.

Iron manufacturing was especially important in Pennsylvania, where it became the leading industry. This state has been the foremost producer of iron in America since 1750. In this part I discuss a few iron villages in Pennsylvania and New Jersey, following a brief description of how ironmakers made iron in early America, 1715 to 1839.

Iron is made from iron ore, which is either mined or gathered from bogs. Three ingredients are needed to transform the ore into iron: fuel, flux, and fire. In early ironmaking, charcoal was the fuel. This fuel had a dual purpose: it provided both heat and carbon. Iron ore is transformed into iron by the process known as smelting. The oxygen in the iron ore combines with the carbon from the fuel to form carbon monoxide, leaving the iron behind.

The collier made charcoal in the following way: he stacked logs in a conical pile with an opening at the top, covered the logs with earth, and built a smoldering fire inside. The heat of the fire caused the logs to release their fluids in the form of steam and heavy oils, leaving charcoal.

Besides charcoal and fire, the other crucial ingredient was flux, such as limestone or oyster shells. This was used to take away the waste matter, called slag.

The mixture of iron ore, flux, and charcoal was heated in a furnace. In the scale house, the mixture was carefully measured (later weighed) and then taken up to the top of the furnace stack and thrown in. This is called "charging the furnace." Once started, the furnace was kept going ("in blast") day and night. The fire was kept hot by the use of forced air, either through bellows or tubs, powered by waterwheels. The nozzle through which the air was forced is known as the *tuyere.*

The heat of the fire melted the iron ore. The slag stayed on the top of the molten mixture and was drawn off periodically through openings in the furnace. The iron itself settled in the bottom of the crucible. Every nine or ten hours the gutterman drew off the iron through a lower opening in the furnace. He guided the molten iron into shallow ditches in the casting or molding house, where it cooled into bars. This iron was called pig iron because the main ditch with its tributaries brought to mind pigs seeking nourishment from the sow.

The need for charcoal and water power in making iron explains why most early iron furnaces were located in forested areas near rivers or streams. It took at least four square miles of woodland to feed a furnace.

Where there were furnaces, there were usually forges. Pig iron tends to be brittle and not of great strength. Workers often transformed it in a forge into the more malleable wrought iron. In the forge, the worker reheated the pig iron in a small furnace and then took out the resultant pasty mass and hammered and shaped it into bars using a tilt hammer. The hammer weighed hundreds of pounds and was powered by a waterwheel. The cams of the waterwheel lifted the huge hammer, and gravity brought it down again.

The United States got off to a good start in iron manufacturing, but failed to keep pace with the new technology. An Englishman named Henry Cort perfected the puddling furnace, which allowed the ironmaker to make wrought iron directly in the furnace (thus skipping the step of making pig iron first and then hammering it into wrought iron). Although this process was patented in 1784, it was not introduced into the United States until 1840. Also around 1840, charcoal was slowly replaced by anthracite coal and coke.

Due to such factors as these, the iron industry developed slowly in the United States. In 1850 the United States produced only 500,000 tons compared to Great Britain's 3 million. Three-fifths of the nation's iron needs were being supplied by iron imports, mainly from Britain. American ironmasters, however, finally came to terms with the new technology, and this spelled the end for the iron villages discussed below.

Hopewell Village

Hopewell Village National Historic Site is located in French Creek State Park, in Elverson, Pennsylvania, which is located southeast of Reading (take I-76 to exit 22) (Open daily 9–5, all year)

Hopewell Village is perhaps the best of the early iron villages, because it gives the most complete story of early ironmaking. In addition to being very informative, the historic site is a beautiful park. A visit here will take at least half a day.

Iron had been produced in this vicinity a century before Mark Bird built a furnace here in 1771. Like many of the early iron furnaces in the area, Hopewell produced cannon and cannonballs for the Revolutionary Army. After the war, the iron industry as a whole fell on hard times. Bird had to sell Hopewell in 1788 to pay off his debts.

Ownership of the furnace, mines, and surrounding five thousand acres of land passed through many hands before finally coming to rest with the Buckley and Brooke families. Then Hopewell went through some lean years, caused mainly by the many lawsuits over land ownership. Indeed, between 1808 and 1816 the furnace was not used at all.

Prosperous years, especially those between 1830 and 1838, arrived in large part due to the excellent management of Clement Brooke. At this time the furnace mainly produced stoves.

In 1836 the Pennsylvania legislature authorized the use of coke in making iron and two years later did the same for anthracite. This spelled the end of an era for the iron village. Stove casting stopped in 1844. The place survived for another forty years, but only produced pig iron. An anthracite furnace was built here in 1853, but lasted only a brief time. Hauling coal over the Schuylkill Canal proved too expensive. The last blast ended in 1883.

The village is typical of the many self-sufficient ironmaking communities in the state. But one thing is certain, the working iron villages never

Hopewell Village, French Creek Park, Elverson, Pennsylvania

looked so green and parklike. Rather, they were usually covered in charcoal dust. You can tour the park at your leisure. You will see the charcoal hearth where the collier burned acres of wood into charcoal. Nearby is a sod-covered hut where he stayed while watching the fire. A short distance away are the coaling shed and charcoal house where workers sorted and stored the fuel. There is also a mammoth furnace, powered by a massive water-wheel. Be sure to see the furnace office and store where the villagers both bought and sold products.

The ironmaster's mansion is a four-story stone structure built between 1771 and 1830. The northwest wing is the oldest part of the house. This was home to the ironmaster and his family, the clerk, and servants. The workers also used the house. For instance, the basement was the dining area for the community's single men.

The village has two double- and two single-tenant houses remaining. The rent for the houses varied from twelve dollars to twenty-five dollars per year. Other buildings on the grounds include the springhouse, smoke-house, and bake oven.

Other Sites to Visit

Hopewell Village is located in French Creek State Park, where people hike, swim, camp, and picnic. Nearby is the Daniel Boone Homestead (see the section on Conrad Weiser). If you are in the area of Cornwall in Lebanon County, Pennsylvania, stop and see Cornwall Furnace (off PA 419). The museum furnace is an excellent one. This iron village was at one time owned by

Robert Coleman, father of Anne Coleman, who was the fiancée of James Buchanan (see the section on Buchanan).

Batsto Village

Located on Route 542 in Wharton Forest (Open daily 10–6, Memorial Day– Labor Day; Mon–Fri 11–5, Sat–Sun 11–6, Labor Day–Memorial Day.

The great thing about Batsto Village is that it is located in the New Jersey Pine Barrens. With so many pine trees the visitor might easily conclude that he/she is in the Deep South instead of in New Jersey. The area has a unique mixture of fauna because an Ice Age glacier stopped just above it. This forced many northern plant species into an area of New Jersey with many southern plants, yielding a special mixture. Another feature of the area is its very sandy soil—the area was once an island. Many of the pine trees are dwarfed and twisted. One explanation for this is that rainwater flows so quickly through the soil that the plants remain dry. Many pine species are fire-adapted and actually require considerable heat before their cones will open and release seeds.

Another treat is to canoe in the area. The rivers are very winding and slow and present a real navigational challenge to the paddler. The water is ale-colored because of the tannic acid from the trees. Tannic acid is a natural inhibitor to many types of bacteria, so water containing it resists spoiling. This is the reason many sea captains took barrels of Pine Barrens water with them on long voyages.

The trip to Batsto Village should take most of the day, especially if it includes hiking in the woods. And now for some background on the village.

Charles Read of Burlington dreamed of becoming the state's greatest ironmaster. And why not dream big, if you are the most politically powerful man in the state? To accomplish his dream, he built forges and furnaces at Etna, Taunton, Atsion, and Batsto, completing the chain by 1768. This extensive building program taxed both his finances and his health, so in 1773 he fled the state altogether. Some say he ended up running a country store in North Carolina.

In 1770 John Cox took over ownership of Batsto Furnace. (After selling the furnace, Cox purchased the Trent House in Trenton.) During the Revolutionary War, Batsto produced many cannon and cannonballs for the cause. Indeed, this iron-producing center was so important to the Americans that Sir Henry Clinton sent a force to put it out of action. However, the invaders had to content themselves with burning Chestnut Neck because they feared being bottled up in the winding Mullica River.

Ownership of the property changed hands many times, starting in the 1780s. The Richards family owned many of the Pine Barrens iron properties. When hard times arrived, the family tried to produce window glass, but this project also failed. Batsto ironworks closed in 1848 because of competition from Pennsylvania anthracite ironworks. The village then became a ghost town.

William Richards built the mansion that exists today at Batsto. It was remodeled, most notably around 1876 by Joseph Wharton of the Wharton School of Economics fame. He bought the place with the idea of using New Jersey water to supply Philadelphia's needs, but the New Jersey legislature blocked his plans.

Since the operation here used bog ore, a few words about how the workers gathered the ore would be helpful. Men would take modified Durham boats (the kind used by Washington in his crossing of the Delaware) and pole and pull these boats through the streams of the Pine Barrens. They would reach into the water to pick up hunks of iron ore deposited on the surface of the water. These deposits are created by the chemical action of the stream's decaying vegetable matter upon the iron salts in the stream beds. The iron rises to the surface of the water, where it oxidizes, piles up in deposits, mixes with mud, and hardens.

There is not much of the ironmaking equipment remaining at Batsto today. Much of the village, however, does still exist. Visit the general store, visitors' center, and craft houses, where craftspeople show their wares. Stop by the woodcarver's house and marvel at some of his absolutely beautiful wooden ducks. Be sure to see the ironmaster's house with its thirty-six rooms. One such is the secret hiding place above the third floor, said to have been used by fugitive slaves running for freedom on the underground railroad. The former slaves entered the room through a false back in one of the closets. They could look through the semicircular window out onto the front of the estate. A prominent feature of the house is the tower, which is eighty-six feet high and contains a water tank. Also visit the trail museum and, armed with the nature brochure, take the walk on the path that heads north along the east side of Batsto Lake and then doubles back. Picnic tables are available.

Other Sites to Visit

Combine your tour of Batsto with canoeing in the Pine Barrens. There are a number of places that rent canoes in the area. You can also visit some of the villages and ruins of other furnaces and forges of the Pine Barrens, such as those at Atsion, but these are not open for tours. The Atsion ranger station has information about canoeing.

A visit to Wheaton Village (Glasstown Road, Millville) reveals a great deal about glassmaking in southern New Jersey. The museum has several beautiful glass collections.

There are two other iron sites in New Jersey open to visitors. Iron used to be produced at Ringwood Manor (Route 511, north to Sloatsburg Road at New York State Line) in the Ramapo Mountains. The manor house there once belonged to Mayor Abraham Hewitt of New York City, son-in-law of industrialist and philanthropist Peter Cooper. The other place is the Deserted Village of Allaire in Allaire State Park, Allaire, on Route 524. The owner was famed marine engineer James P. Allaire, who built the engine cylinders for the SS *Savannah,* first steamship to make the transatlantic voyage. The emphasis there is more on the village itself, since not much of the ironworks (except for one furnace) is left.

19

Anthracite Coal Region

You don't have to travel to West Virginia to learn about coal mining. The coalfields of eastern Pennsylvania are less than a two-hour drive from New York City and less than an hour's drive from Philadelphia. Many of the sites are located in beautiful mountain areas, which adds further enjoyment to the trips. After a very brief introduction to coal, the tours in this section cover three historical areas associated with this valuable fuel: the town of Ashland, to learn about the ways coal was mined; Eckley, to discover how the miners lived; and the town of Jim Thorpe, which is steeped in coal, canal, and railroad history.

There are two basic kinds of coal: hard and soft. Soft coal, also called bituminous coal, is easier to burn, but produces more smoke and dirt. Although soft coal was discovered around 1760, its first important use was not until about 1840, when it began to be burned in ovens to make coke for the iron industry.

Hard coal is known as anthracite coal. Anthracite was discovered as early as 1762, but was relatively ignored as a fuel because no one knew how to burn it efficiently. In 1812 the British blockade prevented fuel from reaching Philadelphia. Josiah White and Erskine Hazard, who owned the Fairmount Nail and Wire Works at the Falls of the Schuylkill near Philadelphia, were determined to find a substitute for their usual fuel. Luckily, a man named Shoemaker arrived with nine wagonloads of anthracite. In desperation, the partners bought some of the fuel and tried to burn it. The black rocks proved very disappointing, although they did provide enough energy to at least keep the factory doors from closing. One day, White tried and tried, without much success, to get a new batch of this coal to burn. Disgusted, he gave up, slammed the furnace door shut, and went home. Less than half an hour later, a worker pounded at his door, screaming, "The mill's afire!" Rushing frantically down to the mill, White found that the buildings were not on fire at all; rather, the fire in the furnace was so hot that it appeared as if the factory were ablaze. Thus, White discovered that the secret of burning anthracite was as simple as closing the furnace door. He not only showed the usefulness of this fuel, but became one of its main promoters.

Once the utility of anthracite was demonstrated, the next problem was transportation. The coalfields were located many miles from the important port cities of Philadelphia and New York. Canals, and later railroads, had to be constructed to transport the black fuel.

Coal Mining at Ashland

Ashland is located in a narrow valley between Mahanoy and Logan mountains. The main street of town climbs a long hill. Row houses on each side of the street give the town a different, intriguing look well worth a visit. The town is especially charming when adorned in red, white, and blue in preparation for a Mummer's parade. What a great feeling of Americana this invokes!

The town was laid out in 1847 and named for the Kentucky estate of Senator Henry Clay. Mining began here with the very inception of the town.

This trip should take an entire day, especially if the tour of Ashland's downtown area is included. The first stop should be the Anthracite Museum. The museum presents a great deal of information about mining that helps the traveler understand the tour of the nearby mine.

Ashland Anthracite Museum

Pine and Seventeenth streets, Ashland, PA (the town is southwest of Hazelton) (Open Mon–Sat 10–6, Sun 12–5, Memorial Day–Labor Day; Tues–Sat 9–5, Sun 12–5, Labor Day–Memorial Day)

The museum has exhibits on the four basic types of mining: drift mining, in which the coal seam slopes upward and is exposed on a hillside; slope mining, in which the slope of the mine follows the downward course of an anthracite seam; tunnel mining, in which a horizontal opening is dug to the coal; and shaft mining, in which vertical openings penetrating one or more levels of rock and coal are made from the earth's surface.

The museum also has information on the anthracite colliery, which includes the entire mining plant: the mine itself, the breaker where slag and rock are separated from the coal, and the transportation network. In addition, the museum exhibits a great variety of the equipment used by the miners.

Pioneer Tunnel Coal Mine

Located in Mahanoy Mountain, down the street from the Anthracite Museum, Ashland, PA (Open daily 10–5:30, May 30–Labor Day; weekends 10–5:30, May, Sept–Oct)

The mine here operated between 1911 and 1931. The type of mining done, a combination of horizontal and drift mining, was particularly difficult. The miners dug a horizontal tunnel to the seam of coal, but, since the seams ran vertically, the miners then had to dig straight up. All the work was by hand because the miners could not get machinery to the worksite. They would dig their way upward into the seam of coal, actually supporting themselves on a pillar of loose coal that they had worked free earlier.

The trip into the mine is by open mine cars pulled by a battery-operated mine motor. Once inside, you may wonder where are the timbers that hold up the roof. The guide's answer is that solid rock does not have to be timbered.

Steam Lokie Ride

Located at the Pioneer Tunnel Coal Mine, Ashland, PA (Open daily 10–5:30, May 30–Labor Day; weekends 10–5:30, May, Sept–Oct)

Take a short (three-quarters of a mile) train ride pulled by an old-fashioned, narrow-gauge steam locomotive, the Henry Clay. The ride along Mahanoy Mountain provides several nice views of the town below. On the way, the guide tells you about two other types of mining done here: strip mining and bootleg mining. During the Great Depression, when two or three fellows found a vein of coal, they filled up a fifty-gallon drum and hand-hoisted it up and down. Then they dumped the coal into burlap bags and took them to town to sell. When the mine owners found the illegal diggings, they dynamited the openings shut.

A disheartening sight are the black areas in the mountains. The guide explains that this is where they dumped fine silt and rock. This has proved too acidic for most trees, except the birches.

Other Sites to Visit

Combine this trip with one to the Eckley Mining Village or the town of Jim Thorpe.

Eckley Mining Village

This tour gives the visitor a good idea of the lifestyles of the miners. The tour should take about half a day.

Visitors' Center

Located northeast of Hazelton, off Route 940, Weatherly, Pennsylvania (open Tues–Sat 9–5, Sun 12–5, all year)

Eckley is just one of hundreds of company mining towns, known as "patches," that existed in the anthracite regions of Pennsylvania. In 1853 Richard Sharpe, Francis Weiss, John Leisenring, and Asa Foster looked for coal in the Eckley area. Finding the area rich in the black fuel, they constructed the Council Ridge Colliery and built the village of Eckley.

The first type of mining done here was underground mining, but as this dwindled, it was replaced in 1890 by strip mining. This did not, however, halt the town's population decline from 1,500 in 1870 to less than 600 in 1920.

At the village a number of miner dwellings can be seen. Most miners rented their homes from the mining company or a local owner. The rents were often very high, and the workers did not get much for their money. The typical dwelling was a duplex, each side having two rooms on the ground floor and one upstairs. The houses were usually of simple construction, clapboarded on the exterior and plastered in the interior. The furnishings were also very simple: a bedstead and a table with four chairs, all crudely made by the colliery carpenter.

Life is never easy for coal miners—that's the nature of the job. But in days not really so long ago, even young boys had to work in the coal industry. For instance, the breaker boys had the job of removing unwanted slag and rock from the coal as it came down a conveyor belt. The museum captions a picture of a dirty, pitiful-looking boy with the words from a folk ballad, "Down in the Bowels of the Earth":

> I'm a little collier lad, hardworking all the day,
> From early morn till late at night, no time have I to play.
> Down in the bowels of the earth, where no bright sun rays shine,
> You'll find me busy at my work, a white slave of the mine.

In the patches, the first villagers were English, Welsh, and German. The Irish came later. The English and Welsh disproportionately held the skilled jobs, while the Irish had a greater proportion of the unskilled positions. The economic disparities, combined with historic animosities from their home-lands, worked to divide many patches into ethnic enclaves. The Irish soon turned to the protective societies they had known in their native country. These societies had helped these subject people combat British control of their country. One of these societies was the Molly Maguires.

To fight the power of the owners, of whom the Reading Railroad was the biggest, the Molly Maguires converted themselves into a "terrorist" organization. Members committed at least 42 murders and 162 felonious assaults and destroyed countless coal and railroad properties. The violence started as early as the Civil War; the Irish of that time were not particularly fond of the military draft. It continued until 1877, when the undercover work of Pinkerton detective James McParlan helped eliminate the Molly Maguire leadership—twenty of whom were hanged.

Eckley was used by Paramount Pictures from 1968 to 1969 to shoot the film *The Molly Maguires*. However, most of the Maguire action actually occurred south of this area, flourishing especially in the towns of Mahanoy City and Pottsville.

Other Sites to Visit

Visit Ashland or the town of Jim Thorpe.

Jim Thorpe

Jim Thorpe is a beautiful Victorian town steeped in mining, canal, and railroad history. It is sandwiched in among mountains and the Lehigh River, which add to the great scenery of the place. The tour here should take all day. Don't miss seeing this scenic mountain town, located north of Allentown, Route 209, off the Northeast Extension of the Pennsylvania Turnpike.

In 1791 anthracite coal was found at Summit Hill, north of the town of Mauch Chunk (present-day Jim Thorpe), on property belonging to Colonel Jacob Weiss. Effective use of this discovery could not be made, however, because of the difficulties inherent in transporting the fuel to Philadelphia over the Lehigh River and then down the Delaware River.

Josiah White and Erskine Hazard leased the land from Colonel Weiss. In 1820 these men started to build the Lehigh Canal in order to get the coal to market. The canal eventually ran seventy-two miles from White Haven in the upper Lehigh River valley to Easton on the Delaware River.

By 1827 the Lehigh Coal and Navigation Company built a switchback railroad to more effectively bring Summit Hill coal to the Lehigh Canal at

Town of Jim Thorpe, Pennsylvania, showing railway station in foreground and Asa and Henry Packer mansions at back center and back right

Mauch Chunk. The cars filled with coal wound their way down to the river by force of gravity, and mules pulled the empty cars back up the hill.

The town further prospered when Asa Packer provided much of the financing for the Lehigh Valley Railroad. The railroad ran from Mauch Chunk to Easton. Packer expanded the line until, at the time of his death in 1879, the railroad consisted of 650 miles of track that ran to New York State and the New Jersey coast.

In 1954 the towns of Mauch Chunk and East Mauch Chunk won a newspaper contest to be the final resting place of the Native American Olympic athlete Jim Thorpe. The towns merged into the new town of Jim Thorpe.

Start the tour at the Visitors' Center in the New Jersey Central railroad station in the center of town. You can catch a train ride here in the summer (see the section on Pennsylvania railroads). Don't miss the 15,100-pound chunk of anthracite coal in the park near the railroad station.

Asa Packer Mansion

Packer Road, Jim Thorpe, PA (Open Tues–Sun 1–5, May 30–Oct 31)

This Italianate mansion constructed in 1861 was the home of local hero Asa Packer. Asa was born in Mystic, Connecticut, in 1805. He came to Pennsylvania as a carpenter's apprentice to his cousin, who lived in Susquehanna County.

Working as both a carpenter and a farmer, he saved his money and purchased coal lands on the upper Susquehanna. This became the basis for his later wealth. The future railroad mogul also ran coal boats on the Lehigh Canal, starting at Mauch Chunk. Not missing a single opportunity, he then turned to building the boats himself. Moreover, he operated several mines at Hazelton.

In 1843 he ran successfully for the state legislature. Once there, he secured an act to create Carbon County with Mauch Chunk as county seat. He was associate judge of the new county for five years. In 1852 he was elected to Congress as a Democrat. He served for two terms.

By 1851 the immigrant from Connecticut had gained enough stock in the Delaware, Lehigh, Schuylkill, and Susquehanna Railroad to control it. The name of the railroad was shortened to the Lehigh Valley Railroad. He could not get support from the Lehigh Coal and Navigation Company for his railroad expansion project, so he proceeded on his own and profited accordingly. Indeed, he became the richest man in Pennsylvania. Among his accomplishments are the founding of Lehigh University in Bethlehem, for which in all he gave $2 million.

The self-made man had seven children. Three died in infancy. Daughter Mary Packer Cummings lived in the house, and it is she who willed the mansion to the borough. In the house itself is a chair from the estate of Robert E. Lee. Also here is an orchestrion, a virtual musical band in a cabinet.

Harry Packer Mansion

Packer Road, next to the Asa Packer Mansion, Jim Thorpe, PA (Open daily 1–5, May 19–Oct 31; or by appointment)

Next-door to the Asa Packer Mansion is the home of Asa's youngest son, Harold. The Second Empire–style mansion was built in 1874 by Asa as a wedding gift for his son and daughter-in-law.

Harry Packer received his college education at the university his father founded, Lehigh University. He eventually became president of the Lehigh Valley Railroad. Tragically, Harry died in 1884 of hereditary kidney failure at the early age of thirty-four.

The mansion now serves as a bed-and-breakfast inn. In the dining room are some beautiful Tiffany stained-glass windows. The main hall doors, complete with etched-glass inserts, weigh 450 pounds each.

St. Mark's Episcopal Church

Race Street, Jim Thorpe, PA (Tues–Sun 1–4; go to the door marked "office")

Asa Packer was one of the founders of this parish and served as a vestry-man for forty-four years. Inside the church are replicas of the reredos (screen) and altar of Windsor Castle that serve as memorials to the great industrialist. The reredos in the main chapel is twenty-three feet high and freestanding. Right in the chapel itself, three craftsmen carved the entire structure in eighteen months. Also here are two priceless Tiffany windows. Craftsmen used a special staining process to represent flesh tones and sheer garments. There are more Tiffany windows in the Mary Packer Cummings Memorial Chapel (a part of St. Mark's). The church has an Otis elevator that the guide said is the second oldest in the country. Workers installed it in 1912 for Mrs. Cummings.

The building itself is a beautiful 1869 Gothic Revival church designed by Richard Upjohn, Sr. The main chapel is built over the mountain floor, and this keeps the room cool.

Stone Row (private)

27-57 Race Street behind St. Mark's, Jim Thorpe, PA

Asa Packer built these sixteen row houses for the engineers and fore-men of the Lehigh Valley Railroad. The builders made the houses distinctive through individual variations. Today, various artists live in them.

Carbon County Jail

West Broadway, a few blocks walk from the train depot, Jim Thorpe, PA

This 1869 jail and courthouse is not open to the public, but is filled with history. In 1877 the jail witnessed the hangings of four members of the infamous Molly Maguires. On the evening of December 2, 1872, mine superintendent Morgan Powell was on his way home from work when he noticed four men approaching him. All of a sudden they attacked, and one assailant shot him within sight of hundreds of houses on the streets of Summit Hill. He died from his wounds several days later. Jack Donahue, the triggerman, and Tom Fisher were two of the men arrested for the murder.

General superintendent John P. Jones had refused to rehire two discharged employees suspected of involvement in various crimes. The former workers swore revenge and applied to Alexander Campbell for aid. The Maguire contact made a deal with a leader from another district to supply two men to murder Officer Yost of Tamaqua in return for two others to kill Jones. Edward Kelly and Michael Doyle waited for Jones on his way to work. He was just two hundred yards from the office when the two men walked up behind him, drew their revolvers, and fired two shots point-blank into his body. The superintendent died within half an hour. Mine officials immediately sent a telegraph message to Tamaqua, and the two men were caught walking along the mountainside.

Large crowds gathered to see the executions. The jailers erected scaffolds in the corridor between the jail and the courthouse. The four Mollies executed were Doyle, Kelly, and Campbell, convicted in the murder of Jones, and Donohue, guilty of the murder of Powell. Contemporary accounts went into great detail about the executions. Campbell and Doyle died without a struggle from broken necks, but it took more than fifteen minutes before Campbell's heart stopped. The other two criminals struggled violently. They finally died of strangulation, Donahue taking two minutes and Kelly eight.

A fifth man, Tom Fisher, was hung later as an accessory to the murder of Powell. It is said that the condemned man made the mysterious handprint on the jail's wall, shouting that this would always remain as proof of his innocence. The outline of the print is still there to this day. (Probably each time a guard told the story, he emphasized the point by placing his hand where the condemned man had placed his, thereby insuring the continued existence of the handprint.)

Jim Thorpe Memorial

One-half mile east of town on PA 903 (North Street), Jim Thorpe, PA

The final resting place of Jim Thorpe (1888–1953) is just off Route 903, where there is a small pull-off area for parking. Born in Oklahoma to a Sac

Indian mother, Thorpe gained fame playing football for the Carlisle Indian School in Pennsylvania. He took the 1912 Stockholm Olympics by storm, winning every event in the pentathlon except the javelin throw. Carved on the granite slab are the words of King Gustav of Sweden when he presented the gold medals to the famous Native American: "Sir, you are the greatest athlete in the world."

Switchback Railroad Bed

Entrance adjacent to the lake at Mauch Chunk Creek Park, three miles west of Jim Thorpe, PA

Thousands of tourists rode the gravity railroad after its industrial use was discontinued in 1870. Today hikers can walk along the ten-mile recreation trail. There is no trace left of the actual switchback railway.

Flagstaff Mountain Park Resort

Ask for directions when in Jim Thorpe

Looking out from the observation platform located here, the visitor can understand why Jim Thorpe is called "the Switzerland of America." In the distance is the entire town and the surrounding area: Mount Pisgah, the Lehigh River, Bear Mountain, and the Lehigh Valley Railroad.

Flagstaff Mountain has been a popular park and resort area since the early days of the town of Mauch Chunk. Such popular bands as those of the Dorsey Brothers, Fred Waring, and Paul Whiteman played at the Rooftop of the World located here.

Other Sites to Visit

Visit Ashland, the Eckley Mining Village, and Bethlehem. The Anthracite Museum at Scranton is located in McDade Park, off Keyser Avenue, West Scranton. Here attention is given to the domestic and industrial uses of coal. Future and alternatives sources of energy are also discussed.

20

Canals

There is a certain romance about canals—a romance captured by the English writer Charles Dickens on a canal-boat trip from Harrisburg to Pittsburgh in 1842. Dickens was very caustic in most of his remarks about the United States, but he fondly remembered his travels on a canal boat:

> There was much in this mode of traveling which I heartily enjoyed at this time, and look back upon with great pleasure. Even the running up, bare-necked, at five o'clock in the morning, from the tainted cabin to the dirty deck; scooping up the icy water, plunging one's head into it, and drawing it out all fresh and glowing with the cold; was a good thing. The fast, brisk walk upon the towing-path between that time and breakfast, when every vein and artery seemed to tingle with health; the exquisite beauty of the opening day, when light came gleaming off from everything; the lazy motion of the boat, when one lay idly on the deck, looking through, rather than at, the deep blue sky; the gliding on at night, so noiselessly, the shining out of the bright stars, undisturbed by noise of wheels or steam, or any other sound than the liquid rippling of the water as the boat went on; all these were pure delights. (Quoted in William H. Shank's *The Amazing Pennsylvania Canals* [York, Pa: American Canal & Transportation Center, 1981], 91.)

This chapter captures a bit of this feeling with visits to the regional canals, many of which are now state parks. While enjoying the history of the canals, you can also hike, bike, picnic, or go boating.

During the early years of the nation, boats and canoes were the major means of inland transportation. As pioneers hacked out primitive roads through the wilderness, stagecoaches and wagons became the main transportation methods. These methods, however, were slow and cumbersome. The few roads that existed were extremely rough, making them difficult to traverse.

Toward the end of the 1700s, Americans turned to a new method of hauling cargo that was much more economically efficient: canals. Canals made a great reduction in the cost of freight possible. A team of horses could pull a 1,200-pound wagon, but a team of mules could pull a 50-ton canal barge.

Between 1792 and 1796 quite a few canals were either being built or were already built in many sections of the United States. It is difficult to discover which are the oldest canals, because the dates of construction often overlap. New England got the jump on the Mid-Atlantic states when, in 1793, Massachusetts built the South Hadley Falls Canal a few miles south of Northampton. Nevertheless, real canal fever did not arrive until the construction of New York's Erie Canal (completed in 1825).

As the Erie Canal pushed the port of New York forward, Philadelphia felt pressured to build a comparable system to stay competitive and win its share of the western trade. The state should have planned an all-rail route between Philadelphia and Pittsburgh. Instead, state officials built a mongrel system of rail and canal that performed poorly. The 395-mile Main Line cost twice as much as the Erie Canal, partly because it had to go over mountains at 2,200 feet above sea level. The system was never a formidable rival and was not commercially successful.

Although Pennsylvania was unable to come up with a rival to New York's canal, the need to transport coal to New York City and Philadelphia provided the impetus for constructing an extensive canal network that extended into the neighboring states of New York and New Jersey.

Lehigh Canal

The Lehigh Canal extended from White Haven to Easton, Pennsylvania. The man responsible for building the canal was Josiah White, the main promoter of anthracite coal. Part of his plan to get Americans to use anthracite was, of course, to get it to them cheaply, and the canals provided the means.

White chartered the canal in 1818, and in 1820 delivered the first coal to Philadelphia via Mauch Chunk. This stretch of canal, known as the lower division, was in operation from 1829 to 1931 and consisted of a series of nine dam-created pools connected by eight canal sections. The upper division of the canal extended from Mauch Chunk to White Haven. It existed from 1838 to 1862, when a flood destroyed it.

Canal Museum

Route 611 (take the first exit off U.S. 22 after crossing the bridge from New Jersey into Pennsylvania, make a left onto Route 611, which leads across the Lehigh River bridge, and take the first left after crossing the bridge), Hugh Moore Park at Easton, PA (Open Mon–Sat 10–4, Sun 1–5, all year)

This is the best museum on canals in the travel area. A video, "Pathways of Progress," gives a good historical introduction; and exhibits explain such technical items as canal locks. Here also are models of some of the canal boats. A talking stove tells the listener about canal travel. It sits in a full-scale

Guard Lock, Canal Museum, Easton, Pennsylvania

model of a canal-boat cabin, complete with beds that fold up out of the way.

At Easton three canals met: the Lehigh Canal; the Delaware Canal, from Easton to Bristol; and the Morris Canal, from Philipsburg, New Jersey (across the Delaware River from Easton), to Jersey City, New Jersey. Workers pulled the boats into the Morris Canal across the Delaware River with a cable system. From the museum grounds, the western end of the Morris Canal can be seen. Look southeast for the stone archway upstream of the railroad bridge on the east shore.

Outside the museum is a six-mile walking path along the Lehigh Canal. In addition, there is a sixty-mile walk along the Delaware Canal. Right outside the museum is dam no. 9, which marks the end of the Lehigh Canal.

A few miles west of the Canal Museum, those interested can ride on the *Josiah White,* a reconstructed canal boat pulled by mules. Also for rent are rowboats and paddleboats to go boating on the old canal. Located across from the Abbott Street Locks is the training gym of Larry Holmes, the Easton native who was once heavyweight boxing champion of the world.

About a mile up from the boathouse is the Locktender's House Museum, recently restored. The first floor displays how a locktender and his family might have lived in the 1890s. The house is right next to the chain dam, guard lock no. 8, and the change bridge. The children of the house would often ice skate on the canal in winter. Another activity was looking for muskrats. Just one of these burrowing animals could ruin a canal.

Other Sites to Visit

See the nearby sites in the towns of Bethlehem and Jim Thorpe. If you are ever in the Reading area, see the Union Canal Towpath at the Tulpehocken Creek Valley Park on Red Covered Bridge Road (near the airport). The hiker can see several locks along the path. The Union Canal connected the town of Reading on the Schuylkill River to Middletown on the Susquehanna.

Delaware Canal

The Delaware Canal, running some sixty miles from Easton to Bristol, Pennsylvania, was started in 1827 and completed in 1832. The canal was state-financed and leased by the Lehigh Coal and Navigation Company when completed. The last paying barge used the canal in 1931. Nine years later, the state renamed the canal and towpath the Theodore Roosevelt State Park.

Delaware Canal

Towpath Landing between New and S. Main Streets, New Hope, PA (Barge rides Tues–Sun 1, 3, 4:30, 6, Apr–Labor Day)

At New Hope is an hour-long barge ride pulled by mules along the Delaware Canal. The ride comes complete with a sing-along. You can also hike along the canal. Be sure to visit the town of New Hope with its many stores dealing in arts and crafts. This is a very popular place and really gets crowded in season. Also in New Hope is the Bucks County Playhouse.

Parry Mansion

Cannon Square, New Hope, PA (Tours Fri–Mon 2–5, all summer)

This mansion has ten rooms, each decorated in a different style. The town got its present name from Benjamin Parry's New Hope mill. This mill is the present Bucks Country Playhouse.

Other Sites to Visit

Take a train ride in New Hope or the one in nearby Flemington, New Jersey. Not far away are the Washington Crossing state parks.

Delaware and Hudson Canal

While the Lehigh and Schuylkill canals served the southern anthracite coalfields of Pennsylvania, the Delaware and Hudson Canal served the northern fields. Two brothers, Maurice and William Wurts, working out of the Carbondale area, sent coal to Philadelphia. Since they faced stiff competition from the two other canals, they decided to supply coal to New York City.

To service New York, they had to build a canal from the coal-fields of the Wilkes Barre–Scranton area to the Hudson River. The Delaware and Hudson Canal was incorporated in 1823 and completed in 1829. It connected Eddyville, near Kingston, New York, with Honesdale, Pennsylvania. This is a distance of 108 miles by canal. To connect Honesdale to Carbondale, workers built a sixteen-mile inclined-plane railroad. Some of the sites to be seen along the canal are listed below.

Roebling Suspension Bridge

The bridge crosses the Delaware River north of Barryville, along Route 97, Barryville, NY

Believe it or not, canal barges filled with coal used to be pulled over this onetime water bridge. In 1849 John Roebling built the 600-foot-long aqueduct for the Delaware and Hudson Canal crossing of the Delaware River. The oldest suspension bridge in the world, it served as a model for the Brooklyn Bridge (also built by Roebling).

The bridge was later used as an automobile crossing. It is now a national landmark and only open to pedestrians. Nearby is a house in which Zane Grey, who wrote numerous Western novels, once lived.

Delaware and Hudson Canal Park

Hoag Road off Route 209, Cuddebackville, NY, a short distance north of Port Jervis (Open Wed–Sun 10–4, all year)

This is a small museum dealing with the history of the canal. It is located near the remains of another of Roebling's aqueducts (this one over the Neversink River). The only remnants of the structure are the stone abutments on either side of the river. On the grounds are the sites of locks 51 and 52.

Delaware and Hudson Canal Museum

Mohonk Road off Route 213 (take the New Paltz exit of I-87, drive west on Route 299/Main Street, turn right/north onto Route 32/North Chestnut Street, pick up Route 213 in Rosendale and travel west), High Falls, NY (Open Wed–Sun 10–4, May–Nov; or by appointment)

This excellent museum dealing with the Delaware and Hudson Canal traces the history of the building of the canal. There are some artifacts and a replica of a canal barge cabin. Especially interesting is the working model of a canal lock. The guide will demonstrate exactly how the lock operated.

Just across the street from the museum is a self-guided tour of locks 16 through 20 of the Delaware and Hudson Canal. The loop walk takes between thirty-five and forty-five minutes.

While in High Falls, you might want to eat at the Depuy Canal House, one of the finest eating places in the Hudson Valley. The building was constructed in 1797 by S. and A. Depuy, who ran a tavern here.

Other Sites to Visit

In the upper Delaware River area visit Fort Delaware and the Minisink Battlefield. Near High Falls visit the towns of New Paltz and Kingston.

Morris Canal

The two New Jersey canals, the Morris and the Delaware and Raritan canals, were basically offshoots of the Pennsylvania canals. They formed part of the vast anthracite canal system. The first canal to be built in New Jersey was the Morris Canal. Construction began at Newark Bay in 1824. The waterway followed the Passaic River to Little Falls, and from there to Boonton, Dover, and the southern tip of Lake Hopatcong, then south to Phillipsburg—a distance of 106 miles or five travel days.

The Morris Canal has the distinction of being the first American canal to climb hills. Professor James Renwick of Columbia University devised a series of twenty-three inclined planes to haul the boats up and down. Workers placed the boats in giant cradles and raised or lowered them by cable (powered by waterfalls) to elevations as high as 100 feet; an ascending boat was counterbalanced by one that was descending. As might be expected, this procedure could be dangerous. One poor woman and two children were killed at Port Colden when a chain broke, sending the boat crashing into them.

The canal was handicapped from its very beginning because the locks were too small. They could not accommodate the big boats used on the Lehigh canal. This allowed the younger Delaware and Raritan Canal to grab most of the coal business. This canal ran for forty-three miles from Bordentown to New Brunswick. Workers also constructed a feeder canal from Raven Rock to the canal at Trenton. There are beautiful sections of the canal park where you can walk, especially the sections from Stockton to Washington's Crossing and from Kingston to Bound Brook. Canoeing is also available in certain locations along the waterway.

Waterloo Village Restoration

Take I-80 to exit 25, Stanhope, then Route 206 north to the second light and turn left onto Waterloo Road. The village is two miles up on the left. Waterloo, NJ (Open Tues–Sun 10–6, Apr 15–Sept 30; Tues–Sun 10–5, Oct 1–Dec 31)

Waterloo provides a romantic picture of life in a canal town. The settlement took its original name, Andover, from an English town. The town itself was the center of industrial, commercial, and social activity for northeast Warren and southern Sussex counties. Brigadier General John Smith owned and operated a blast furnace here. He decided to rename the foundry Waterloo in celebration of Napoleon's defeat by the British in 1815. The town followed suit. The descendants of General Smith managed the village industries, including a number of mills, a store, and a tavern. When the canal was finally dismantled in 1927, Waterloo fell into decay. Restoration began after World War II.

In addition to touring the many village buildings, look for the remains of one of the inclined planes. Take a short hike up the hill across from the canal. At the top of the hill are the stone remains of the inclined plane. There is a nice view looking back to the blacksmith shop and the bridge. Walking past the crest of the hill, look for the unrestored canal bed.

The Museum of the Canal Society of New Jersey, located on village grounds, has a model of one of the canal's inclined planes. Here also is a model of a Morris Canal hinge boat, joined together at the middle by pin joints to permit the long boat to pass over the tops of the inclined planes.

At the Grist Mill, the miller demonstrates how a corn shaker drops corn down between two grinding stones. The top stone often weighed as much as 2,400 pounds. Corn shakers chattered as they worked, and so the millers

Blacksmith Shop, Waterloo Village, Waterloo, New Jersey

often referred to them as "damsels." (A person in the audience spoke up at this and said the millers must have all been a bunch of "mill" chauvinists.)

Various musical groups often perform at Waterloo, so the traveler may want to combine a picnic with some musical entertainment.

Lake Hopatcong State Park

South end of Lake Hopatcong (exit 28 off I-80, Shippenport Road, turn right/north onto Lakeside Boulevard), Mount Arlington, NJ

To the left of the beach is a huge iron waterwheel, from plane no. 3, which operated the chains, later wire cables, that pulled the boats up. At the gate control house, near this old turbine, one can see the locks under water at the edge of the lake. Just west of the pumping station and the turbine, the broad declivity was the pathway of the old canal, which continued on toward Lake Musconetcong. In the park is the gatekeeper's and paymaster's house, built about 1826 and now occupied by the Lake Hopatcong Historical Society (call for appointment).

Stephens State Park and Saxton Falls

Take Waterloo Road south to the Stephens section of Allamuchy Mountains State Park, Andover, NJ

Not far from Waterloo Village is Saxton Falls. Beside the falls is guard lock no. 5, once used to adjust water levels for the canal. A sign on the dam says: "A dam was erected here about 1830 as a feeder for 30.6 miles of the canal between this point and the Delaware River. An average of 34.17 cubic feet per second of water was taken for this purpose. This was drawn from storage in Lake Hopatcong, Cranberry Lake, and Bear Pond. This land, including 3.33 miles of right of way, was acquired from Nathaniel Saxton."

Other Sites to Visit

The closest sites to visit are in Morristown. See the sections on the Revolutionary War winter quarters, Speedwell Village, and Thomas Nast.

21

Railroads

Who does not have fond memories of playing with or watching toy loco-motives pulling plastic cars through tunnels or around curves? Unfor-tunately, fewer and fewer of us have had real life experiences with trains as they continue to decline in favor of the automobile. Sales of toy trains also seem to be declining relative to electric racing cars.

And yet the romance of the train lives on. From Storm King Mountain you can watch trains whiz by on both shores of the Hudson River. Most people seeing the trains are not aware that the two tracks were part of a rail-road war that raged between the two mighty empires of the New York Central and Pennsylvania railroads.

In the early days of the railroad, there were literally hundreds of rail-road companies. Over time, however, these merged into just a few powerful companies. Following a brief history of the larger railroads in the region is a list of the railroad museums and train rides available.

The English took the lead in railway developments. In 1803 the English-man Richard Trevithick put into operation the first locomotive to do actual work. In the United States, charters were being granted to build railroads, but horses, not steam engines, provided the motive power. In 1821 New Jersey granted a charter to John Stevens of Hoboken to build a railroad across the state. The resultant horse-drawn Camden and Amboy Railroad was the earliest railroad in the region. In 1825 Stevens ran a steam locomo-tive on a small circular track laid at his great Hoboken estate, Castle Point. Although it was never commercially applied, this was the first steam engine in the United States to run on tracks.

The first locomotive to run commercially on a track in the United States was the British locomotive, the Stourbridge Lion. The Delaware and Hudson Canal Company sent Horatio Allen to England to determine if the company should replace horse power with steam power. Allen brought back the Stourbridge Lion and first ran it in 1829. Unfortunately, it was too heavy for the rails and had to be used as a stationary power source.

Allen moved on to Charleston, South Carolina, where he designed a railroad locomotive known as the Best Friend of Charleston for the Charleston and Hamburg Railroad Company. In 1831 his locomotive drew the first regularly scheduled passenger trains carried by rail. In the same year the locomotive John Bull ran on the Camden and Amboy Railroad, which connected Philadelphia to Perth Amboy, New Jersey. A steamboat completed the journey to New York City.

Railroad building proceeded rapidly in the 1830s with the emergence of myriads of small railroads. For instance, by 1840 there was a chain of ten short connecting railroads from Albany to Buffalo, New York. You can imagine the confusion when moving passengers and materials from Albany to Buffalo over track owned by so many companies. In 1853 Erastus Corning consolidated the chain of ten railroads that connected Albany with Buffalo into one railroad called the Central Railroad. This railway served the northern tier of New York counties. The Erie Railroad (which reached Lake Erie in 1851) served the southern tier.

Cornelius Vanderbilt, the great steamboat tycoon, knew that the New York Central would eventually want access to New York City. In preparation for this, he acquired both the New York and Harlem (extending from New York City to Chatham) and the New York and Hudson River (extending from New York City to Poughkeepsie) railroads. The Central came to depend on Vanderbilt's lines to provide access to New York City.

Then, in 1867, Vanderbilt suddenly stopped all Central trains from using his lines. This caused such economic hardship for the Central that it agreed to consolidate with the New York and Hudson River Railroad into the New York Central and Hudson River Railroad. This consolidation gave Vanderbilt control of a route all the way from New York City to Buffalo. Vanderbilt also tried to gain control of the Erie Railroad, but failed (for more information, read about Lyndhurst in the section on the Hudson River mansions).

The great rival to the New York Central and Hudson River Railroad was the Pennsylvania Railroad (incorporated in 1846). By 1858 this railroad could send a passenger train from Philadelphia to Pittsburgh. In 1871 the Pennsylvania Railroad took over the United New Jersey Railroad and Canal Company, which included the Camden and Amboy Railroad. This gave the Pennsylvania Railroad access to New York City.

As the two great railroad conglomerates formed, they started to invade each other's territory. The New York Central began to build the South Pennsylvania Railroad, which paralleled the Pennsylvania mainline from Reading to Pittsburgh. In retaliation, the Pennsylvania Railroad began buying bonds of the New York, West Shore, and Buffalo Railroad, which extended from Buffalo to New York City.

As the battle lines were drawn, financier J. P. Morgan, banker to the Vanderbilts and a railroad mogul himself, stepped in. With the so-called Corsair Compact, the financier got the two railroads to stay in their own backyards. In 1899, under Morgan's leadership, the two railroad giants created a virtual duopoly in eastern railroad transportation with clearly defined territories. For instance, in Pennsylvania the New York Central had the anthracite coal regions, while the Pennsylvania had the bituminous regions.

In 1968 the New York Central and Pennsylvania Railroads, the once-warring giants, merged into the Penn-Central Railroad. In 1976 virtually all railroads in the Northeast merged into the Conrail Corporation. The following railroads merged into the Conrail system: Penn-Central (composed of the Pennsylvania, New York Central, and New York, New Haven, and Hartford); Erie Lackawanna (composed of the Erie and the Delaware, Lackawanna, and Western); the Central of New Jersey; Lehigh Valley; and Reading.

Before discussing railroad sites, a brief introduction will help the reader more readily appreciate the different types of locomotives. Identification is relatively easy because locomotive types are determined by wheel arrangements. For instance, the earliest locomotives were 0-4-0 arrangements, meaning no wheels in the front or back, but two pairs of drive wheels in the middle (making four wheels in all). A 2-8-4 Berkshire type means there is one pair of wheels in the front, four pairs in the middle, and two pairs in the rear.

It is important to note the wheel arrangements because progress in making larger and stronger locomotives is associated with a greater number of locomotive wheels. Moreover, different work purposes called for different wheel arrangements. Some of the more common types of steam locomotives are American (4-4-0); Atlantic (4-4-2); Ten-Wheel (4-6-0); Pacific (4-6-2); Hudson (4-6-4); Twelve-Wheel (4-8-0); Mountain (4-8-2); Northern (4-8-4); Mastodon (4-10-0); Southern Pacific (4-10-2); Union Pacific (4-12-2); Columbia (2-4-2); Mogul (2-6-0); Prairie (2-6-2); Consolidation (2-8-0); Mikado (2-8-2); Berkshire (2-8-4); Decapod (2-10-0); Santa Fe (2-10-2); and Texas (2-10-4).

Pennsylvania and Delaware Sites

Franklin Institute

Twentieth Street and Benjamin Franklin Parkway, Philadelphia, PA (Open Mon–Fri 9:30–5, Sat–Sun 10–5, all year)

In this huge institute of science there is a large room devoted to railroad locomotives. The museum has an 1838 model of one of the earliest locomotives ever built, the Rocket. In 1829, locomotive trials were held near Rainhill Bridge, ten miles from Liverpool, England. George and Robert Stephenson's Rocket proved to be the most dependable and practical engine. The locomotive became the father of future locomotives, and the Stephensons became the world's outstanding locomotive builders. Also on display is a Baldwin No. 60000, a 4-10-2 locomotive. It was built in 1926 at the Baldwin Locomotive Works, once located on Spring Garden Street between Fifteenth and Broad streets, not far from Philadelphia's City Hall. The huge engine moves back and forth about ten feet—not a long ride, but the size of this monster makes the experience worthwhile. In addition, there is a Reading Railroad 4-4-0 locomotive used until 1883. The room also has many models of important locomotives in railway history.

The Stourbridge Lion
Route 6, Honesdale, PA

A gravity railroad was constructed at Honesdale to run a course of thirty miles from Valley Junction to Honesdale. At Honesdale, workers loaded the coal onto barges of the Delaware and Hudson Canal Company. By the 1840s, the workers were mining more coal than the gravity railroad could handle. So the Pennsylvania Coal Company constructed its own gravity railroad in 1847–1850 with the help of James Archbald. The railroad transported coal from Port Griffith (near Pittston) to Hawley, Pennsylvania, on the Lackawaxen River. A locomotive road did not replace the gravity railroad until 1885.

There are a number of sites connected with gravity railroads. In Scranton a Pioneer gravity railroad car used on the Pennsylvania Coal Company Railroad is located in Nay Aug Park behind the Everhart Museum. The car carried passengers from Pittston to Hawley from 1850 to 1884.

In Honesdale there is a replica of the Stourbridge Lion enclosed in housing built especially for it. Along with the replica of the first commercial locomotive in the United States is the Eclipse, one of the original passenger coaches used on the gravity railroad. On certain days in the summer and fall, the town of Honesdale sponsors train rides (see below). In the town of Hawley (off Route 6) there is another Pioneer Coach. From 1850 to 1885 the car operated from Port Griffith to Hawley—a forty-seven-mile route.

Stourbridge Line Rail Excursion
742 Main Street, Honesdale, PA (Open May, July–Sept, Dec—call ahead)

The Wayne County Chamber of Commerce has a fifty-mile, four-and-a-half-hour round trip from Honesdale to Lackawaxen. The line was once a part of an Erie Railroad branch, the Lackawaxen and Stourbridge.

Steamtown, U.S.A.
Former Delaware, Lackawanna, and Western Railroad Station, 700 Lackawanna Avenue, at intersection with Jefferson Avenue (exit 53 of I-81), Scranton, PA (Trains run Mar–Oct)

While touring the gravity railroad sites of the Delaware and Hudson Canal, you may want to take the twenty-six mile, one-and-one-quarter-hour round trip from downtown Scranton to Moscow, Pennsylvania, and back. Purchase your tickets at the former Delaware, Lackawanna, and Western Railroad station (now a hotel). A number of locomotives are exhibited on the tracks. The car we rode in had wicker seats that reverse direction. The interior was red with a white roof. On the trip itself the most memorable sight was the monstrous auto junkyard that went on and on.

Steamtown is located on the grounds of the repair yards of the Delaware, Lackawanna, and Western. The organization boasts a collection of forty locomotives and over one hundred pieces of rolling stock. Here also are a warehouse, railroad shops, and office buildings.

Blue Mountain and Reading Railroad

Tuckerton Road, between Route 61 and U.S. 222, Temple PA (Open Tues–Sun 10–4, Memorial Day–Labor Day; weekends 2–4 Mar–Memorial Day and Labor Day–Oct)

Take a twenty-six-mile, one-and-a-half-hour round trip on former Pennsylvania Railroad tracks from Temple (near Reading) to Hamburg. Plans are being made to restore those parts of the Schuylkill Canal that run parallel to the railroad line.

Railroad Museum of Pennsylvania

Route 741, opposite the Strasburg Railroad, Strasburg, PA (Open Mon–Sat 9–5, Sun 11–5, all year)

This is the best railway museum in the region. It is possible to follow the development of Pennsylvania Railroad locomotives as they grew more powerful and fancier. Some of the many locomotives in the museum are a replica of the Stevens Locomotive of 1825; a replica of the John Bull 2-4-0 locomotive that ran on the Camden and Amboy Railroad, an early precursor of the Pennsylvania Railroad; a 2-8-0 H6-class locomotive, which was the most numerous and long-lived type of locomotive used by the Pennsylvania Railroad; a 4-6-0 G5 used to pull commuter trains; and a GG1 electric locomotive, no. 4800, which logged nearly five million miles in forty-five years of service.

On the second floor are excellent displays of railroad memorabilia. Among the items are paintings by Grif Teller and dinnerware from the dining cars. Especially enjoyable are the advertising antics of "Miss Phoebe Snow," a fictional character who represented the Lackawanna Railroad and always dressed in white.

Strasburg Railroad

Route 741 in Strasburg, PA (Open daily 10–3, May–Oct; variable times Mar–Apr, Nov)

Several different types of locomotives are used to take passengers on a nine-mile, forty-five-minute round trip from Strasburg to Paradise. The station is located directly across from the Railroad Museum of Pennsylvania, providing a wonderful railroading day. The train ride itself goes by farms of the Amish. If you are lucky, you will catch a glimpse of these farmers at work with horses instead of tractors.

Gettysburg Railroad

Located in the center of Gettysburg on Constitution Avenue, off North Washington Street, Gettysburg, PA (To Biglerville: weekends 1–3, June–Oct; Mon–Fri 11–3, July–Aug; to Mt. Holly Springs: variable Saturdays, July–Oct)

This line offers two trips. There is a sixteen-mile round trip from Gettysburg to Biglerville and a fifty-mile round trip (reservations are needed) from Gettysburg to Mt. Holly Springs. The track once belonged to the Reading Railroad.

Rail Tours, Inc.

Railroad depot at junction of U.S. 209 and Broadway, Jim Thorpe, PA (Open weekends 1–4, Memorial Day–Labor Day and Sundays in Sept)

This is an eight-mile, thirty-five-minute round trip from Jim Thorpe to Nesquehoning over Panther Valley Railroad track, which was once a Jersey Central branch line. There is a small gift shop and a toy railway display. (See the section on Jim Thorpe for a tour of the town.)

Wanamaker, Kempton, and Southern Steam Railroad

Routes 143 or 737, just north of I-78, twenty miles west of Allentown, Kempton, PA (Open Sat 1–4, May–Oct; Sun 1–4, Apr and first two Sun of Nov)

This is a six-mile, forty-minute round trip train ride over a line belonging to the Reading Company's Schuylkill and Lehigh branch. Passengers can detrain at Furhman's Grove for a picnic and then reboard.

New Hope Steam Railway and Museum

Just off Bridge Street (Route 179) in the center of New Hope, PA (Open Sat 1:30–3:30, Apr–Oct)

This is a nine-mile, one-hour round trip on a former Reading Railroad branch line. The trip takes passengers from New Hope to Lahaska, past the

Wilmington and Western Railroad ride, Greenbank, Delaware

curved trestle featured in the movie serial the *Perils of Pauline*. Combine this pleasant train ride with the canal-boat ride in New Hope.

Wilmington and Western Railroad

Greenbank Station, junction of Routes 2 and 41, four miles southwest of Wilmington, Greenbank, DE (Open Sun 1–5, May–Oct)

Available is an eight-mile, one-hour round trip from Greenbank Station to Mt. Cuba Picnic Grove. The line goes over a portion of the former Baltimore and Ohio's Landenberg Branch. The Wilmington and Western Railroad built the twenty-mile track between Wilmington, Delaware, and Landenberg, Pennsylvania, in 1872 to provide service to the communities and industries of the Red Clay Valley. In 1883 the B & O Railroad acquired the line. The car we rode in was made for the Lackawanna line and has yellow stripes against a blue background. Inside are wicker seats. The ride itself is mostly through wooded areas.

New York and New Jersey Sites

Catskill Mountain Railroad

Twenty-two miles west of Kingston on Route 28, Mount Pleasant, NY (Open weekends 11–5, Memorial Day–Columbus Day)

This six-mile, forty-five minute round trip travels from Mount Pleasant to Phoenicia along Esopus Creek. The track formerly belonged to the Ulster and Delaware Railroad, later the Catskill Mountain Branch of the New York Central. In the summer at the Mount Pleasant station, you can rent an inner tube and ride with it on the train to Phoenicia. Then you can tube back on Esopus Creek to Mount Pleasant. The tubing hours are timed with the release of water from the dam upstream.

Delaware and Ulster Rail Ride

Forty-three miles west of Kingston on Route 28, Arkville, NY (Open Wed–Sun 10–6, late May–early Nov)

Located close to the Catskill Mountain Railroad, the Delaware and Ulster Rail Ride has a choice of train rides of three different lengths, the longest one being a fourteen-mile, one-and-one-quarter-hour round trip from Arkville to Highmount. The ride provides some very pretty views of the Catskill Mountains. The track belongs to the former Delaware and Ulster Railroad.

Trolley Museum

1 Roundout Landing, East Strand area of Kingston, NY, on the Roundout Creek waterfront (Open weekends 10–4, in season)

This museum offers a trolley excursion that is a two-mile, half-hour round trip on former Ulster and Delaware track from the museum site to Kingston Point. A highlight of the trip is the view of the Kingston lighthouse in the Hudson River. At present the line uses a gasoline-powered Brill car built in 1919. This is a young museum and should improve with time.

Black River and Western Railroad

Intersection of Church Street and Central Avenue at Liberty Village, Flemington, NJ (Open weekends mid April–Nov; Tues–Fri, July–Aug)

This train runs from Ringoes to Flemington and can be boarded at either location. The trip takes about one hour. The track is a former branch of the Pennsylvania Railroad. The conductor told us that originally the train ran from Lambertville, where it would pick up goods brought there via canal, to Flemington. At Ringoes there are a number of locomotives on display and a very small museum. After the ride, walk around the Liberty Village shopping area. Also visit some of the many retail outlet stores in Flemington. The town is not far from New Hope, where you can take another train ride or, if you prefer, the canal-boat ride.

New Jersey Museum of Transportation

Allaire State Park, Route 524, Wall Township, NJ (a short distance west of Garden State Parkway Exit 98 and one mile east of I-95, Exit 31) (Open daily 10–5, July–Aug; weekends Apr, Sept–Oct)

The Pine Creek Railroad consists of a one-and-one-half-mile loop track (three-foot-gauge line) in Allaire State Park. The ride lasts for about ten minutes. The train ride provides a nice addition to a visit to the old ironmaking community located at Allaire State Park.

Refueling a locomotive at Allaire State Park, Wall Township, New Jersey

Whippany Railway Museum

Route 10 and Whippany Road, Whippany, NJ (Open Sun 12–4, Apr–Oct)

This museum has a dozen pieces of rolling stock and a collection of railway items.

22

Maritime History

In the 1500s the English may have been disappointed that their new lands had no gold or spices, but North America did have an abundance of codfish, which Catholic Europe consumed in enormous quantities. Indeed, fishing was the continent's first industry and remained a central one for centuries. Codfishing was so important that a wooden image of the codfish was hung in the Boston assembly chamber. It is still there to this day.

Long Island has several fishing museums available for viewing. Two interesting ones are the East Hampton Town Marine Museum (Bluff Road, Amagansett) and the Suffolk Marine Museum (Suffolk County Park, Montauk Highway, 27A, West Sayville). The former concentrates on the different types of fishing, while the latter specializes in explaining the oyster trade, once dominated by the town of West Sayville.

The fishing industry gave rise to another early American industry, shipbuilding. The new industry expanded quickly, especially in Philadelphia. Between 1727 and 1766 Philadelphia's yards built 737 ships. By the time of the American Revolution the city was the leading seaport in America and the third most important shipbuilding center in the world, after London and Liverpool. New York City did not surpass Philadelphia until the early 1800s.

This part of the section on the Industrial Revolution covers three maritime topics: whaling, the China trade, and the advent of steam.

Whaling on Long Island

Whales were abundant at the time of the first settlements of English North America. For instance, in the town of Brookhaven, Long Island, settlers could find these huge creatures any day they went to look for them.

Long Islanders are credited with being the first settlers to turn whaling into a regular business. This happened as early as the 1640s. The towns of the island began to divide themselves into wards to look for stranded whales. The whales, once on shore, were cut into small pieces and their blubber *tried out,* or boiled, in big iron try pots. The resultant oil was used for many purposes, especially for lamps and candles.

It was not long before the islanders procured boats to go after offshore whales. By 1687 there were seven companies engaged in whaling on the east end of Long Island. As the whales along the coast became scarce, whalers acquired larger boats. These gradually developed into great floating factories designed to reduce large numbers of whales into barrels of oil.

The greatest years for whaling were between 1820 and 1850. After 1847 the industry started a gradual decline. The primary reason was the vast depletion of these great mammals caused by extensive whaling. Other, less important reasons were the California gold rush of 1849 (which took ships away from the whaling trade); the drilling of oil in Pennsylvania in 1859; the destruction of many whaling vessels by Confederate ships; and several ice disasters. Whaling hung on until the 1920s in the United States, but only on a very limited scale.

Long Island has a proud whaling history. In this section we visit places on the island connected with this history: Sag Harbor and Cold Spring Harbor. At the towns' whaling museums, you learn everything you ever wanted to know about whaling and whales: the types of whales, the ships and boats used to catch the giant mammals, the lifestyles of the whalers, and life in a whaling port. The first stop is Sag Harbor and the second is Cold Spring Harbor. Both towns have a certain ocean atmosphere that is different from inland towns.

Sag Harbor was one of the world's preeminent whaling ports and helped earn Long Island whalers a global reputation. In 1845 there were sixty-three vessels whaling, with over a thousand employees and a total capital of $2 million.

Hemmed in by hills, marshes, and the waters of Gardiners Bay, Sag Harbor was necessarily restricted in its development as an eighteenth- and nineteenth-century maritime community. The town's growth was also hindered by a great fire in 1817 and another one in 1845 that destroyed fifty-seven shops, stores, and warehouses.

The picturesque little village of Cold Spring Harbor was a thriving whaling port from 1838 to 1858. The town is now known for its many antique shops.

Sag Harbor Whaling and Historical Museum

Main and Garden streets (from the Montauk Highway, turn left/north onto Bridgehampton Harbor Turnpike, which turns into Sag Harbor Turnpike and then into Main Street), Sag Harbor, Long Island, NY (Open Mon–Sat 10–5, Sun 1–5, May 15–Sept 30)

This is the former home of Captain Benjamin Huntting. Notice the roof of the building with its wooden harpoons and blubber spades. The Greek Revival structure, designed by Minard Lafever in 1845, houses whaling tools; scrimshaw; antique (and modern) fishing rods, reels, and lures; and paintings. Outside is a replica of a whale boat from the whaler *Concordia*.

Custom House

Main and Garden streets, across from the Whaling Museum, Sag Harbor, Long Island, NY (Open Tues–Sun 10–5, June–Sept)

This is a simple Federal building, constructed in 1789 when the town became a United States port of entry for ships of the West Indies trade. It originally stood opposite the Whalers' Church. Its owner, Henry Packer Dering, was the first official collector of the port under the new government. George Washington personally appointed him to the position. He held the post from 1790 until his death in 1822. His job was to record the names of all ships entering and leaving the port, along with their cargoes, tonnage, and any fees collected. The whaling museum has his original appointment book.

In 1820 writer James Fenimore Cooper came to Sag Harbor to visit relatives. He had married a cousin of the Derings. Dering himself owned several ships and became partners with Cooper in still another shipping venture. Their ship, the *Union,* made the first sailing to be financed by selling shares in a ship union. This innovation made it possible for even the cabin boy to be a capitalist, making a profit from the ships' voyages. While waiting for his ship to return, the romantic writer wrote the novel *Precaution* and gathered material for two later books about whaling: *The Pioneers* and *The Sea Lions.*

The house illustrates the lifestyle of a comfortable eastern Long Island family. Dering, however, must have been crowded in this house with his wife and nine children. The interior is very simple, almost spartan by contemporary standards. Youngsters will enjoy examining the little wooden mousetrap.

Oakland Cemetery

Jermaine Avenue and Suffolk Street, Sag Harbor, Long Island, NY

Here stands a monument representing a broken and splintered mast, a memorial to six young whaling captains lost at sea. In the cemetery lie more than thirty-six such captains—the oldest, incidentally, was only thirty years old—killed while whaling.

Presbyterian Church

Union Street, Sag Harbor, Long Island, NY

Known as the Whalers' Church, this building is the dominating landmark of Sag Harbor. The architect is thought to have been Minard Lafever. Notice the Egyptian Revival styling, characterized by tall slitlike windows highlighting the facade. The steeple was made unusually tall so that it could serve as a landmark for returning whalers. Unfortunately, the hurricane of 1938 toppled it.

Whalers' Church, Sag Harbor, New York

Whaling Museum Society

Main Street (Exit 45 of the Long Island Expressway, north on Woodbury Road, bear right on this road and continue, then turn left/north onto Harbor Road, which changes into Main Street), Cold Spring Harbor, Long Island, NY (Open Tues–Sun 11–5, all year)

This museum was founded in 1942 by the scientist Dr. Charles B. Davenport and Dr. Robert C. Murphy, who sailed aboard the whaling ship *Daisy* from New Bedford, Massachusetts. Over four hundred pieces of scrimshaw are on display, along with ship models, shells, and a fully rigged whaling boat from the *Daisy*. Six sailors manned the whale boat, which is thirty feet long and six feet wide. A beautiful diorama of the city in its 1850s heyday is a must-see.

A walk through the town is recommended. At 208 Main Street, near the whaling museum, is the home of Captain Manuel Enos. The poor fellow and his entire crew disappeared at sea aboard a Chilean whaler. At 75 Main Street is the Conklin or Seaman's Railroad House. Originally home to the Conklin family, this structure later became the Seaman's Railroad House. The house provided temporary boarding for sailors and travelers getting off at the railroad station. It was also headquarters for the local stagecoach line. At the corner of Shore Road and Main Street, in front of the Whaler's Monument Library Park, is a slate-tablet memorial to the whalers of Cold Spring Harbor.

Other Sites to Visit

In the Suffolk County Historical Society Museum (300 West Main Street, Riverhead, Long Island, NY), there is a small display on whaling. The Southampton Historical Museum Complex (Meeting House Lane, Southampton, Long Island, NY) contains the house of whaler Captain Rogers. On the grounds is a building with many whaling tools, as well as other items. You can go on a whale-watching voyage on a seventy-two-foot boat, the *Finback II,* owned by the Okeanos Ocean Research Foundation (216 East Montauk Highway, Montauk, Long Island, NY; cruises leaving daily 10–4, spring–fall), which aids stranded or injured whales. See the Geographic Cross-Reference for a listing of other sites to see on Long Island.

Philadelphia-China Trade

Following the Revolution, American merchants began to look for new markets to replace the lost British ones. Another motivating factor to search for new markets was the uncertain policies of the often warring European nations. China appeared to be an ideal substitute. Trade with China began on a grand scale three months after the British left New York City. In 1784 the *Empress of China* sailed from New York City. The ship brought to China the ginseng root, which grows wild in the woods of New England. The Chinese thought the root to be an aphrodisiac. The merchant vessel brought back Chinese tea, as well as other goods. The demand for ginseng was soon satiated, so the Americans had to look around for something else the Chinese might want. That something else was American furs.

To aid the China trade, clipper ships, especially designed for speed, were built. The first clipper, the *Sea Witch,* sailed for China in 1846. Although these ships were originally designed for this trade, the discovery of gold in California in 1849 and later in Australia created a scarcity of ships and drove the demand for express freight sky-high.

No matter how romantic these ships were, they flourished scarcely more than half a decade. Too much emphasis was placed on speed and not enough on cargo space. Windjammers, which were slower but could carry much more cargo, soon replaced the clippers.

One of the important merchants in the new overseas trade was the wealthy Philadelphian Stephen Girard. To learn more about this man, visit the museum he set up in his own honor. This is a short visit and should be combined with other maritime Philadelphia sites.

Stephen Girard Collection

Founder's Hall, Girard and Corinthian avenues, Girard College, Philadelphia, PA (Open Thur 2–4; or by appointment)

Girard (1750–1831) was a Frenchman born blind in his right eye. At age fourteen, he went to sea as a cabin boy. After only six voyages, his employers took the almost unprecedented step of licensing him as a captain though he was not even twenty-five years old.

Arriving in New York with a consignment of sugar and coffee, he decided to stay, and so hired out first as a mate and then as captain. He saved his money and became half-owner of a vessel. The ship put into Philadelphia one day because of rough seas and to avoid capture by the British. The young captain stayed in Philadelphia, largely because the war forced him to abandon the sea for a life of merchandising.

In 1777 he married Mary Lum, daughter of a Kensington shipbuilder, in Philadelphia's St. Paul's Episcopal Church. They lived in Mount Holly, New Jersey, in the still-existing, but private, house at 211 Mill Street.

The couple started a small store in their house. Apparently, the marriage was not a happy one. The story goes that her male customers found her so attractive that they hung around the store. Later, when the British occupied the town, she flirted with several soldiers. Her behavior was in part the result of being pushed away from her husband by his rather morose and stern temperament. The final blowup occurred when the Frenchman entered the store one day to find a soldier stealing a kiss from his wife across the counter.

The bitter and frequent arguments between the couple turned the husband into a cynic, while the wife went mad. In 1790 Mary Girard was deemed a lunatic and committed to a hospital. She died in 1815, and the widower moved back to Philadelphia. The death of his wife partly accounts for his somewhat lonely life. (In addition, his only child died in infancy.)

He became a citizen of Pennsylvania and engaged in the West Indies trade. At his height, he owned six vessels. In 1784 Girard's ship the *United States* sailed from Philadelphia for China. It was also the first American ship to venture to India and, consequently, opened the trade with that country. His vessels were also at the head of the East India trade. And, in 1796, his ship the *Voltaire,* opened the trade with the Baltic ports and Russia.

In 1812 he purchased Thomas Willing's Bank of the United States building on Third Street to be used as his private bank. Indeed, it became known as Girard's Bank. Like Robert Morris before him, he actually floated a war, this one the War of 1812. When the Treasury could only sell a small part of a $16 million bond issue, Girard and two other men subscribed for the entire remainder. He can be seen as the successor to Willing and Morris as the financial leader of Philadelphia. By 1813 he was the first millionaire merchant in the country and, by the time of his death in 1831, the wealthiest man in the United States.

This self-made man could be very self-sacrificing. During the yellow fever epidemic of 1793, he spent so much time in a local hospital caring for the sick that he neglected his businesses. Moreover, he was the first systematic philanthropist in America. In his will he left $2 million for a school for poor, white, orphan boys, which later became Girard College. It was the largest bequest up to that time. The will spelled out the smallest details on how the school should be run. He also left money to improve Philadelphia's waterfront and strengthen its police. Girard relatives contested the will itself, but the Supreme Court held in favor of the deceased.

Just inside the main entrance to Founder's Hall, you will see a life-size statue of the maritime millionaire. Near the statue, his body lies in a sarcophagus. Also nearby is the Girard Museum. In the collection are, as the will stipulated, his books, furniture, silver, porcelain, financial records, and private papers.

Other Sites to Visit

A must stop for one interested in seagoing vessels is Penn's Landing in Philadelphia. The outstanding vessel is the USS *Olympia* (see the section on this vessel). In addition, you can see the USS *Becuna,* a submarine; the 1904 ironclad *Lightship Number 79,* known as "Old Barney"; the 1883 Portuguese barkentine *Gazela Primeiro;* and the 1907 *Moshulu,* the largest steel sailing ship in the world. From the landing, you can take a boat ride around Philadelphia. Also visit the Maritime Museum of Philadelphia at 321 Chestnut Street. This museum contains some mementos from the sinking of the *Titanic,* as well as many ship models. The Franklin Institute also has some exhibits on shipbuilding.

The Advent of Steam

When we think of the steamboat, we usually imagine a romantic time of well-dressed women with parasols and fancy-suited gentlemen talking sweetly on the deck of a Mississippi riverboat. Or we think of Mark Twain's descriptions of life on the Mississippi. The romance of the steamboat, however, was also evident in the Mid-Atlantic region. After all, Robert Fulton built and demonstrated the steamboat in New York. Just as on the Mississippi, small boys along the Hudson and Delaware rivers knew the boats by their colors and shapes and the owners by the house flags that flew above the pilothouses.

Despite the unromantic name, an attractive feature of steamboating was the safety barge towed along behind a steamboat. Safety barges had no engine rooms, so passengers did not have to worry about explosions. The absence of engines allowed more room for travelers. Most of the barges had two decks, surmounted by an open promenade. They were usually lavishly ornamented with paneled walls and carpets. Travelers could enjoy a sumptuous meal while the band played.

There are no cruises available on steamboats today, but there are many places along the Hudson and Delaware rivers offering extended boat rides. But why not take one from historic Kingston, which at one time was home base to many steamboats and towboats? Combine the boat ride from Kingston with visits to several museums that have steamboat displays and a walking tour (a map of the Rondout river port area is available). You can easily spend a day here. But first, let's look briefly at the development of steamboats.

Steamboats were at first relatively slow, but this changed over time. For instance, it took Fulton thirty-two hours to make the journey from New York City to Albany, but by the 1830s the journey took only seven hours.

Besides being slow at first, the boats were also dangerous. Take the case of a prominent architect. From the dock at Newburgh, friends of America's foremost landscape architect, Andrew Jackson Downing, wished him a safe journey. They later learned that his boat had caught fire and wrecked itself on the riverbanks at Riverdale in the Bronx. Downing drowned trying to save other passengers. Ironically, the great landscaper had reminisced with a friend that as a boy he used to swim back and forth across the river and that, if one had to die, the best way would be by drowning. Despite such casualties, the steamboats did get better and safer over time.

Although considerable progress in improving steamships was made in the early 1800s, steam vessels were not used for transatlantic voyages until 1838. Instead, the steamboats were primarily used for ferrying local passengers. These boats had the regularity of the coach and were as comfortable as the sloop.

Hudson River Maritime Center

1 Rondout Landing (Kingston Exit of I-87, enter traffic circle and exit for Chandler Drive, continue straight down Broadway, which heads downhill and curves to the right, and then breaks to the left onto Lower Broadway, turn left onto East Strand), Kingston, NY (Open 10–4, all year)

In the nineteenth century, Kingston was one of the state's most important river ports. The port section known as Rondout Creek was once a very busy place. (Pick up a walking guide to Rondout while in the area.) The town also became the base for steamship and towboat lines. The Delaware and Hudson Canal ended here. Workers transferred the anthracite coal from the canal to riverboats, which shipped the coal south to New York City. Other transported products were Ulster County bluestone and locally manufactured cement and brick.

Rondout Creek had boatyards at Rondout, Wilbur, Connelly, and Ponkhockie. Many of the steamboat men lived in adjacent Sleightsburg.

Some of the famous boats operating from Rondout were the *James W. Baldwin, Thomas Cornell, City of Kingston, Henry E. Bishop,* and *Mary Powell.* The museum here has a small display on Hudson River ferryboat travel. Outside is an old tug, the *William O. Benson,* named in honor of one of Kingston's most famous river men.

At one of the museums associated with the Senate House in Kingston there is a small display on steamboats, including the steering wheel from the city's speed queen, the *Mary Powell.* It was this boat that brought back the body of George Armstrong Custer following his death at the Battle of the Little Big Horn (1876). Also in the museum is a painting of the *City of Kingston* steamboat by James Bard, who painted many a steam vessel.

The *Mary Powell* was built in 1861 in Jersey City for its owner, Absalom Anderson. The boat ran daily back and forth to Manhattan. Anderson was very proud of his boat's speed. The story spread that he would hire a little boy, whose sole job was to shoo away the flies from the railings so the boat would not be slowed by the extra weight. Another favorite story was that the owner would mix the boat's paint with whale grease to help it slide through the water. In fifty-six years of service the boat never lost a passenger and was always on time. Still another tale states that the boat was so punctual that the cadets at West Point could time their formations by the sound of the ship's bell.

Other Sites to Visit

See the section on the stockade area of Kingston for other sites in the area. You can take a two-hour boat ride on the Hudson River aboard the *Marion T. Budd.* Hudson River Cruises operates from May to October. (The phone number is 914-255-6515.) On the trip you see the Kingston-Rhinecliff Bridge and the Esopus Light on a tiny rocky island, and you can catch glimpses of Hudson River mansions.

When visiting Long Island, be sure to see the American Merchant Marine Museum (Steamboat Road, United States Merchant Marine Academy, Kings Point). This will round out your maritime history. The museum has many ship models covering the development of transatlantic steam vessels. The highlight of the museum's collection is the Hales Blue Riband Trophy, a gilt award last won in 1952 by the SS *United States* for the fastest transatlantic crossing by a passenger liner. Here also is the National Maritime Hall of Fame, established in 1982. Each year, four individuals and four vessels that have made outstanding contributions to the maritime industry are inducted.

P A R T

EIGHT

The Civil War Period

The conflict that cost the most American lives was the Civil War, 1861–1865. The North fought this war because the continuation of slavery meant the perpetuation of two separate societies—societies with different economies, different ways of life, and different values. Slavery, besides being morally wrong, was just not compatible with the new industrial order and had to be eliminated.

In the region there are just a few places connected with this crucial event to visit. Fortunately for the North, most of the battles took place in the South. Nevertheless, one is constantly reminded of this important conflict by the hundreds of memorial statues dedicated to Northern Civil War veterans found in towns and cities throughout the region.

This section begins with the home of Pennsylvanian James Buchanan, who was president of the United States when sectional tensions mounted to the point where federal troops in the forts of Charleston Harbor found themselves in a very dangerous position. In the next chapter we tour the Gettysburg battlefield, where the most important battle of the war occurred. The last chapter concludes with Fort Delaware, which housed Southern prisoners of war.

23

President James Buchanan

Visiting President Buchanan's home is a special treat because it looks much the same as it did when he lived here. In the Victorian house there are many items from his years of diplomatic travel: rugs from Persia, wallpaper from Japan, and lace curtains from France. And, of course, there are the many gifts he received from various heads of state. The house and carriage house (which contains Buchanan's old Germantown wagon) will take more than an hour to tour. Most people probably would not make a special trip just to see the house, but since the site is located in Lancaster County, many Pennsylvania Dutch attractions are available.

James Buchanan was born in 1791 at Stony Batter, near Mercersburg, Pennsylvania. He attended Dickinson College in Carlisle. Following graduation, he studied law in Lancaster and was admitted to the bar in 1812. He began his political career with elections to the Pennsylvania legislature in 1814 and to the United States House of Representatives in 1820.

In 1819 he became engaged to Anne Coleman, daughter of Robert Coleman, who owned many iron properties and was one of the country's first millionaires. Unfortunately, the young lawyer became so involved in his work that he neglected his fiancée. They quarreled, over what we probably will never know. She either felt that he did not really love her or that he was marrying for her money, or both. So she released him from the engagement.

Anne Coleman became depressed and was sent to Philadelphia to recuperate. She stayed with her elder sister, Margaret, wife of Judge Joseph Hemphill. (You can visit Hemphill's mansion located in Fairmount Park.) While there, she either became ill and died or committed suicide. Many people blamed Buchanan for her death. Anne's father certainly did. He refused to let the former fiancé attend the funeral service.

This event is often cited as an explanation for why the future president never married. In fact, he was the only president to remain a bachelor. It may also explain his heavy involvement in politics. He once said, perhaps a bit too modestly, that he "never intended to enter politics . . . but as a distraction from a great grief which happened at Lancaster when I was a young man . . . I accepted a nomination." Ironically, the affair had the net result of increasing his law practice. Potential clients felt that here was a young man who would sacrifice his own personal interests for their sakes.

In 1832 he became minister to Russia under President Jackson. Upon his return, in 1834 he successfully ran for the United States Senate. In hindsight, it was a good thing that he was out of the country when Jackson's attack on the banking system became a white-hot controversy. Pennsylvania backed Jackson's enemy, bank president Nicholas Biddle, and this would have forced Buchanan into open conflict with the president.

By campaigning hard in his home state for James K. Polk, Buchanan helped the Democratic candidate win the 1844 election. President Polk rewarded him by appointing him secretary of state. Both men agreed on annexing Texas and taking New Mexico and California from the Mexicans. However, the president did not trust Buchanan, and they often feuded. Nevertheless, Polk retained him as secretary of state, considering him an able man.

Wheatland

1120 Marietta Avenue (Route 23), west of the intersection with President Avenue (from Lancaster take Route 340 west until it branches out onto Marietta Avenue), western outskirts of Lancaster, PA (Open daily 10–4, Apr–Nov)

The Pennsylvania bachelor had been a leading contender in both the 1844 and 1848 Democratic presidential nominations. He looked forward to running again at the 1852 convention and began to look for a house to match a man of his ambitions. His old house was just too crowded, because he now had charge of a growing number of nieces and nephews. One of his favorites was Harriet Lane, the daughter of his sister, Jane Buchanan Lane.

In December 1848 he purchased a Federal brick mansion in Lancaster known as Wheatland. It had been built in 1828 for William Jenkins, president of the Farmers' Bank. The new owner moved into the house after leaving his cabinet post.

Buchanan was not nominated by the 1852 convention. Instead, the delegates chose Franklin Pierce, who went on to win the presidential election. Pierce appointed Buchanan minister to Great Britain, partly as a reward for his efforts and partly to remove him from the political scene for the next Democratic convention. As the 1856 election campaign drew near, the minister, still wishing to be nominated, asked to be recalled from Britain. He did not get his wish until the eve of the convention. Although his opponents thought this would keep him out of the race, the timing was actually fortunate. The disastrous results of the Kansas-Nebraska Act (which had turned Kansas into a battleground over the issue of the extension of slavery) left all the candidates dirtied except the former minister, who had been out of the country.

Upon receiving the presidential nomination, he conducted the entire campaign from his study, with politicians and ordinary folk coming to Wheatland. It may not have been much of an effort, but it was enough to elect him. The voters chose him because he was seen as a cautious man who would not rush the nation into war.

While in the White House, his niece, Harriet Lane, served as surrogate first lady. The president let her determine all matters of social protocol. Some have described this "glamorous blonde" as the most beautiful of all White House hostesses. At Wheatland you can see the Chickering piano her uncle gave her so she could entertain guests. Upstairs in her bedroom is her Episcopal kneeling perch and a petticoat table complete with a mirror to make sure her slip did not show.

Buchanan has often been accused of weakness for not letting the South know that secession would mean war. An Andrew Jackson he was not. He was an agrarian-minded man who approached the growing problem as one to be solved through the correct interpretation of the law. This often led him to support the Southern side on those issues for which that region had legal backing. He tried to get the Supreme Court to solve the slavery issue legally, but its Dred Scott decision of 1857 (declaring that Congress had no right to deprive slaveholders of their "property" without due process of law) just made matters worse. The legalist approach was not going to work, and it effectively paralyzed the president.

Following Lincoln's election in 1860, he retired from public life. These, however, were not happy retirement days. Many Republicans blamed him for starting the war, and worse, for aiding the secessionists. Several Masons stood guard at Wheatland for the early part of the war to protect the former president from harm. In order to clear his name against many of the grossly unfair charges, the former president wrote a history of his administration. He also initiated a biography of himself to be written by friends, but none was published while he lived.

At Wheatland he greeted groups that came to honor him. The home livened with the 1866 marriage of Harriet Lane to Henry E. Johnston in the mid-Victorian parlor. Two years later, the ex-president died at his beloved home.

Other Sites to Visit

Next-door to Wheatland is the Lancaster County Historical Society. It has changing exhibits along with a great many historical documents. While visiting Lancaster, tour the Pennsylvania Dutch sites in the area. Also consider touring the Gettysburg battlefield (see the next chapter). When in Philadelphia on a weekday, stop and see the Civil War Library and Museum (located at 1805 Pine Street), which has many items, including a collection of weapons, Custer's flag from the Battle of Gettysburg, Lincoln's life mask made two months prior to his assassination, many of General Grant's personal belongings, and the shawl worn by Jefferson Davis as he tried to escape at the end of the war.

24

Gettysburg

This battle site requires a little extra driving to get to, but it is a must-see for any traveler. Touring the now quiet fields amid the numerous stone monuments from both the North and South is a very moving experience. The tragedy of Americans killing Americans adds to the impact of this place of carnage. The conflict was the single most important battle of the war, often referred to as the turning point. Moreover, the battle was the occasion for the recitation of one of the most beautiful and moving pieces of English prose ever written: Lincoln's Gettysburg Address.

Gettysburg is a major tourist area. One could easily spend many days here visiting the countless ancillary museums and other attractions connected with the battle.

In terms of battle successes there were actually two Civil Wars. Thanks to Ulysses S. Grant, the North was largely winning the one in the west. Thanks to Robert E. Lee, the South was holding its own in the east. For the eastern front, Lincoln kept searching for a fighting general who would keep constant pressure on the Southern forces, which, compared to their Northern counterparts, were vastly undersupplied.

Lee had won most of the battles that had taken place on Southern soil, partly because he usually held the defensive position. The North suffered terrible losses by attacking dug-in Southern troops. Such, for example, was the case at the Battle of Fredericksburg in December 1862. When Lee went on the offensive north of Virginia, he had little success. His first foray led to the bloody Battle of Antietam in Maryland in 1862. His second trip north, this time into Pennsylvania, went no better, as we shall see.

Lee had just come off a victory at the Battle of Chancelorsville, May 1863. The victory, however, had cost the life of one of the South's outstanding generals, Stonewall Jackson, who was mistakenly shot by one of his own soldiers. Because of the defeat, the North replaced the losing general, Joseph Hooker, with General George Meade.

The primary reason for Lee's Pennsylvania foray was to collect supplies for his ill-equipped army. He also planned to capture Harrisburg. On June 28, 1863, the Southern commander, located a mile east of Chambersburg, had his army stretched in a forty-five-mile crescent, with General James Longstreet at the southern tip at Chambersburg and Lieutenant General Richard S. Ewell (Stonewall Jackson's replacement) at the northern tip at Carlisle (southwest of Harrisburg) and York (southeast of Harrisburg). Major General Ambrose P. Hill, known as A. P. Hill, was located to the east of Longstreet's forces.

Much to Lee's surprise, the Northern army had been on a long march and was now at Frederick, Maryland. Meade was rushing north to prevent the enemy from crossing the Susquehanna River and opening the way toward Philadelphia.

Lee quickly decided to consolidate his scattered forces at Cashtown (eight miles west of Gettysburg). Unbeknown to him, the town of Gettysburg was held by Major General John Buford and three brigades of federal cavalry. Meanwhile, Meade was taking up defensive positions just south of Gettysburg behind a stream called Pipe Creek.

On the morning of July 1, Southern troops under Hill were walking from Cashtown to Gettysburg to get their shoes repaired. They ran into Buford's pickets just northwest of the town, and the fight was on. From this chance encounter each side gradually threw in its forces until a full-scale battle developed. Neither side chose the Gettysburg location, but both forces were in the area and their collision was inevitable.

Visitors' Center

Gettysburg National Military Park, Taneytown Road (from Lancaster take Route 15 south, Route 140 north, turn right onto Hunt Avenue, turn left onto Taneytown Road), Gettysburg, PA (Open daily, 8–5, all year)

Here is an electric map that outlines the troop movements with words and electric lights on a huge relief map of the battlefield area. It is a good way to get an overview. Near the Visitors' Center is the Cyclorama Center, which presents a ten-minute film and views of the *Cyclorama*—a spectacular painting by Paul Philippoteaux of a climactic part of the battle known as Pickett's Charge.

I always like to start touring battlefields chronologically so the action can be followed logically. This is not always the most convenient or most economical way to see a battlefield, but it is better to do some extra traveling in order to more fully appreciate and understand the battle itself. Pick up a good battlefield map at the Visitors' Center. Start your tour where the battle began, at McPherson Ridge just off Route 30 (Chambersburg Pike).

To help you understand the battle before traveling to Gettysburg, draw a crude map by making a battle clock. The center of the clock is the town center, where York and Carlisle streets intersect. Carlisle Street heads due north (12:00). McPherson Bridge is at 9:30, the Eternal Light and Oak Ridge at 11:00, Barlow Knoll at 1:00, Culp's Hill at 4:30, and Cemetery Hill at 5:45. There are two main ridges, which run north to south parallel to each other. Draw a line extending down from the outer rim of the clock at the 6:00 position to represent Cemetery Ridge. Draw a similar line just below and to the east of the McPherson Ridge position. This is Seminary Ridge.

July 1: The First Day

McPherson Ridge

Corner of Reynolds Avenue and Route 30, Gettysburg, PA

As the Southern soldiers gaily walked toward town they ran into Buford's pickets, and the battle commenced. Major General Henry Heth, commanding A. P. Hill's leading division, came forward and met the leading division of Major General Abner Doubleday's I Corps.

Meade had earlier sent Major General John F. Reynolds to scout the situation at Gettysburg. By the time he arrived, the fighting had already begun. He quickly took command of the Union forces. Tragically, he recklessly exposed himself at the forefront of the action at the eastern edge of McPherson's Woods and was promptly killed.

Eternal Light Peace Memorial

Off North Confederate Avenue, Gettysburg, PA

Located northeast of McPherson Ridge, this memorial, dedicated in 1938 on the seventy-fifth anniversary of the battle, marks the area where Major General Robert Rodes's Confederate division arrived in the early afternoon to threaten the Union forces.

Oak Ridge

Off North Confederate Avenue (has observation tower), Gettysburg, PA

Rodes arrayed his men here on Oak Ridge (just to the southeast of the Eternal Light), preparing to link up with Hill's troops to drive the Yankees from the battlefield. However, Northern troops repulsed the attack with heavy Confederate losses. At the same time, Hill's troops to the west pushed the Union soldiers back onto Seminary Ridge, just east of McPherson Ridge.

Barlow Knoll

Howard Avenue, located between Route 34 and Harrisburg Road, Gettysburg, PA

Here Confederate troops under Major General Jubal Early arrived in the afternoon to rout the Union defenders. Northern troops fled south through the town.

Lee arrived on the battlefield around noon. He witnessed the developing Southern victory as his forces pushed the Union troops completely out of town and south to Cemetery Ridge. He also saw that there was a weakness to the North's Cemetery Ridge position. Looking at a map from south to north, the Union positions looked like an inverted fishhook, with the curve in the hook turning to the right. The hook's straight line was Cemetery Ridge, the curve Cemetery Hill, and the barb Culp's Hill. If the Confederates under Ewell could take the high ground at Cemetery Hill, the Union forces would be extremely vulnerable.

If Lee had still had Stonewall Jackson, the South probably would have taken Cemetery Hill and pushed the Northern forces further south away from Gettysburg. Lee's message to Ewell, however, read: "Attack that hill if practicable." The message confused the field commander, who thought this left the attack to his discretion. By the time he had gathered his scattered forces, it was too late for an assault. Lee must also share part of the blame. Suffering from an attack of dysentery, he performed under par in communicating with his field commanders.

July 2: The Second Day

The Confederates lost valuable time in pursuing their victory of the first day. It was already late afternoon before their first assault began. When they did attack, they did so along the whole fishhook line. By that time, the Union army had brought up reinforcements and had dug into defensive positions.

Culp's Hill View

East Confederate Avenue (observation tower available on Culp's Hill), Gettysburg, PA

At dusk, Ewell's forces tried unsuccessfully to take this hill. If they had succeeded, the entire Union position on Cemetery Ridge would have been endangered.

Spangler's Spring

South of Culp's Hill, Geary Avenue, Gettysburg, PA

Repulsed at Culp's Hill, the Confederates seized this spring. They lost it to the North the following morning.

Cemetery Hill
Slocum Avenue, Gettysburg, PA

This is the hill Lee wanted Ewell to capture on the first day of battle. On the second day, Union forces repelled a Confederate assault that reached the crest of the hill east of the road. Drive past the Visitors' Center to the southern part of the battlefield park. This is where the heaviest fighting took place on the second day of the battle.

Little Round Top
Sykes Avenue, Gettysburg, PA

Union forces under Major General Edgar Sickles occupied the southern part of the fishhook position, with their furthest southern extension at Little Round Top. The commander thought he saw a better position for his troops to his front and, without waiting for permission from Meade, abandoned the hilltop. He spread his troops on the plain to the west, from Devil's Den through the Wheatfield to the Peach Orchard. This left an opening for the Confederates. Fortunately for the Union forces, General G. K. Warren, chief engineer of the Army of the Potomac, saw the exposed position on Little Round Top and summoned troops to defend it.

Devil's Den
Warren Avenue, Gettysburg, PA

From their positions on Seminary Ridge, Southern troops under Longstreet attacked Sickle's positions at Devil's Den, the Wheatfield, and the Peach Orchard. They pushed the Union defenders from the boulders at Devil's Den. From here, their sharpshooters fired on Little Round Top.

The Wheatfield
Sickles Avenue, Gettysburg, PA

For four long hours the battle raged between Seminary and Cemetery ridges. The fighting surged back and forth without any real pattern. At the end of the fighting the Southern forces had control of the plain in front of Cemetery Ridge, but the Union forces still held the ridge itself.

The Peach Orchard

Wheat Field Road, Gettysburg, PA

Longstreet pushed Sickle's men from this area back to Cemetery Ridge.

July 3: The Third Day

After two days of fighting the Union forces still held strong defensive positions on Cemetery Ridge. Lee decided to do what many a Union general had disastrously failed to do. He threw troops across an open field at heavily entrenched enemy forces. He himself had defeated this tactic on several occasions, so what in the world possessed him to order such an attack?

As in classical tragedies, the fault in the hero was hubris. Lee thought that the Army of Northern Virginia could take any position once it had set its mind to do so. This pride was to cost him the battle.

General George Pickett of Longstreet's corps had arrived with a fresh division of five thousand troops. Lee strengthened this division and, on the morning of July 3, hurled it against the Union lines.

Virginia Memorial

West Confederate Avenue, Gettysburg, PA

The Southern commander watched Pickett's charge from here on the morning of July 3. He thought a barrage of early morning artillery fire would soften the Union defensive lines. However, the bombardment proved ineffective because the shots landed far behind enemy lines.

Confederate troops then lined up in battle formation and began the assault known as Pickett's Charge. The Union artillery had an easy target—massed troops in an open field. Lee watched as Brigadier General J. J. Pettigrew's division gave way before the brutal cannon fire. The Confederates crossed Emmitsburg Road and came into musket range. Incredibly, a few hundred crossed the Union lines. The attack failed, and only half of the troops in the battle returned. As they retreated, Lee told them: "All this has been my fault."

As you stand by the Virginia Memorial looking out over the open area toward the Union positions, think how fortunate you are not to have been a Southern soldier on that July 3 morning.

High Water Mark

Hancock Avenue, Gettysburg, PA

You are now looking from the Union lines at the ground over which the Confederates attacked. It must have been a frightening and awe-inspiring sight to watch thousands of Confederate troops mass in battle formation. Notice the nearby clump of trees reached by Pickett's men. This spot became known as the High Water Mark of the Confederacy. For the Confederates it was all downhill from here.

Following the failure of Pickett's Charge, the rebels, having lost a third of their initial strength, retreated south. Never again would Lee engage in an offensive campaign. Meade did not pursue the Confederates. This infuriated Lincoln, who desperately wanted to quickly crush the rebels.

Gettysburg National Cemetery
Across from the Visitors' Center, Gettysburg, PA

Governor Andrew Curtin of Pennsylvania was distressed that many of the battle dead lay in inadequate graves or were not buried at all. So he commissioned David Wills, a local attorney, to buy land for a proper burial site.

The cemetery was dedicated on November 19, 1863. Lincoln gave a two-minute speech, following a two-hour oration from the famous speaker Edward Everett. It is Lincoln's words that we remember. The president wrote the first draft in Washington and revised it at the home of David Wills.

Other Sites to Visit

At the Visitors' Center, pick up tickets to tour the Eisenhower National Historic Site. There is a train ride available in downtown Gettysburg. And, of course, don't miss the Pennsylvania Dutch sites in Lancaster County.

Fort Delaware and Finns Point

Fort Delaware and Finns Point are to be cherished as two of the few sites in the region connected with the Civil War. Children especially enjoy seeing the massive fort that to them appears more like a giant playground. The fort is reachable only by boat (another thrill for the kids) from Delaware City, Delaware, while Finns Point is located in New Jersey near the town of Salem. To see both sites will take an entire day.

Fort Delaware
Pea Patch Island (from the first exit of I-95 after passing over the Delaware Memorial Bridge, travel south on Route 9 into town, turn left at traffic light onto Clinton Street, to Delaware State Park dock on the canal), Delaware City, DE (Pick up tickets at the boat dock in Delaware City, Delaware.)

(Boats leave 11 A.M.–4 P.M. Sat, Sun, and holidays, last weekend in Apr–last weekend in Sept)

After the War of 1812 the federal government constructed a fort on Pea Patch Island in the Delaware River, one mile from Delaware City, Delaware. According to popular legend, the island got its unusual name when a boat carrying peas ran aground on the 178-acre mud flat. The peas sprouted and changed the flat into an island. The masonry fort, built in 1819, lasted until 1831 when it was destroyed by fire.

It was not until 1849 that Congress appropriated funds for a new fort. The workers finished building the pentagon-shaped structure by the end of 1859. It was made of solid granite blocks and bricks and surrounded by a thirty-foot moat. The first troops arrived in February 1861.

Even with the eruption of the Civil War, life at the fort was extremely quiet. This changed in April 1862 with the arrival of 258 Confederate prisoners fresh from the Battle of Kernstown near Winchester, Virginia. The prisoners stayed in wooden barracks inside the fort. Captain Augustus A. Gibson, the fort's commander, and his men were extremely disappointed that they were to be jailers rather than fighters for the Union cause.

As more prisoners arrived, additional barracks had to be constructed on the parade ground and then on the grounds north of the fort. In July 1863, following the Battle of Gettysburg, the number of prisoners on the island reached an all-time high of 12,595.

The death rate at the prison was alarming. Disease was the number one cause. During a smallpox epidemic, 861 prisoners died within three months. In all some 2,400 Confederates died here.

The highest-ranking prisoner was Lieutenant General Joseph S. Wheeler, who was the leader of cavalry in the western theater. Lee con-

Fort Delaware, Delaware City, Delaware

sidered him, along with J.E.B. Stuart, one of his two outstanding Confederate cavalry leaders. Fighting Joe had been wounded three times while participating in two hundred engagements and eight hundred skirmishes. His services ended with his capture near Atlanta, where his troops had been just about the only ones opposing Sherman's march to the sea. Other important prisoners included Burton S. Harrison, private secretary to Confederate President Jefferson Davis, and Governor Francis Lubbock of Texas.

At the fort are huge cannons from the Spanish-American War. They were installed in 1896 on the eve of that conflict. During World War I, the fort was garrisoned, but was deactivated in 1919. The fort finally closed in 1944. Also here is a small museum that has exhibits of old bottles, coins, clay-pipe fragments, bullets, and many other items. There is also a model of the island as it looked in 1864. Upstairs are other displays, including some uniforms. Excess moisture has seriously marred some of the displays.

Finns Point National Monument

Just north of Fort Mott (off Route 49), Finns Point, NJ (which is northwest of Salem and not far south of the Delaware Memorial Bridge)

As early as 1837, the federal government erected gun emplacements at what was called Finns Point Battery, at Finns Point, New Jersey, opposite Pea Patch Island. A total of 2,400 prisoners who died at Fort Delaware are buried in the Finns Point national cemetery. With so many dead, one would expect to find a great many headstones, but apparently they buried the bodies helter-skelter and no one could identify the graves individually.

In 1896 the government built elaborate, large-gun emplacements with connecting tunnels and named the fortifications Fort Mott in honor of General Gershom Mott, commander of the New Jersey Volunteers in the Civil War. Children have a great deal of fun climbing on the embankments, but this can be a bit dangerous if they are not watched.

The guns here were twelve-inch breach-loading rifled coastal-defense guns, mounted on disappearing carriages. The gunners would load their weapons in the lowered position, safely behind the fortifications. They then raised the cannon. When fired, the recoil would return the weapon to its lowered position.

Other Sites to Visit

Combine this tour of Civil War sites with a tour of Wilmington, Delaware. See the sections on the Hagley Museum and the Du Ponts of Delaware. Also see the sections on Swedish and Quaker settlements in the Delaware River valley. Not far from Wilmington is the Brandywine Battlefield.

PART

NINE

Post–Civil War Period

The Civil War cleared the way for the dominance of the industrial way of life in the United States. The industrial society of the North now held clear sway over the agricultural society of the South. This new industrial order brought many changes to the lives of Americans. One change was the concentration of vast amounts of wealth in the hands of a few men as their companies swallowed other firms. The business methods of the new industrialists were often harsh and brutal, which explains the origin of the term *robber baron* as applied to the new entrepreneurs. Another massive change was the influx of people from rural farms to urban factories. The workers usually found factory conditions to be very harsh with long working hours at low wages.

The first chapter in this section covers tours of the areas where the wealthy and near-wealthy lived and/or played: the mansions of the Hudson River valley; the home and laboratories of the inventor and industrialist Thomas Edison, a wealthy man much influenced by the robber baron ethics of the times; and the resorts of the rich and not so rich, including Cape May and Mohonk Mountain House.

The next chapter describes sites that demonstrate the political and cultural responses to industrialism: the homes of the political cartoonist Thomas Nast, the newspaperman Horace Greeley, and the "honest" president Grover Cleveland; the USS *Olympia;* and sites connected with the painter Thomas Eakins.

After the Civil War, a number of architectural styles predominated. The Second Empire style (1855–1885) is often called the Grant style because so many buildings in Washington, D.C., were built in this one style during his presidency. Its chief feature is its mansard (dual-pitched, hipped) roof with dormer windows (vertical windows sticking out from a sloping roof) on the roof's steep lower slope.

In the 1880s, the Queen Anne style (1880–1910) became popular. This style avoided a solid-wall appearance. Instead, the emphasis was on asymmetrical facades. Another prominent feature was the porch, usually extending along one or both side walls. Towers were also common in this style. If there is a round tower on a house, the style is probably Queen Anne, although the towers can also be square or polygonal.

With architects taking the dominant role, architects, interior decorators, and artists cooperated on many building projects in a trend known as the American Renaissance. The proponents of this style wanted a monumental architecture with huge European-type mansions. Quite a few of the persons working in this tradition found their inspiration in classical imagery and themes. Many were trained at the Ecole des Beaux Arts in France. Designer Louis Comfort Tiffany was a key figure in the movement.

Richard Morris Hunt, who designed many of the mansions for the wealthy in New York City and Newport, was the first American designer of buildings to be trained at the Ecole des Beaux Arts. Beaux arts architecture emphasized neoclassical elements with the return of two-story-high columns. Another feature is the use of statuary on outer walls.

The firm of McKim, Mead, and White also designed many of the mansions in Newport, often in the neoclassical vein. Stanford White, an especially talented member of the firm, designed houses in many different styles, including beaux arts and Italian Renaissance. The sexually active architect gained lasting notoriety when he was murdered by sadist Harry K. Thaw, inheritor of a massive Pittsburgh fortune. Thaw married Evelyn Nesbit, whose beauty was held in such great esteem that she became the model for the Gibson girl. White's death followed the husband's discovery that the architect had had a brief affair with Evelyn before she married.

In interior decoration the styles of the post–Civil War period have been designated Late Victorian (1870–1900). This term encompasses many revivals of older furniture styles, including the Renaissance, Rococo, and Colonial. A rough generalization is that French styles dominated during the federal and romantic periods, and English styles inspired furniture makers in the post–Civil war era.

Compared to rooms of other periods, Victorian rooms have a surplus of objects. The rooms look as overstuffed as the couches and chairs. (One of the best rooms to illustrate this is the library-den of the gorgeous Ballantine House, associated with the Newark Museum at 43 Washington Street, Newark, New Jersey.) Filled with reds and browns, the rooms are slightly dark because of the use of heavy drapes.

The Renaissance Revival style (1850–1885) adopted ideas from the Italian Renaissance. Borrowing from the Baroque, the primary emphasis is on overblown decoration rather than design. This was the first style to be mass-produced by the new furniture factories, especially those in Grand Rapids, Michigan.

William Morris, an English designer, produced simple, sturdy furniture styled after medieval English designs. He was a leading figure in the arts and crafts movement, which held that the new mass-produced factory furniture had led to a decline in furniture quality and craftsmanship.

Charles Eastlake, influenced by Morris, became the chief exponent of the English arts and crafts movement. The Eastlake style (1870–1890) is characterized by geometric ornamentation. The designer preferred straight lines to curves, and his furniture had medieval outlines, but with ornamentation borrowed from the Gothic, the Japanese, and the abilities of the new factory machines.

A latter style in the period was Art Nouveau. Its curved shapes were based on plants, waves, and flowers. This style became popular in the 1890s and lasted until 1915. Tiffany was one of the leading exponents of this style. He specialized in lamps and other glassware, but also designed many prestigious interiors.

If you visit a number of houses from the same time period, you will develop some favorite interior features. For instance, notice the wall covering known as lincrusta (used as a substitute for leather) and the hand-painted stenciling used as wall decoration. You will start regarding these as old friends and fondly remember the houses where you have seen them.

25

The Great Concentration of Wealth

Most of us learned about the great wealth and influence of the robber barons from our American history classes. A tour of the opulent Hudson River Valley mansions of several major industrialists should make those history lessons come alive. Then visit the laboratories of the famous (and wealthy) inventor Thomas Edison to learn more about this eccentric and talented man. The wealthy often vacationed in the popular seaside resort of Cape May or amid the breathtaking scenery of the great mountain houses. The last two sections in this chapter describe these vacation spots.

Hudson River Valley Mansions

The Hudson is a very beautiful and famous river. Much history has taken place along its banks, and New York City's wealthy often built their houses here. The area provides unique opportunities to enjoy both the splendor of the mansions and the beauty of the river. It is not possible to cover all the Hudson River mansions, but we will take a look at three outstanding ones: Lyndhurst, home of Jay Gould; the Vanderbilt Mansion, built by Frederick William Vanderbilt; and the Mills Mansion, once belonging to the Livingston family. To see all three mansions will take an entire day. The tour is highly recommended. These three mansions are not the only representatives of the mansions of the wealthy in the Hudson River Valley, but they belonged to notable characters of the post–Civil War period. The three are also related in that members of the Livingston and Gould families feuded with Cornelius Vanderbilt, who helped break Robert Livingston's Hudson River steamboat monopoly and fought Jay Gould for control of the Erie Railroad.

Lyndhurst Mansion

635 South Broadway (Route 9), 0.4 of a mile north of Sunnyside Lane, which leads to Washington Irving's house, Tarrytown, NY (Open Tues–Sun 10–5, May–Oct, Dec; Sat–Sun 10–5, Jan–Mar, Nov)

In 1838 General William Paulding, a former New York City mayor, had Alexander Jackson Davis build this gorgeous mansion in Gothic Revival

Lyndhurst Mansion, Tarrytown, New York

style. The architect used Sing-Sing marble for the exterior. He also designed much of the furniture for the house in this same style, using carved oak leaves and acorns for the motif.

In 1865 George Merritt, a New York merchant with a patent on a boxcar spring, bought the estate and hired Davis to make modifications. This time the architect used Hastings limestone for the outer surface. The two different types of stone are clearly visible on the building's exterior. On the estate grounds, Merritt also built the largest private greenhouse in the world.

In 1880 the robber baron Jay Gould purchased the Hudson River estate as a summer home. He fell in love with the greenhouse and would walk there every morning after breakfast and in the evening. Gould's rise to power and wealth makes an interesting and somewhat sordid story. He was a boyhood chum of the future naturalist John Burroughs in the small Catskill town of Roxbury. One man believed in and led a simple life, while the other came to be the richest man in the United States (1881–1884).

The future robber baron became a surveyor as a means of escaping Roxbury. (Although why anyone would want to escape from this town with its picture-perfect main street, especially in the fall, may be hard for the reader to understand emotionally.) He later went into the tannery business with Zadoc Pratt, after whom the town of Prattsville is named. Gould used the profits from the business to invest in various ventures, all without his partner's knowledge. When Pratt finally discovered what was happening, his scheming partner bought out his share of the business.

Gould repeated the same pattern with his next partner in the tannery business, again using company funds to speculate. This second partner, thinking he was bankrupt, committed suicide. Subsequently, the robber baron's business became so tied up in legal battles that he had to abandon the tannery altogether. Changing residences, he set himself up as a leather merchant in New York City. With the money from this business venture, he purchased the Rutland and Washington Railroad. When he sold it, he became a rich man.

He later bought into the Erie Railroad—enough so that he became a member of the board of directors (1867). Soon a battle began between Vanderbilt and Gould, Daniel Drew, and Jim Fisk, Jr., for control of the railroad. As Vanderbilt bought up more and more Erie Railroad stock, his competitors illegally kept cranking out new shares for him to buy.

When the enraged Vanderbilt obtained a contempt order against the three, they fled to Jersey City, where they stayed in a hotel surrounded by armed guards. Drew weakened and tried to reach a separate agreement with the trio's opponent, but this attempt failed. Seeking vengeance, Gould and Fisk made peace with their old enemy. The two men got control of the Erie Railroad and Vanderbilt got his $4.75 million back. Gould eventually engineered Drew's bankruptcy.

Gould and Fisk next became involved in an attempt to corner the gold market. This plan, of course, depended on the government not selling its gold reserves. Gould thought he had President Grant under his thumb through his connections with the president's brother-in-law. Even when the plot unraveled, the slippery one received advance warning. This enabled him to survive the ensuing financial panic (Black Friday of 1869) that ruined so many others.

In 1872 a stockholders' uprising finally forced him to relinquish his control of the Erie Railroad. However, by that time he had bilked the company of millions of dollars. He and his friend Russell Sage then manipulated the stock of the Pacific Mail line to their benefit. The industrialist used some of the money from this venture to buy enough stock in the Union Pacific Railroad to give him control of that line. An additional conquest was the Western Union telegraph company. With one success after another, he seemed unstoppable. But then he got a piece of bad news: he had tuberculosis. In addition, he had become one of the most hated men in the United States. As a precaution, he maintained a small army to protect himself and his family from threats on their lives.

Gould, like John D. Rockefeller, loved to spend his leisure time with his family, which included five children. The family at first was not accepted into society, but Gould really did not care that much. Only once did they have a party at Lyndhurst where society turned out (with the exception of the Vanderbilts).

In 1892 the man from Roxbury died of tuberculosis. He passed most of his fortune on to his children. Helen took over the mansion on the stipulation that she take care of her younger siblings. Congress awarded her a gold medal for her work among the sick and wounded during the Spanish-American War. George Jay, the eldest child, built a mansion in Lakewood, New Jersey. Howard wanted to marry an actress, Odette Tyler, but sister Helen was so opposed that the couple had to cancel their marital plans. Howard later built a mansion at Sands Point, Long Island (see the section on Long Island's Gold Coast), while Helen founded the New York University Hall of Fame in the Bronx.

Helen did not marry until she was forty-four years old. In 1913 she wed Finley Shepard in the Lyndhurst drawing room, amidst the beautiful Tiffany windows that her father had installed.

On your tour of the mansion, notice the picture of Gould's yacht. He used the ship to commute back and forth to New York City. The robber baron refused to take the train because his rival, Vanderbilt, owned the railroad that ran by the Lyndhurst property. Also don't miss the gorgeous Tiffany windows in the art gallery/billiards room. In this beautiful room hang art works that belonged to the Goulds. The room also has a musician's gallery.

Be sure to walk around the expansive grounds. A map identifying the trees and their locations is available. The Croton Aqueduct Trail (following the route over which water from the Croton Reservoir flowed to New York City) crosses through the property.

Vanderbilt Mansion National Historic Site

Route 9 (six miles north of Poughkeepsie), north of Hyde Park, NY (Open daily 10–6, Apr–Oct; Thur–Mon 9:30–5, Nov–Mar)

This was the summer home of Frederick William Vanderbilt, a grandson of Cornelius Vanderbilt. When Cornelius Vanderbilt died in 1877, he left most of his estate to just one of his offspring, William Henry. When William Henry died in 1885, control of the bulk of the Vanderbilt empire was split between two of the four sons, Cornelius and William Kissam. Cornelius received $67 million and William Kissam $65 million, while the other two sons received $10 million each.

Frederick William only received $10 million because he had angered his father by falling in love with Louise Anthony Torrance, who was twelve years older than Frederick William and married to his first cousin. The father ordered the young man to break off the affair, but the son pursued the relationship anyway. In 1878, following the father's death and Louise's divorce, the two married.

In 1876 Frederick William graduated from Yale's Sheffield Scientific School and then worked in the various departments of the New York Central Railroad. By the time of his death in 1938, he held directorships in twenty-two railroads.

In 1895 he bought the old Langdon place, which is not far from the FDR home in Hyde Park. Colonel Walter Langdon's wife was Dorothea Astor, daughter of John Jacob Astor. Vanderbilt hired the architectural firm of McKim, Mead, and White to remodel the house into a three-story Italian Renaissance mansion with columns on all sides of the building. While the mansion was under construction, the workers erected a temporary house for the owner and his wife. This pavilion was later used by male guests. Also in the pavilion were the servants' quarters.

The new owner's brothers also built fantastic mansions: George Washington erected Biltmore, near Asheville, North Carolina; Cornelius constructed the Breakers at Newport, Rhode Island; and William Kissam built Marble House in Newport.

Frederick William was able to quadruple the $10 million he had inherited through hard work and a frugal life (at least by Vanderbilt standards). He was an introvert, often sneaking out of the house when his wife entertained. The industrialist's only real luxury was his love of yachting. He financed several entries in the America's Cup races.

He and his wife would usually stay at their Hyde Park mansion from Easter until after the Fourth of July. On winter weekends the couple stayed in the pavilion. Sometimes they would have Franklin and Eleanor Roosevelt over to visit. They also invited the naturalist John Burroughs to their home. He lived just on the other side of the Hudson, in West Park. Mrs. Vanderbilt gave him a dog, which he named Nip. The dog became the writer's favorite pet until, one day, responding to his master's call, the beloved animal slipped off a bridge to his death.

The mansion with its Louis XIV and XV interior decoration has more of the feeling of Europe than of the United States—in keeping with the American Renaissance movement's search for monumental architecture and interiors. Louise Vanderbilt's bedroom is more befitting a French queen than the wife of an American industrialist. In fact, it was deliberately designed to look like a French queen's bedroom. The bed is cordoned off from the rest of the room by a low barrier with attached Corinthian columns. Moreover, French paintings are inset on the bedroom walls. For those who like woodwork, Frederick William's study is paneled in Santo Domingo mahogany, and his bedroom has woodwork of carved Circassian walnut with bed and dresser designed as part of the overall paneling.

Mills Mansion

Old Albany Post Road off Route 9 (just north of the Vanderbilt mansion), Staatsburg, NY (Open Wed–Sat 10–5, Sun 1–5, late May–Labor Day; Wed–Sat 12–5, Sun 1–5, after Labor Day–late Oct)

Between 1792 and 1797 Morgan Lewis and his wife, Gertrude Livingston, built a summer home on the then 1,600-acre piece of property. Gertrude was a sister of Chancellor Robert Livingston. Morgan was the son of a signer of the Declaration of Independence, a Princeton graduate, a law student under John Jay, General Gates's chief of staff at the Battle of Saratoga, chief justice of the New York Supreme Court (1801–1804), and governor of New York State (1804–1807).

The red-brick farmhouse was enlarged to accommodate daughter Margaret, her husband, Maturin Livingston, and their twelve children. Their home, called Staatsburg House, burned in 1832. A Greek Revival house was immediately built as a replacement.

By the year 1875 the estate had passed into the hands of one of Margaret's sons, Maturin Livingston II. He, in turn, passed the property on to his daughter, Ruth. Ruth Livingston married Ogden Mills, whose father was an extremely wealthy Californian. It has been said that Ruth and Ogden were the models for Judy and Gus Trenor in Edith Wharton's *House of Mirth*. Farming done here provided food for the estate and the Mills's New York City mansion. In 1895 the couple commissioned the firm of McKim, Mead, and White to enlarge and remodel the Greek Revival house into a neoclassical, beaux arts mansion. Today, six massive two-story columns grace the front of the building.

Just as in the Vanderbilt mansion, the interior of the Mills mansion is decorated in the styles of French kings Louis XIV, XV, and XVI, typical of the American Renaissance movement of the period. Don't miss seeing the dining room with its eighteen-foot-high ceiling, gilded plaster work, and Flemish tapestries. In the house are pictures of the two daughters, Gladys and Beatrice. They were good friends of Theodore Roosevelt's irascible daughter, Alice.

On the death of Mr. and Mrs. Ogden Mills, the estate passed to their son Ogden Livingston Mills, who was secretary of the treasury in the Hoover administration. After he died, his sister, Mrs. Phipps, deeded two hundred acres of the property to the state.

The mansion is set in the Mills-Norrie State Park, where visitors can picnic, hike, and boat. The mansion property is beautiful, with a huge back lawn sloping down to the river.

Other Sites to Visit

See the sections on the lords of the manor, Washington Irving, Franklin and Eleanor Roosevelt, and Samuel F. B. Morse. The Hudson River Museum at 511 Warburton Avenue, Yonkers, has tours of the John Bond Trevor mansion known as Glenview (built in 1876). The interior of this mansion is very lovely.

Thomas Edison

This is another highly recommended tour. The Edison laboratories are extensive and very interesting, while the inventor's mansion is impressive. It will take a day to see all the sites.

Thomas Edison has been called the world's greatest inventor and the world's worst businessman. It may come as a surprise to some that he is placed here in a section on the concentration of great wealth and robber barons, but he was an industrialist as well as an inventor. Moreover, he learned a great deal from the robber barons with whom he worked.

He was born in 1847, the last of seven children, in the small canal town of Milan, Ohio. In 1854 the family moved to Port Huron, sixty miles northeast of Detroit. At the age of twelve the young boy got a job hawking newspapers and sundries on the train from Port Huron to Detroit. He used part of the baggage car to house his collection of chemicals. When this led to a chemical fire, he transferred his collection to his home basement. Not one to be stopped, he set up a press in the baggage car to produce his own newspaper.

Edison became a part-time operator in the telegraph office. He was fired from myriads of jobs for experimenting with the office equipment and had to keep moving on as people learned of his reputation.

In 1869 he came to New York, where he manufactured telegraphic devices (for which he took out several patents). Competitors to the Vanderbilt-controlled Western Union, which virtually monopolized the industry, turned to him for new inventions to give them a technological edge against Vanderbilt. They even set the inventor up with a laboratory in Newark.

Western Union officials responded by trying to woo him to their camp. Soon the inventive genius found himself working for rival telegraphic firms. Jay Gould, always looking to best Vanderbilt, bought a telegraph company in order to compete with Western Union. Edison worked for a short time with this infamous robber baron.

In 1871 he married Mary Stillwell. The marriage was not a happy one because the inventor ignored his wife and children for his work. Poor Mary led a very lonely life indeed. Her husband didn't even have to come home to sleep. He could sleep anywhere and often did. When he tired at work, he would often create a makeshift bed by simply clearing off space on a laboratory table. One of the strangest places he ever slept was curled up in the broom closet beneath the stairs. Many people thought the workaholic did not sleep much, but careful studies have revealed that he slept an average amount. The impression that he got very little sleep stemmed from his habit of working late into the night. However, his frequent catnaps sustained his night owl routine.

Edison Memorial

Christie Street (Exit 131 off the Garden State Parkway, south on Lincoln Highway/Route 27, turn right onto Christie Street), Menlo Park, NJ (Open Tues–Fri 12:30–3:30, Sat–Sun 12:30–4:30, June–Aug; Tues–Fri 1–3, Sat–Sun 1–4, Sept–May)

Unable to save money, Edison and his wife decided to leave the more expensive Newark for Menlo Park about twelve miles to the south. His father came to supervise construction of the one hundred-foot-long, two-story wooden building that became the hub of the new invention factory. The laboratory was constructed in 1876 and proved to be a forerunner of the industrial research laboratory. Its effective life was short (1876–1881), but this period saw the birth of two of Edison's most famous inventions.

In 1877 the inventor faintly reproduced sound through a speaker. From this start he designed the phonograph. He demonstrated his new machine to President Rutherford B. Hayes, and the nation hailed him as its greatest inventor.

Edison next turned his attention to the search for a filament that would burn long enough to make an electric light bulb commercially successful. For sixteen hours in the fall of 1879 he was able to keep lit a piece of cardboard that had been boiled in sugar and alcohol and then carbonized. The excitement over the new invention was worldwide.

At this time, the man from Ohio was considered the world's greatest inventor. He was also one of the world's richest men—his inventions had made him a fortune. He formed companies to manufacture electric light bulbs and to install electrical systems in businesses and homes. These endeavors eventually blossomed into today's General Electric Company.

The New Jersey location became less and less the center of activity. Already by 1881, the inventive genius had moved his operations from Menlo Park to Manhattan. Henry Ford, who virtually worshiped Edison, wanted to create a monument to him. In the late 1920s he had the Menlo Park laboratory facilities dismantled and moved to Dearborn, Michigan, where workers reassembled them.

The residents of Menlo Park, also wishing to honor the man, constructed a wooden tower. This was soon destroyed. The citizens then erected a concrete tower. In the base of the tower is the eternal light. The light from the twelve-volt bulb is so weak that visitors sometimes think it has burned out. In the building next door are displays dealing with Edison's inventions, including a model of the original tinfoil phonograph.

Glenmont

Accessible only by ticket and bus transportation from the Edison Laboratories, West Orange, NJ (Open Wed–Sun 9:30–3, all year)

In 1884, Mary died at the age of twenty-nine, leaving her husband with two boys and a girl. He soon began to court Mina Miller, eighteen years his junior. In 1886 the widower married the young woman. They honeymooned in Fort Myers, Florida, where Edison had recently constructed a laboratory.

Playroom in Thomas Edison's home, known as Glenmont, West Orange, New Jersey

About this time the newlywed bought a place of permanent residence in West Orange. The twenty-three-room brick-and-timber Queen Anne mansion, called Glenmont, had been built for Henry C. Pedder by architect Henry Hudson Holly. Pedder had gotten the money for the estate through embezzlement from his employer, the Arnold Constable department store. As part of his punishment, the government confiscated the mansion.

The house is very ornate, showing extravagant signs of the wealth acquired by its first owner: stained-glass windows, animal skins on the floor, detailed carvings (particularly flowers on wood), stenciling on the ceilings, and leather-bound books that the owner never opened. At home, Mina treated her husband like an absolute monarch, fussing over him like a devoted servant. The family's favorite room was the more simply styled living room on the second floor, where her husband would study while she sewed. However, the workaholic did not actually spend that much time in the house.

Edison Laboratories

Main Street, between Alden and Lakeside streets (from Exit 147 of the Garden State Parkway, travel south on Parkway Drive, turn left/west onto Park Avenue, turn right/north onto Main Street), West Orange, NJ (Open Wed–Sun 9:30–3, all year)

In 1887 the inventor caught pneumonia and pleurisy and was near death. While ill, he dreamed of building the world's greatest laboratory. He imagined that a larger version of the Menlo Park facilities would enable him to be even more inventive. As pointed out by Robert Conot in his book *A Streak of Luck,* things did not turn out that way. The laboratory was just too large and impersonal. Edison preferred to hire men who would be subservient to him and work under his direction. Therefore, the only progress made was on those projects in which he became personally involved.

Nevertheless, the years from 1888 to 1892 saw a new burst of creative energy. At the laboratory he worked to improve the phonograph, which had been commercially unsuccessful. The revitalized machine created a sensation. Unfortunately, he also tried to separate iron from crushed rock with a powerful magnet. The inventor was a very stubborn man and would not abandon the project even after it was clear it was unworkable. He poured more than $3 million and many years of labor into the scheme.

In 1888 he developed a crude version of a movie projector called the kinetograph. This early device was improved upon and renamed the kinetoscope. Kinetoscope parlors, which consisted basically of peepholes, were an immediate sensation when opened to the public in 1894. However, the novelty quickly wore off. What the world needed was a motion-picture projector that could project pictures onto a screen.

Thomas Armat developed the first practical projector, and Edison got control of the new invention and made it a commercial success. This opened the way for the creation of the movie business. Edison built the world's first motion-picture studio, called the Black Maria because of its resemblance to a police paddy wagon. (There is a reconstructed version of the studio on the laboratory grounds.) Edison monopolized the early film industry to such an extent that he helped force its move to southern California. Out West the new industry could develop without the great one's censorship and domination.

Many of the industrialist's businesses were in trouble. Henry Ford often lent or gave him money. The two went on several camping trips, along with Harvey Firestone and the naturalist John Burroughs. On one of the library walls are pictures of the naturalist and his West Park cabin, Slabsides.

The great man died at Glenmont in 1931. Both he and Mina are buried on the mansion grounds.

Edison's library is very interesting. Amid his ten thousand volumes he would often watch his films. He took so many catnaps here that his wife finally got him a cot. He smoked up to a dozen cigars a day and also liked to spit tobacco juice directly onto the floor. Edison's wake was held in the library.

The tour of the laboratories includes a visit to the "hay fever room," so called because Edison used goldenrod as a possible substitute for commercial rubber. All the machines in the machine shop derived their power by connecting and disconnecting from one of two powerful, constantly running pulley systems on either side of the room.

Other Sites to Visit

For nearby sites to visit see the section on President Grover Cleveland.

Cape May

Cape May is a very charming beach town. Its large and concentrated collection of Victorian houses brings the past to life for the history-minded visitor. It is highly recommended. You can easily spend several days here. The best way to see the town is on foot, although a trolley tour is available. It is easy to get around given the town's wide streets and plentiful parking.

Cape May boasts for itself the title of the oldest seaside resort in the United States, although Newport, Rhode Island, is probably the oldest. However, during the early 1800s, in terms of sheer numbers of visitors, Newport placed a poor third to Cape May and Long Branch. The town was reachable by boat from Philadelphia and Baltimore, which accounts for much of the resort's growth. In 1851 Cape May attracted some 120,000 customers, and by 1856 there were twenty-four hotels in the small village.

The town's history as a summer resort can be traced to an 1801 advertisement in a Philadelphia newspaper, in which Postmaster Ellis Hughes let it be known that he "has prepared himself for entertaining company who use sea bathing, and he is accommodated with extensive house room, with fish, oysters, and crabs and good liquors."

Some of the famous people who visited the resort were Presidents Lincoln, Grant, Pierce, Buchanan, and Harrison; Horace Greeley; John Wanamaker; and many members of Congress and leaders of society. Unfortunately for the visitor interested in history, two disastrous fires in 1869 and 1878 consumed most of the hotels visited by the famous. The town had to rise literally from the ashes, doing so at the height of Victorian times. And yet, we should be grateful for this very sequence of events for it has left us with a treasure trove of great Victorian houses.

By the 1890s the resort had already reached its zenith and was no longer a serious competitor to Atlantic City for the Philadelphia trade. Atlantic City's main competition came from Asbury Park.

Stephen Decatur Button (1813–1897) designed many of Cape May's houses, so a brief note on this architect is in order. He was born in Preston, Connecticut, and lived on his family's farm until the age of sixteen. He trained for five years as a carpenter and then studied architecture for two years. He gained some fame in the American South, where, among other buildings, he designed the Alabama statehouse. In 1848 he returned north to work in Philadelphia. He first came to Cape May in 1863 to work on assignments for Philadelphia clients. He designed more than forty buildings in the town. A typical Button creation has a center hall, front porch (a possible Southern influence), and flat roof.

Start your Cape May visit at the Cape Island Presbyterian Church (1853) on the corner of Lafayette Street, west of Bank Street. (To get there take the Garden State Parkway to its end and continue straight ahead on Lafayette Street.) At the center you can pick up information on the town and arrange accommodations if needed. The sites below are arranged in geographical order heading down Washington Street to Hughes and Columbia Streets and then to the area by the beach.

Emlen Physick House

1048 Washington Street, north of Madison Avenue, Cape May, NJ (Open Tues–Sat 11–4, July–Aug)

Completed in 1881, this nineteen-room mansion was designed for Dr. Emlen Physick by Philadelphia architect Frank Furness. Furness was a student of Richard Morris Hunt and later taught architect Louis Sullivan, who in turn taught Frank Lloyd Wright. Furness also designed some of the furniture in the house. Still other pieces are in the Eastlake style.

The Physick family is a famous one in Philadelphia history. Emlen's

Emlen Physick House, Cape May, New Jersey

grandfather, Philip Syng Physick, became known as the father of American Surgery. (You can visit the Hill-Physick-Keith House at 321 South Fourth Street in Philadelphia.) Dr. Emlen Physick never married and never practiced medicine. Instead, he was a gentleman farmer and animal breeder. He lived in the house with his mother and maiden aunt. Animal lovers will be pleased to hear that at one time he had fourteen dogs on the property. The house museum displays a collection of Victorian costumes, books, toys, furniture, and many other items. Please note the woven willow screen above the stairs in the hall; the vestibule ceiling covered with lincrusta; and the stenciling on one of the bedroom walls.

Vondrick Cottage

726 Corgie Street, south of Madison Avenue, Cape May, NJ (Tours available)

This Gothic structure built around 1865 is one of the few remaining small, private Victorian homes in Cape May.

Victorian House (George Allen House)

720 Washington Street, south of Jefferson Street, Cape May, NJ

This Italianate villa–style house was built between 1863 and 1864 for George Allen, a Philadelphia merchant.

J. Stratton Ware House

653 Hughes Street, south of Franklin Street, Cape May, NJ

This house is in the Gothic Revival style of the 1860s.

Joseph Hall Cottage

645 Hughes Street, Cape May, NJ

Another Gothic Revival house, this one built in 1868.

Baltimore Hotel (Girls' Friendly Society)

642 Hughes Street, Cape May, NJ

This wooden hotel is the way most of the inns looked in earlier days. The Episcopal Church uses the 1867 building as a summer holiday residence for young women.

Chalfonte Hotel

Corner of Howard Street and Sewell Avenue, Cape May, NJ

Built in 1876, this is the oldest of Cape May's still-standing hotels. Lieutenant Colonel Henry Sawyer had it constructed in the ornate Italian style. The former carpenter spotted the disastrous 1878 fire from the hotel's cupola.

The hotel catered to generations of wealthy Southern families, despite the unpleasant experiences the colonel had during the Civil War. The wounded Sawyer became a prisoner in the hands of the Confederates. He and another officer were sentenced to death by hanging as retaliation for the unrelated deaths of two rebel captains. Sawyer's devoted wife raced to Washington for an audience with President Lincoln. The sympathetic leader acted immediately to warn the Confederates that if they executed the two soldiers, the North would respond by executing General William Lee, son of Robert E. Lee, and another Southern officer.

The South reacted slowly, and the poor condemned men, unaware of the efforts being made on their behalf, waited in daily fear of the gallows. Finally, in March 1864, the men gained their freedom in the war's first prisoner exchange. Sawyer saw further action with the New Jersey cavalry and received two more wounds before his unit was discharged.

Mainstay Inn

635 Columbia Avenue, corner of Stockton Place, Cape May, NJ (Guided tours and afternoon tea are available in season)

This Italianate-style inn is considered by some to be Stephen D. Button's finest Cape May design. It was built in 1872 as a gentlemen's gaming club and was known as Jackson's Clubhouse. It has one of the cape's finest interiors.

The Abbey

Columbia Avenue and Gurney Street, Cape May, NJ

In 1869 architect Button built this Gothic revival summer place for the coal baron John B. McCreary. It is now a bed-and-breakfast inn, but the first-floor rooms can be toured.

Baldt House

26 Gurney Street, Cape May, NJ

Built in 1871, this is considered the most original of Button's Stockton Place row houses (the others are 16, 18, 20, 22, 24, 28, and 30 Gurney Street). It still has the wood acroterion (ornament at the apex of the pediment) capping the building. The cottages were called Stockton Place because they were across the street from the Stockton Hotel.

Colonial Hotel

Corner of Beach Drive and Ocean Street, Cape May, NJ

This hotel was built in 1894 for the Church brothers, Will and Charles, after Cape May had passed its heyday. When completed, the hotel bragged of its many modern conveniences, including steam heat, gaslights, electric bells for room service, and the town's very first elevator.

John Philip Sousa stayed here. Henry Ford and Louis Chevrolet also roomed here when they raced their cars on the beach in 1905. Not only did some other car win the race, but an ocean wave swamped Ford's car. To get enough money to return to Detroit, Ford sold his then unknown automobile to Daniel Focer. When Ford made it big, Focer's became the first Ford agency in the United States. In the summer of 1915, a coming-out party for Baltimore society's Wallis Warfield, later duchess of Windsor, was held at the hotel.

There is no television, radio, or air conditioning in the rooms. But this can be advantageous if you use the quiet time to relax.

Congress Hall

Bordered by Perry Street, Congress Place, Congress Street, and Beach Avenue, Cape May, NJ

This is the third structure on this site. The first hotel was built in 1816 and destroyed in an 1828 fire. Rebuilt, it was dubbed Congress Hall because, at the time, the owner, Thomas Hughes, was running for Congress. This second hotel was destroyed in the great fire of 1878. The current building was constructed shortly afterward.

Postmaster General John Wanamaker (the Philadelphia department store baron and one of the founders of Cape May Point), told President Benjamin Harrison of Cape May's wonders. Friends of the president built a cottage for him and his family at Cape May Point in 1889–1890. The president set up his working headquarters in Congress Hall in the summers of 1890 and 1891. Although Mrs. Harrison died in 1892, the former president continued to spend his summers at the point until 1896.

John Philip Sousa and the Marine band played here. The great conductor composed the "Congress Hall March" for the occasion.

Seven Sisters

10, 12, 16, 18, and 20 Jackson Street, between Jackson and Perry streets and near the intersection with Beach Avenue, Cape May, NJ

Five of the seven identical houses designed by architect Stephen D. Button.

The Pink House

33 Perry Street, corner of Carpenter's Lane, Cape May, NJ

This is the Eldridge Johnson house built around 1880. The color of this most elaborately decorated cottage in Cape May gives the house its name. It is often featured as an illustration of gingerbread woodwork.

Joseph Evans House

207 Congress Place, near the corner of Congress Street, Cape May, NJ

In 1881 Stephen D. Button built this house, which has two-story verandas in both the front and the back with lots of prominent brackets.

E.C. Knight House

203 Congress Place, Cape May, NJ

Also designed by Button, the house was built in 1882–1883 in the same style as the Joseph Evans House.

Wilbraham Mansion

133 Myrtle Avenue, corner of Park Boulevard, Cape May, NJ (Tours available)

This house started out as a simple 1840 farmhouse. In 1900 John W. Wilbraham, a wealthy Philadelphia industrialist, expanded and Victorian-ized it.

Other Sites to Visit

Visit the Victorian houses in Cape May Point or drive to the south New Jersey towns of Salem and Greenwich. Or tour the iron village at Batsto in the New Jersey Pine Barrens. There is a ferry to Lewes, Delaware. The sixteen-mile run takes about eighty minutes and is a nice change of pace. Driving through Delaware, notice how flat and heavily agricultural the southern part of the state is.

The Great Mountain Houses

One of the most beautiful sites in the region is the Mohonk Mountain House, which is situated by a mountain lake. It is gorgeous in any season and is a must stop for those inspired by beauty. To add to the enjoyment, this mountain house is the only survivor of the once-great mountain houses of the past. History thus adds to the romanticism of the setting. The resort has been true to its past and has no modern conveniences such as televisions and radios. So if you stay here, it is like going back in time to enjoy those simple repasts that Victorian visitors enjoyed. The emphasis is on the natural, and there are many hiking trails in the area. You can easily spend the whole day here. Don't miss it!

As discussed in the section on Thomas Cole, the mountain houses were built to accommodate the increasing number of people vacationing locally in the mountains. The Catskill Mountain House may have been the earliest such hotel, but it was followed some years later by many others. All the hotels have disappeared except for the Mohonk Mountain House.

Mohonk Mountain House

New Paltz Exit of I-87, Route 299 west through New Paltz (turns into Main Street), take the first right turn after the bridge onto Springtown Road; one-half mile ahead, bear left onto Mountain Rest Road and proceed 3.5 miles to the entrance; New Paltz, NY (Open all year)

This mountain house is located near New Paltz in the Shawangunk Mountain range. The Quaker Smiley twins established the hotel starting in 1870. They greatly expanded it over the following years. The oldest extant section is the Rock Building from 1879, and the newest is the 1910 dining room extension. The interior is rather plain, in keeping with the Quaker emphasis on the simple life, but the woodwork, especially on the main staircase, is very attractive.

Strict Quakers, the Smiley twins banned alcohol, playing cards, and dancing. Instead, they emphasized voluntary prayer, daily nature walks, lectures, evening concerts, golf (at a later date), bowling, boating, horseback riding, and fishing—activities still available. Or you can just sit in the rocking chairs on the porch by the lake and enjoy good conversation. Children love to stand by the porch railing and feed the fish in the lake. From the Albert K. Smiley Memorial Towers (a twenty-minute walk), you can look toward the Hudson River and see the town of New Paltz or look west and see the water towers and the rooftops of the remains of the hotel at Lake Minnewaska.

Visit the Mohonk Mountain House for the day and picnic on the property by obtaining a grounds pass for a reasonable fee at the entrance gate. Or make reservations for lunch and/or dinner. Of course, you can always stay overnight at the hotel itself.

Mohonk Mountain House, New Paltz, New York

Lake Minnewaska
Route 299 to Routes 44-55, New Paltz, NY

Alfred H. Smiley established two mountain houses (known as Wildmere and Cliff House) at Lake Minnewaska, not far from the Mohonk Mountain House. The Cliff House, closed in 1972, was destroyed by fire in 1978. The only remaining structure on the site is the water tower. Wildmere remains, but a recent fire damaged the structure. The hotel is in very bad shape and is scheduled for destruction. This will be a real shame as the hotel by the lake creates a beautiful sight. You can swim or canoe in the lake. The bottom is clearly visible through the crystal blue water. Or you can hike on the many trails in the area.

Other Sites to Visit

Nearby is the town of New Paltz, where you can see the old houses on Huguenot Street. Or travel farther north to Kingston.

Political and Cultural
Responses to Industrialism

Along with their vast wealth, the industrialists wielded considerable political power. Indeed, some of them literally bought favorable legislation, which led to further corruption. By the time of the two presidential terms of Ulysses S. Grant, corruption was rampant.

Chapter 26 discusses the political and cultural responses to industrialism and growing corruption. One idea was to expose the situation to the public. To illustrate this, we visit the home of Thomas Nast, the famous political cartoonist who lived in Morristown, New Jersey.

Another proposal was that of civil service reform. The main issues in the presidential election campaigns in the early post–Civil War years largely revolved around this issue. We can investigate this when visiting the home of Horace Greeley in Chappaqua, New York.

Related to the search for civil service reform was the search for an "honest" man to throw the rascals out. This search explains the election of Grover Cleveland as president in 1884 and 1892. The section on Cleveland describes a visit to Caldwell, New Jersey, to see the house in which he was born. As seen by his example, it would take more than simple honesty to provide an effective answer to political corruption.

Of the various "isms" that came into existence as a result of industrialism, one of the most important forces was imperialism. We consider the emergence of the United States as a world power by visiting Admiral Dewey's flagship, the USS *Olympia,* at Penn's Landing in Philadelphia.

A more effective answer to the problems of the concentration of wealth in a few hands and the resultant political corruption would not come until followers of the Progressive movement came to power. Part 10 will describe sites connected with this movement.

Along with the harsh realities of the industrial order came the death of romanticism. In the last section we deal with the new, more critical trend in art: realism. We visit the art museums of Philadelphia to see the works of the great realist painter, Thomas Eakins.

Thomas Nast at Morristown

You are dead wrong if you think that political cartoons are just for the reader's enjoyment and have no political aftereffects. Just how wrong can be shown by a visit to Morristown, where the political cartoonist Thomas Nast lived. One day a year his house is open. If touring at this time, the sites in this chapter will take a day to see. If not, the trip should take about half a day. The sites here are rather modest ones, unless you have a particular interest in Nast. But there are many other sites in Morristown to tour.

In the latter half of the nineteenth century, Morristown was a fashionable summer resort. Many of New York City's wealthiest people came here, drawn by the rural setting and healthy climate. By 1902 one hundred millionaires lived within three miles of the town green.

One of the most famous of the men drawn to the town was Thomas Nast. He deserves a great deal of the credit for making political cartooning respectable. His cartoons became so important that he himself was a virtual political institution, with people anxiously awaiting what he had to say (or draw) on any given topic. In addition to his political accomplishments, he made the elephant and the donkey the symbols for the Republican and Democratic parties, respectively, and even provided the current look for Santa Claus.

Villa Fontana (private)

50 Macculloch Avenue, at the corner of Miller Road (from South Park Place and South Street at the town green, turn left/east onto South Street, turn right/south onto Miller Road, and turn right onto Macculloch Avenue), Morristown, NJ (Open once a year around Christmastime for tours; call Macculloch Hall at 201-538-2404 for information)

David Rockwell built this house in 1866. From 1872 to 1902 it was the home of the famous political cartoonist. The house has green shutters, with a Palladian window on the second floor, and a mansard roof.

The cartoonist was born in 1840 in Germany, but his family moved to New York City when he was six years old. At the age of fifteen he was hired as an artist for the newly created *Frank Leslie's Illustrated Newspaper*. He stayed there for three years, then moved on to the *New York Illustrated News*.

At the start of the Civil War, he married Sarah Edwards of New York. Shortly afterward, he took a job with Harper's Weekly—a job that would last for over a quarter of a century.

During the war, Nast became a fierce partisan of the Northern cause. A stern moralist, he drew strong ethical statements for the North and against the South. He was especially fond of depicting the atrocities committed by the latter. In 1864 his drawings helped defeat the Copperhead peace movement (composed of Republicans and northern Democrats seeking a settlement with the South) by stressing that the party's platform meant surrender. This helped reelect Lincoln.

After the war, the cartoonist drew his first true political cartoons to oppose the reconstruction policies of President Andrew Johnson. In doing so, he turned to the caricature.

Thomas Nast's home, known as Villa Fontana, Morristown, New Jersey

In 1869 he started his campaign against the Tweed ring, which was steal-ing millions of dollars from New York (city and state). The leading thief, William Marcy Tweed, even tried to bribe Nast to stop him from drawing cartoons of the ring leaders. Tweed was eventually arrested and sentenced to twelve years in jail. He escaped to Spain, but the Spanish police soon caught him, thanks to the fat man's easily recognizable shape and a Nast car-toon circulated for means of identification. Based on this cartoon, the Spanish authorities thought Tweed was a child kidnapper. They returned the ringleader to the United States, where he died in his jail cell.

The same year that the cartoonist moved into Villa Fontana, he helped defeat Democrat Horace Greeley's attempt to win the 1872 election against Republican U. S. Grant. Nast's cartoons were so nasty that some people partly blamed him for the losing candidate's death shortly after the election.

As the issues of the Civil War faded, the stern moralist lost much of his fire. He found it difficult to adapt his cartoon style to more subtle issues. And being a strong Republican, he had trouble dealing with the scandals arising from the Grant administrations. His work grew weaker and weaker and he drew less and less with the passing years.

In an attempt to get enough money to start his own newspaper, in 1884 the cartoonist suffered a financial disaster when an investment he had made turned out to be fraudulent. Two years later, at the age of forty-six, the great moralist finally left *Harper's*. He shifted from newspaper to newspaper, and again tried unsuccessfully to establish his own. Needing money, in 1901 he accepted President Theodore Roosevelt's appointment as the American con-sul to Guayaquil, Ecuador. He died there of yellow fever in 1902.

Macculloch Hall

45 Macculloch Avenue, Morristown, NJ (Open Sun, 2–5, all year)

Across the street from Villa Fontana is Macculloch Hall, which has changing exhibits of Nast cartoons on the second floor. The hall was built in 1810 by George Perrot Macculloch, who later planned the Morris Canal (completed by 1831). The future canal builder was born in India. Orphaned at age nine, he went to Edinburgh for his education. He later became a merchant in the trade between England and France. With the coming of the Napoleonic Wars, he emigrated to the United States, choosing Morristown because of its many French immigrants. In 1810 he purchased twenty-five acres of land in the town.

The left wing of the present house was built in 1810, the center portion in 1812, and the right wing in 1814. From here the proud owner operated George Macculloch's Latin Academy, a private school for boys. Mrs. Louisa Macculloch established the Charitable Female Society of Morristown, which she led for thirty-three years. The house later became an important center of Republican leadership in New Jersey when a United States senator, Jacob Welch Miller (Macculloch's son-in-law), occupied it.

The General Porter House (private)

1 Farragut Place, Morristown, NJ

Around the corner from Villa Fontana is the former home of General Fitz John Porter. In the Civil War, he was in charge of the Fifth Corps of the Union army at the Battle of Gaines Mill. He also served at Malvern Hill. He was court-martialed for refusing to obey orders while serving under Major General John Pope in the disastrous second battle of Bull Run. An 1886 act of Congress finally exonerated him.

Following the departure of the Tweed ring, Porter reorganized the Department of Public Works in New York City and was later that city's police commissioner. Robert Porter, the general's son, married the daughter of Thomas Nast.

Other Sites to Visit

Drive around Morristown and see the fancy houses that once belonged to millionaires (many of which are found on Woodruff Road off Whippany Road, Normandy Heights Road, and Route 24 to South Street, while others are around the Loantaka Brook Park, along Spring Valley and Kitchell roads); tour Revolutionary War sites in Morristown; or visit Speedwell Village. You may also want to stop at the Morris Museum (6 Normandy Heights Road), which specializes in natural history. Still another stop is Acorn Hall (68

Morris Avenue). This Italianate house, stressing the Victorian period, is headquarters of the Morris County Historical Society.

Horace Greeley at Chappaqua

To tour these sites, travel to the village of Chappaqua in Westchester County, New York. In the town are several sites associated with the life of Horace Greeley of "Go West, young man, go West" fame. To see all the sites listed should take more than half a day. The sites are modest ones, but, combined with a walk in Greeley's woods, they can make an enjoyable visit.

Greeley was born on a farm in the year 1811 near the town of Amherst, New Hampshire. He was able to read by the age of three and was outstanding in school. While the future reformer was progressing nicely, his father was doing so poorly that he had to flee to escape debtor's prison. The family later joined him in Vermont, where they spent some very rough days eking out a living.

In 1831 Greeley set off to make his fortune in New York City, where he and a partner set up a small printing establishment. About three years later he and two partners started the *New-Yorker* magazine. In just three more years, the magazine had nine thousand subscribers (more than any other American literary magazine of its time). In 1836 the future presidential candidate married Mary Cheney, a schoolteacher.

In the 1840s Moses Beach's *Sun* and James Gordon Bennett, Sr.'s *Herald* sold for a penny, so Greeley decided to bring out a penny Whig paper. The result was the *New York Tribune*. In the paper he supported all types of reforms. Indeed, he was somewhat of a professional reformer, albeit a conservative one. For instance, while he supported the call for a ten-hour work day, he was hardly a friend of the worker.

In 1853 the Greeleys moved to a small farm just east of the village of Chappaqua. Here the newspaperman could indulge his interest in agriculture. He would try out the latest techniques and then write about them for his readers.

Chappaqua Historical Society

South Greeley Avenue (from the Chappaqua Exit off the Saw Mill River Parkway, travel east on Route 120 and turn right/south onto South Greeley Avenue), Chappaqua, NY (located on the grounds of the Bell School, just south of the downtown area) (Open Wed 1–4, all year; or by appointment)

The Chappaqua Historical Society is located in a quonset hut on the grounds of what was once the Greeley farm. This House in the Woods was located a short distance southeast of the Bell School. Unfortunately, in 1875 the house burned to the ground. Some of the items in the historical society's collection are the walnut desk and Victorian armchair used in the *New York Tribune* office; a pine hooded cradle; and a marble bust of the famous editor by Ames Van Wart.

The great reformer was not particularly content in Chappaqua. He lacked a very important ingredient for happiness: a calm, supportive family life. He was a workaholic and tended to neglect his family, which in turn may have contributed to his wife's nervousness. She became a constant complainer with a very bad temper. This further drove the poor man from home. His wife stayed most of the year at Chappaqua; he stayed in New York, returning to the village on Saturdays. Another reason for sadness in the family was that only two of their nine children survived to adulthood.

In the political realm, the newspaperman became increasingly dissatisfied with the Whigs' conservatism on the slavery issue. Another reason for disenchantment was that the *New York Times,* established in 1851, had replaced the *Tribune* as the party's main political mouthpiece. Out of a sense of alienation, he worked to establish the Republican party.

Although Greeley often sought political office, being a liberal conservative always placed him too far to the left for the conservative Whig party, or later, the Republican party. What could one make of a conservative who hired Karl Marx at the beginning of the 1850s to write interpretations of European developments for the *Tribune?*

Perhaps Greeley's greatest contribution to American society was his abolitionist stance. He was so identified with the cause that, during the 1863 draft riots in New York City, the rioters tried to hang him. Fortunately, they did not find him, but they did damage the *Tribune* offices. During the riots, a mob threatened to attack the House in the Woods. Consequently, Mrs. Greeley wanted to move to a less-isolated location. In 1864 they bought the House on the Main Road (Main Road is now King Street).

Horace Greeley Gift Shop
100 King Street, Chappaqua, NY (Open during normal business hours)

The family's House on the Main Road is now a gift shop. It was their country home from 1864 to 1873. In the gift shop there are a few reminders of the past, such as the engraved portrait of Greeley over the mantle in what was once his music room.

The liberal conservative did not share the great enthusiasm that swept U. S. Grant into the presidency in the 1868 election. And when the new president supported the more conservative faction in New York Republican politics, Greeley bolted from the party he had helped found. While he distanced himself from the party, a similar revolt swept Missouri in 1870, giving birth to the liberal Republican movement. One of their chief concerns was civil service reform, which they saw as a means of limiting political corruption. The liberals held a national convention in Cincinnati in 1872 and nominated Greeley as their presidential candidate. The Democrats also accepted him as their candidate, knowing this was their only hope of defeating Grant.

Church of St. Mary the Virgin

South Greeley Avenue, Chappaqua, NY (just south of the Chappaqua Historical Society)

In July 1872 Greeley held an outdoor banquet reception for the delegates to the Democratic National Convention. He held the gathering in the hemlock grove that he had planted himself. You can visit this grove, which today is located alongside the Church of St. Mary the Virgin (dedicated in 1906). You can also walk in Greeley's Woods to see the waterfall over the dam erected by the presidential candidate. Pick up the path beside the hemlock grove.

The election campaign was so nasty that Greeley remarked that he wondered at times if he was running for the presidency or the penitentiary. The cartoons of Thomas Nast were especially hurtful. To make a long story short, Grant easily won the election.

The exhausted candidate died very shortly after the election. There were a number of causes. He was subject to nervous reactions to stress that would incapacitate him. This nervousness had already begun during the campaign. Moreover, his wife had died shortly before the election. Finally, his paper, the *Tribune,* had suffered during his campaign, and he felt himself no longer in control of it. In short, he no longer cared to live and gave up the fight.

Rehoboth (private)

33 Aldridge Road (on the hill behind the Bell School, overlooking Chappaqua; about a block northeast of the gift shop, turn right onto Prospect Street and right again onto Aldridge), Chappaqua, NY

In 1865 Greeley built on his farm a concrete barn, one of the first such structures in the country. In 1891 his daughter, Gabrielle, married the Reverend Frank M. Clendenin. The following year, she converted the barn into a residence. The new country home was christened Rehoboth, the Hebrew word for "broad place."

The Clendenin family is buried behind the Church of St. Mary the Virgin, which was erected in memory of Muriel Morton Clendenin, one of Gabrielle's daughters. The land and the money for the church came from the Clendenin family.

Statue of Greeley

Saw Mill River Road (on the west side of the Saw Mill River Parkway, opposite the Chappaqua Railroad Station), Chappaqua, NY

Many of us have whizzed by this area while driving on the Saw Mill River Parkway. Some have even caught a glimpse of a statue on the west side of the road. If you are like me, you were curious, but always too busy to stop. Now we all know. The statue was inaugurated in 1914.

Other Sites to Visit

A short distance to the west is Sleepy Hollow territory. In White Plains and North White Plains there are sites connected with the Battle of White Plains.

Grover Cleveland

The house in which Grover Cleveland was born is occupied by a family, who also give tours of the house. This sometimes makes for an interesting visit, if you catch them at an inopportune time. But don't let this discourage you, for they will gladly show you the Cleveland house museum, which has quite a number of possessions of the former president. The visit does not take long—perhaps an hour or so. The house itself is very simple and not much to look at. But you should enjoy seeing the many Cleveland mementos that help bring the man and his times to life. The political career of Grover Cleveland illustrates one of the proposed solutions to the problem of corruption caused by the great concentration of wealth in the hands of relatively few men. Not fully understanding the economic forces producing corruption, American voters sought a simple solution: find an honest man to be president. They had given the majority of their votes to such a man in the election of 1876—Democrat Samuel J. Tilden, who had fought many legal battles against Boss Tweed. But, through election fraud, the victory went to Rutherford B. Hayes.

Hayes worked to combat some of the more corrupt aspects of the Grant administration, even pushing for civil service reform. Partly because of this, the professional politicians did not like him. In turn, Hayes did not like being president and chose not to run for a second term.

A liberal Republican dark horse, James A. Garfield, won the next presidential election. Unfortunately, he was soon assassinated by a disappointed office seeker. (The mortally wounded president was taken to Long Branch, New Jersey, where he died. There is a statue of him in the town.) Vice-President Chester A. Arthur became president. He had been made vice-president because he was a favorite of New Yorker Roscoe Conkling's Republican machine. He proved, however, to be a big disappointment to the machine politicians when he became somewhat of a reformer. One of the more important measures passed under Arthur was the 1883 civil service reform sponsored by George Pendleton. This law set up a civil service commission; made it a requirement to hold open competitive examinations for all appointments; and forbade the payment of money by civil service appointees to the federal officials who hired them.

Arthur proved too much of a reformer for the Republican conservatives, known as Stalwarts, and not enough of one for the Republican reformers, known as Half-Breeds. The Stalwarts succeeded in getting their man nominated as the presidential candidate. However, James G. Blaine was a man with a very shady past. This was the last straw for liberal Republicans, known as Mugwumps, and they proclaimed that they would support the Democrats if they came up with a decent man.

And find a decent man the Democrats did. In fact, the single outstanding feature of Grover Cleveland was his integrity. This former mayor of Buffalo had been chosen governor of New York largely because of this trait, and, fortunately for him, the nation was looking for an honest man in 1884.

During the campaign, the Republicans revealed that the Democratic candidate had an illegitimate son by a widow, Mrs. Maria Crofts Halpin. The charge almost derailed his campaign, but he limited the damage by forthrightly acknowledging the revelation. The widow had kept company with several men in Buffalo, so Cleveland had not been sure the child was his. He accepted parentage, however, reasoning that it would be easier on him than on any of the other suitors, who were all married. This was a noble, if somewhat foolish, act from an honest, but naive, man.

Evidence of corruption hurt Blaine during the campaign, as did his failure to denounce immediately the remark of a supporter that the Democrats were the party of "Rum, Romanism, and Rebellion." This remark cost him the support of many Irish-Americans.

Cleveland won and, soon after assuming office, in a White House ceremony, he married Frances Folsom, daughter of a former law partner.

The president received the Democratic nomination again in 1888, but lost to Benjamin Harrison. The main campaign issue was the rate of tariffs. Cleveland supported lower rates. Out of office, the ex-president settled in New York City and practiced corporate law. His party again turned to him for the 1892 election. This time he defeated Harrison in a dull contest with no new issues.

His second term in office was miserable. The depression of 1893 wreaked havoc on the economy and on his plans. He refused to intervene, believing the economy would right itself in time. This inactivity and the continued sufferings of the people made the president extremely unpopular, and he eagerly awaited the end of his term. Upon its completion, he settled in Princeton, New Jersey (see the section on Woodrow Wilson's Princeton for information about Cleveland's later years.)

Grover Cleveland Birthplace

207 Bloomfield Avenue (Route 506), between Arlington and Forest avenues, just west of the Essex County Jail (from Exit 149 of the Garden State Parkway, travel west on Route 506–Bloomfield Avenue), Caldwell, NJ (Open Wed–Fri 9–12, 1–6, Sat 9–12, 1–5, Sun 1–6, all year)

This is the house in which Cleveland was born in 1837. His father was minister to the Presbyterian Church located about a mile away. The young lad lived in this house until the age of four, when the family moved to Fayetteville, New York, near Syracuse.

At age thirteen, he and his family moved to Clinton, New York, where his father became director of the American Home Missionary Society. The young man studied for entrance into Hamilton College, but could not financially afford further education after his father died. He finally found his future occupation when, in 1855, his uncle in Buffalo got him a table in an outer room of a law firm. Some four years later, he was admitted to the bar.

The future president became involved in local politics while becoming one of Buffalo's leading lawyers. In 1881 he became the city's mayor. He won election to the governorship of New York the following year and, two years later, received the Democratic party nomination for the office of the presidency.

The house is filled with mementos of Cleveland's long career. Here is the bedroom where he was born, the cradle that rocked him, his desk when he served as mayor of Buffalo, another desk from his Princeton years, and many of his personal belongings. There is certainly enough to make a visit worthwhile.

Other Sites to Visit

Nearby is the Montclair Art Museum, South Mountain and Bloomfield avenues in Montclair (open Tues–Sat 10–5, Sun 2–5, Sept–June). Also visit the Thomas Edison laboratories and house in West Orange.

USS *Olympia* at Penn's Landing

Visit Penn's Landing, Philadelphia, to see the Spanish-American War flagship of Admiral Dewey. The ship itself is very beautiful, especially the woodwork in the officers' quarters. This trip can take an entire day because there are many ships to see at the landing.

Besides being a thing of beauty, the warship provides an opportunity to learn about another phase in American history: the Spanish-American War. This war marked the emergence of the country as a world power, imitating, though to a lesser extent, the actions of the European powers.

Eight-inch guns of the USS Olympia, *Penn's Landing, Philadelphia, Pennsylvania*

The conflict with Spain also marks the emergence of the great power of the press. It is highly debatable whether the war would have occurred if it were not for the mighty press barons: James Gordon Bennett, Sr., with his *New York Herald;* Joseph Pulitzer with the *World;* and William Randolph Hearst and his *Journal.* These papers warred with each other for subscribers, and journalistic ethics became a casualty.

Journalists vied with each other in exaggerating the atrocities committed by Spanish officials in their attempts to quell Cuba's fight for independence. The term *yellow journalism* came to signify reporting that is irresponsible and inflammatory. The description certainly fits the press's handling of the Cuban revolution. William Randolph Hearst provided the classic quote from the period in his response to the painter Frederic Remington. The young artist cabled from Cuba that, since he could find no signs of war to paint, he wished to return to New York. Hearst wired back: "Please remain. You furnish the pictures and I will furnish the war."

American sympathy with Cuba and antipathy toward Spain rose to such a fever pitch that President McKinley felt compelled to send the USS *Maine* to the island. The ship arrived in Havana harbor in January 1898. There it exploded in February for reasons that never became known. Of the 350 men aboard the vessel, 252 were killed.

Two months later, President McKinley signed a joint resolution that amounted to a declaration of war against Spain. Within five days the Americans had a triumphant victory, provided by Admiral Dewey and his seven vessels at Manila Bay in the Philippines. The admiral led his fleet from Mirs Bay along the China Coast to Manila Bay. Making ready for battle, he left the open bridge for the conning tower. There he told Captain Charles V. Gridley: "You may fire when ready, Gridley." In the seven-hour battle that followed, the American fleet destroyed ten Spanish vessels and the Cavite naval yard. Nearly four hundred Spanish naval personnel were killed or wounded. Spain lost half its fleet and was swept off the Pacific Ocean. All this the admiral accomplished with the loss of only one American life, and that from a heart attack.

USS *Olympia*

Penn's Landing, off Delaware Avenue, from Market to Spruce streets, Philadelphia, PA (Open daily 10–4:30, all year)

The ship was launched in November 1892. It is a protected cruiser, smaller than the heavier armored cruisers produced at that time. The ship carried four eight-inch rifles, ten five-inch rapid-fire guns, fourteen six-pounder quick-firing rifles, and six one-pounders, along with a crew of 33 officers and 395 enlisted men.

The ship's later history included a tour as the summer cruise ship for the Naval Academy at Annapolis; use as a barracks ship; and a role in the 1918 Allied anti-Bolshevik intervention force sent against the Soviet Union. In 1921, sailing from France, the ship brought back the remains of the American Unknown Soldier to Arlington National Cemetery. The wooden casket used in the mission can be found on the upper deck.

In the ship's museum there is a model of the USS *Maine* and a picture of the war Congress, along with uniforms of the soldiers who fought in the war. Here also are some items from the Philippine insurrection. President

McKinley leaned toward annexation of the Philippines. Emilio Aguinaldo led an insurgent force to stop this. He launched a vehement assault on American forces starting in February 1899. The war to put down the guerrillas lasted for three years and actually cost more than the entire Spanish-American War itself.

Hundreds of Americans and thousands of Filipinos lost their lives, but the Americans were able to set up a colonial administration in the Philippines.

Other Sites to Visit

There are many ships to visit at Penn's Landing. One is the USS *Becuna,* a World War II submarine. Also here is the Museum of the Port of History, which has changing exhibits. You may also want to ride the trolley that runs nearby.

Thomas Eakins of Philadelphia

Romanticism dominated the arts between 1830 and 1865. However, in the later part of this period, a trend toward greater realism began. One can see the emerging realism in the works of Herman Melville. Several changes in the United States helped bring about the weakening of the romantic spirit. The primary change was the triumph of the industrial over the agricultural way of life. At least in its early stages, the new industrial order, compared to farming, was not "romantic." In fact, some writers, such as Karl Marx, became so upset by the rising capitalist societies that they called for revolution to overthrow the newly emerging order. Furthermore, the brutality of the Civil War—the war that cleared the way for the triumph of the new industrial order—also did a great deal to knock much of the romance out of romanticism. It was hard to be "romantic" after Shiloh and Antietam.

In concert with the above changes, the new scientific ideas of Charles Darwin weakened the religious basis of romanticism. Nature, seen by romantics as a reflection of God, was now increasingly seen as a battleground for the survival of the fittest.

Contemporaries used the revolutionary ideas of Darwin both as a self-congratulatory ideology and a critical philosophy. On the one hand, the newly emerging captains of industry adopted a new philosophy, known as social Darwinism, which was a corruption of Darwin's ideas. This doctrine held that industrialists dominated industry because they were the fittest of the competitors in the struggle for economic domination. Much of the religious thought of the period gave its blessing to the new industrial philosophy by saying that God worked through this struggle.

On the other hand, the intellectuals gave voice to the philosophy of realism. This trend opposed the spirit of self-satisfaction then current. Realism in literature and the arts was critical of the social and economic problems of Victorian society and the new industrial order, even though the realists still tended to be optimistic about the future.

To learn more about realist art, travel to Philadelphia to see the paintings of Thomas Eakins, an outstanding American painter. If you take the time to look at other paintings in addition to those of Eakins, this is easily a day trip.

The future realist was born in Philadelphia in 1844. After graduating from high school, he started to draw at the Pennsylvania Academy of Fine Arts and, possibly, at classes sponsored by the Philadelphia Sketch Club. At one time he considered becoming a physician and attended anatomy classes at Jefferson Medical College.

From 1866 to 1870 he studied painting at the Ecole des Beaux Arts in Paris. Not long after his return, the young artist exhibited his works. *The Champion Single Sculls* (commonly known as *Max Schmitt in a Single Scull*) was one of the paintings hung at the Philadelphia Union League. Despite mixed reviews, Eakins continued to paint sculling and sailing works. In 1874 he began teaching at the Philadelphia Sketch Club, where his classes were very popular.

Jefferson Alumni Hall

Locust and Eleventh streets, Thomas Jefferson University and Medical College, Philadelphia, PA (Open days, all year)

Thomas Jefferson University and Medical College owns one of the most controversial portraits of nineteenth-century American painting. Ask the guard at Jefferson Alumni Hall to show you the way to the Thomas Eakins Gallery. Here hangs the infamous *Portrait of Doctor Gross,* along with the *Portrait of Benjamin Howard Rand* (his first formal portrait, painted in 1874) and the *Portrait of Professor William Smith Forbes* (1905).

Eakins wanted to paint an outstanding portrait for the upcoming 1876 Centennial Exposition to be held in Philadelphia. While attending lectures on anatomy at the medical college, he became familiar with the chair of surgery, Professor Samuel Gross. The result of this acquaintanceship was the notorious painting, which shows the doctor during an operation. This was far too realistic for contemporary tastes. Especially upsetting was the blood on the doctor's hands. The young realist had several pictures displayed for the centennial celebration, but the officials rejected his portrait of Dr. Gross. (A statue of Dr. Gross stands in the plaza of the college.)

He exhibited the Gross painting (no pun intended) in New York under the auspices of the Society of American Artists and met harsh criticism there. The Philadelphia Academy of Fine Arts refused to hang the picture. Never shrinking from controversy, Eakins met more criticism when he defiantly painted bold nudes for his William Rush series. (You can see some of William Rush's sculptures at the Fairmount Water Works.)

Pennsylvania Academy of Fine Arts

Corner of Broad and Cherry streets, Philadelphia, PA (Open Tues–Sat 10–5, Wed 10–7, Sun 11–5, all year)

Frank Furness designed this architectural treasure for the Pennsylvania Academy of Fine Arts. The interior is fantastic, with huge skylights to brighten the halls. The architect's intent was to overwhelm the visitor with the grand scale. He succeeded. There are several paintings by Eakins in the museum. Not sharing the artist's concerns for absolute realism, children may not like seeing the body casts made from a corpse the painter used to study anatomy.

The artist started as a teaching assistant at the academy in 1876, the year it opened. He was controversial from the start. He wanted to hire life models, not from houses of prostitution, as was the practice, but from other walks of life. He even wanted to advertise for the models in the papers, which further upset the academy's committee members. In response to the ensuing furor, he left his classes and set up his own school in 1877. This so badly hurt attendance at academy classes that school officials asked him to return.

At this time he developed a keen interest in photography. Inspired by Eadweard Muybridge's work on the study of motion, he decided to paint trotting horses in his *A May Morning in the Park*. This 1879 painting is the first to show animals in rapid motion as they actually move.

In the same year, he became professor of drawing and painting at the academy. Four years later, at nearly forty years of age, he married one of his students, Hannah Susan Macdowell. They moved into a studio at 1330 Chestnut Street.

The new professor drew criticism for his carefree use of nudes. He often had his students model nude for each other and even took nude photographs of them to use in his paintings. The final straw came in 1886 when, to show the origin of a certain muscle, Eakins removed a male model's loincloth in a ladies' life class. The board of directors asked for his resignation, and he complied. Many of the academy students followed him into organizing the Philadelphia Art Students' League.

Eakins was a social gadfly fighting against the self-satisfaction of Victorian society. The Victorians pretended that all was right with the world, but obviously this was not true. The artist wanted to be realistic and show the world as it was. He was not popular, precisely because his contemporaries were not interested in seeing this world.

Following a trip out West, he painted Walt Whitman's portrait at the poet's Camden residence (you can see the painting at the academy). The two

Detail of Pennsylvania Academy of Fine Arts

unconventionals got along very well. The artist then taught classes at the Art Students' League in Philadelphia and New York until 1897. At this time, he started producing boxing and wrestling works. Toward the end of his life, he specialized in portraits of prominent clergy. His last known work was *Portrait of Dr. Edward Anthony Spitzka* (1913–1914). He died in 1916.

Eakins's near brutalism and extreme scientism were too advanced for his time. Nevertheless, his wonderful paintings did influence artists to come, especially those urban realists of the ashcan school.

Philadelphia Museum of Art

Twenty-sixth Street and Benjamin Franklin Parkway (from downtown, travel west on Vine Street), Philadelphia, PA (Open Tues–Sun 10–5, all year)

The museum has a room devoted to the city's native son. The paintings cover his career, including sculling pictures, sketches for the *Portrait of Doctor Gross,* a work dealing with William Rush, motion-study pictures, boxing and wrestling works, and portraits. The visit here is highly recommended.

Other Sites to Visit

There are two other sites in Philadelphia connected with the painter. On the front of the Woolworth's store on Chestnut Street, close to Thirteenth Street, is a bronze tablet marking the site of his studio. He painted here from 1884 to 1900. At 1729 Mount Vernon Street is his boyhood home. It is now owned by the Philadelphia Museum of Art, which uses it as a study center. See the Geographic Cross-Reference for a list of the numerous sections dealing with Philadelphia.

PART

TEN

The Progressive Era

The post–Civil War period was dominated by the problems of the growing concentration of wealth and power in the hands of a few men. In the previous section I discussed several proposed, but ultimately unsuccessful, solutions to correct this situation. Two other responses to industrialization and its problems were populism and socialism.

Populism was primarily a defensive reaction of farmers and ruralites to increasing industrialism. Its greatest political spokesman was William Jennings Bryan, who ran unsuccessfully for the presidency in the elections of 1896, 1900, and 1908. However, an effective solution was not going to come from the field of agriculture, which would decline to less than 5 percent of the American work force.

Socialism, like populism, was another occupationally specific movement—tied to the growth of blue-collar occupations (or, to use their lingo, the working class). And, like populism, its occupational base dwindled over time. The percentage of the labor force involved in blue-collar occupations continues to decline relative to white-collar jobs. The socialist movement wanted government to play a much stronger role in the direction of the economy, some even preferring a centrally controlled, planned system. Socialism in the United States never had the success that Populism enjoyed. The hostility of religious Americans to any brand of socialism, combined with the country's great wealth and opportunities for upward mobility, made it extremely difficult for that movement to thrive here. This atmosphere also forced the American labor movement to be very cautious in its actions. Socialism in the United States will be discussed in the chapter on the 1913 labor strike in Paterson, New Jersey. In this section I discuss how the United States finally came up with a more effective answer.

The solution arose out of progressivism, which was a liberal conservative movement. Proponents of this philosophy believed in the new industrial order, but realized that government had to take a more active role in regulating some of the more flagrant abuses. The new era began with the presidency of Theodore Roosevelt and lasted through the presidencies of William Howard Taft and Woodrow Wilson. It ended in a wave of post–World War I conservatism.

Before the era ended, however, the Progressives accomplished many reforms. Perhaps one of the most important was the introduction of the federal progressive income tax, which eventually made it impossible for most people of wealth to afford the kinds of mansions one sees along the Hudson River or in Newport, Rhode Island. Other democratic reforms were also introduced, such as the initiative, referendum, direct primary, and popular recall of elected officials.

In the first chapter of this section, we visit Sagamore Hill, the home of President Theodore Roosevelt, to learn more about the Progressive Era. In the next chapter we consider the rise of another Progressive president, Woodrow Wilson, through a tour of Princeton. That some people still had a great deal of wealth in the early days of the twentieth century can be seen on the trip to Wilmington, Delaware. The section's third chapter describes a tour of three mansions belonging to the Du Ponts. The disparity in wealth created resentment in the nation, which spilled over into labor strikes and the growth of the American labor movement. In the final chapter, we visit Paterson, New Jersey, to see the sites associated with the 1913 strike.

Much of the architecture and interior decoration of the Progressive Era can be seen as a continuation of the American Renaissance movement. In architecture there was a return to more traditional styles: the Georgian Revival, Dutch Colonial, and Spanish Colonial. Architectural innovations included the prairie architecture and natural houses of Frank Lloyd Wright and the emphasis on curves in art nouveau.

27

Theodore Roosevelt at Oyster Bay

Theodore Roosevelt, so filled with boundless energy, was one of the most colorful presidents the United States has ever had. We try to catch some of this spirit by visiting the former president's home in Oyster Bay, Long Island. Combined with lunch, the visit can last three-quarters of a day. Visit other sites on Long Island to make it a longer trip. The tour is highly recommended. Besides having the chance to learn more about this fascinating man, you will see his absolutely gorgeous Queen Anne house. Especially beautiful is the piazza overlooking a large expanse of open land. The grounds themselves are very lovely and make for a very enjoyable stroll.

In today's world, many people see Theodore Roosevelt as a bit too macho and imperialistic. His emphasis on strength partly stemmed from his insecurity over having a puny, unhealthy body as a child and the security of knowing that he had transformed that body into an extremely strong one. (An attempted assassination failed when, after going through a thick overcoat, the bullet lodged in his powerful chest muscles.) If presidents were judged solely on strength, he would certainly be number one. Considering his role in foreign affairs, it must be remembered that he lived in a time of European imperialism that dwarfed similar activities of the United States.

On the positive side, the nation owes Roosevelt a great deal because he was the first president to carry out some of the ideas of the Progressive movement. He thought that government should take a more active role in regulating the giant industrial companies that had developed since the Civil War. In addition, he believed in strengthening the bargaining position of lower-income groups. Roosevelt is also remembered for his love of the great outdoors and his conservation efforts.

The future president was born in 1858 in a brownstone town house (which you can tour) at 28 East Twentieth Street in Manhattan. In 1872 Theodore's father bought a home in Oyster Bay, Long Island. On the island the boy developed his interest in natural history to the point where he wanted to be a naturalist when he went to Harvard.

Soon after college graduation, he married Alice Hathaway Lee, daughter of an exclusive Boston family. He then attended Columbia University Law School. In 1882 he won election as a Republican state assemblyman.

In 1884, Alice gave birth to a baby girl, also named Alice. The new mother lapsed into unconsciousness and died the day after childbirth. On that very day, the future president's mother also passed away. Roosevelt finished his assembly term, but dogged by painful memories, escaped into Dakota Territory for two years to be a rancher-cowboy. Upon his return east, he ran for mayor of New York City, but lost to Peter Cooper's son-in-law, Abraham Hewitt of Ringwood Manor. Not long after the election, he married Edith Carow.

President Benjamin Harrison appointed Roosevelt to the Civil Service Commission in Washington, D.C. There, the New Yorker followed the rules so impartially that he was reappointed after the second presidential election of Democrat Grover Cleveland. While winning the admiration of Democrats for his impartiality, he also earned the distrust of many Republicans.

Back in New York City, he became president of the police board. It seems an ironic position in which to gain a social conscience, but this job awakened him to some harsh realities. Two of his associates helped in this process: Jacob Riis, the photographer and author of *How the Other Half Lives,* and Lincoln Steffens, author of the muck-raking book *The Shame of Our Cities.* Seeing the poverty around him, he became convinced of the need for at least some government intervention.

As in his work for the civil service, Roosevelt's independence and unpredictability got him into trouble with the Republicans. To get rid of him, Thomas Platt, the boss of the state Republican party, convinced President McKinley to get "that damn cowboy" out of New York. And that is how the hero of this story became assistant secretary of the navy.

The Spanish-American War began in 1898. Anxious to see action, Roosevelt accepted the post of second in command of the First Cavalry. He recruited so many cowboys and other men he had known from his Dakota days that the press dubbed the unit the Rough Riders. The cowboy returned from the war a national hero for his exploits at San Juan Hill, really Kettle Hill. This helped convince the Republican party in New York to run him for the governorship, which he won in the 1898 election.

Upon the death of Vice-President Garret Hobart (from Paterson, New Jersey), the position of vice-presidential candidate became available. A popular groundswell gave Roosevelt the spot on the ticket. In 1900 when McKinley was reelected, the war hero became vice-president of the United States. He catapulted into the presidency upon the assassination of McKinley in September 1901.

Although he was no radical, Roosevelt did work to break up some of the giant business monopolies, such as the Northern Securities Company. This monopoly, created by J. P. Morgan, E. H. Harriman, James J. Hill, and Rockefeller, would have dominated all rail traffic west of Chicago.

In 1904 the people elected the war hero president in his own right. Near the end of his term, he worked for the election of William Howard Taft, whom he felt would carry on the progressive policies of the Roosevelt administration.

Back porch of Theodore Roosevelt's Sagamore Hill home, Oyster Bay, New York

The now ex-president became terribly disillusioned with Taft's presidency, and decided to run in the next election as a candidate for the progressive Bull Moose party. Unfortunately for the Republicans, this split the party, giving Democrat Woodrow Wilson the victory in the 1912 election.

Sagamore Hill National Historic Site

20 Sagamore Hill Road (Exit 41 of the Long Island Expressway, NY 106 north to the town of Oyster Bay, take Route 16, turn right at East Main Street, left onto Cove Neck Road, and right onto Sagamore Hill Road), Oyster Bay, Long Island, NY (Open daily 9:30–5, May–Oct; daily 9:30–4:30, Nov–Apr)

This house was built for Roosevelt's daughter, Alice, to give her a proper home. (Alice became a very colorful figure in her time, known for her outspokenness. The president, commenting on his daughter's behavior, once said that he could either control Alice or be president of the United States, but that he could not do both.) Completed in 1885, the house was used only intermittently until Roosevelt's marriage to Edith Carow. Besides being stepmother to Alice, Edith bore five children.

This house was the summer White House during the years 1901 to 1909. If ever a house reflected its owner's personality, this one surely does. You can almost feel the vigorous man's presence in the Trophy Room with its walls covered with stuffed animal heads (that is, if you are not shocked or sickened by the overwhelming number of these heads). The room was the family room where all would gather after dinner. He wrote his account of

Detail from Theodore Roosevelt's Sagamore Hill home, Oyster Bay, New York

the Spanish-American War, *The Rough Riders,* as well as many other books, articles, and speeches, in his gun room on the third floor. The master bedroom contains modern Gothic furniture by Frank Furness and Daniel Pabst and provides a good view of Oyster Bay from its small porch.

While serving in the armed forces during World War I, Quentin, the youngest son, was killed in 1918. His father never fully recovered from the shock, and died shortly afterward (1919). Be sure to see the room in which he died.

In addition to his home, tour the Roosevelt Museum, which contains some memorabilia. The museum is housed next-door in the former home of one of Theodore Roosevelt's sons. The museum workers run a video on the president made for the old TV series "Biography" with Mike Wallace.

Other Sites to Visit

See the Geographic Cross-Reference for a list of Long Island sites.

28

Woodrow Wilson's Princeton

If you care about the world of ideas, it is always exhilarating to be around universities. It is fun just to walk around and drink in the college atmosphere. This is especially true along Princeton's Nassau Street. On campus the university buildings themselves are very handsome. One structure that catches many people's eye is the somewhat overpowering Romanesque hodgepodge known as Alexander Hall.

And if you are interested in history, what better way to look at Princeton than through the eyes of one of its most famous alumni, Woodrow Wilson. If you include a walk along Nassau Street and having lunch, this trip can easily take all day.

Woodrow Wilson, like Theodore Roosevelt, was a conservative Progressive who became president of the United States. Both men believed in their God and in themselves with an absoluteness that is hard to imagine in these days of secular humanism. There, however, the similarities between the two men end. One of the biggest differences between the two was that Roosevelt had one of the most robust bodies of any United States president, and Wilson had one of the weakest. Wilson was constantly plagued by various ailments. Another big difference was Wilson's occupation: university professor. Americans don't usually elect professors to the office of the presidency, which makes Wilson's rise especially interesting.

Woodrow Wilson was born in Staunton, Virginia in 1856. His father was a Presbyterian minister, which may partly account for the son's moralistic outlook on life. In 1875 the young man started his college education at the Presbyterian-founded Princeton College, where his father had received his B.D. degree. He settled in Mrs. Josiah Wright's boardinghouse on Nassau Street. From the second floor he could look out over the campus.

Bainbridge House

158 Nassau Street (take Washington Road Exit of U.S. 1, travel north on Washington Road, find a parking place at the junction with Nassau Street), Princeton, NJ (Open Tues–Sun 12–4, all year)

Pick up a tour map and see changing exhibits on the town.

Witherspoon Hall (private)

Just south of Alexander Hall or southwest of Nassau Hall, Princeton, NJ

In his sophomore year the young Virginian moved into Witherspoon Hall. Here he helped organize what became locally known as the Witherspoon Gang. The men would meet to discuss current events and, at times, break into song. In their junior year many of the gang, along with Wilson, joined the Alligator Club, one of the many dining clubs on campus.

Following his graduation in 1879, the future president studied law at the University of Virginia at Charlottesville. He had to withdraw in December 1880 because of ill health. He traveled to Atlanta, Georgia, where he obtained admission to the bar. An oversupply of lawyers at that time forced him to abandon the profession.

He attended graduate school at John Hopkins University to study history and political science. He decided, however, not to pursue the doctorate. Instead, he married the daughter of a Presbyterian minister and became a teacher at the all-female Bryn Mawr College outside of Philadelphia. The young professor saw this job only as a steppingstone to the next teaching position—he wanted to teach men, not women.

Realizing that he needed the doctorate for future teaching promotions, he proposed, and John Hopkins accepted, his already published book, *Congressional Government,* as his dissertation. The doctorate made it easier for him to escape Bryn Mawr after three years of service. He accepted a position at Wesleyan University in Middletown, Connecticut. In September 1890, he returned to Princeton as professor of jurisprudence and political economy.

Wilson House (private)

72 Library Place (off Stockton Street), Princeton, NJ

For six years the Wilsons lived here, virtually across the street from the Morven mansion. During this time, Wilson, with his gift for public speaking, established himself as the leader of the younger professors working for educational reform. This earned him the enmity of Francis Patton, president of the college. The young professor pushed through several reforms, such as raising entrance requirements and introducing an honor system.

Wilson House (private)

82 University Place, Princeton, NJ

The Wilsons bought a wooded lot adjoining the property they were renting. On it they built a house, moving into it in the spring of 1896. Mrs. Wilson worked with the architect on the details of this English Norman

Prospect House, Princeton University, Princeton, New Jersey

country house, half-timbered with stucco. They designed a study with high windows as her husband's special retreat. On the walls of the study were pictures of the men Wilson admired most, including Daniel Webster, Gladstone, Walter Bagehot, Edmund Burke, and his own father.

Prospect House (private)

On campus near the intersection of Prospect Avenue and Washington Road, Princeton, NJ

Wilson became the thirteenth president of Princeton College in June 1902. He moved into this house, the president's house, upon assuming office. Here he and his wife frequently dined with faculty. The Tuscan villa designed by John Notman now serves as a faculty dining place. Don't miss the gardens behind the house.

Walk east to Seventy-nine Hall, which was erected by the class of 1879. Look through the arch up Prospect Avenue. Lining the entire street are the exclusive dining clubs against which the new college president fought so bitterly. At the head of Prospect Avenue is the Woodrow Wilson School, which houses rooms for the study of public affairs.

Prospect Avenue

Off Washington Road, Princeton, NJ

The new president began a series of battles that ultimately led to his embittered defeat. The first of these was his proposal to establish residential colleges, or quadrangles. He wanted all undergraduates to live together, regardless of their year in school. This would throw upperclassmen and lowerclassmen together, along with instructors.

This plan would have upset the private club system at Princeton. The clubs started as eating clubs in 1855 as a protest against the poor quality of the food being served. (The food must have been pretty bad, for the students protested by grabbing the tablecloths with all that was on them and throwing them out the windows.)

The clubs were the most important social institutions on campus. Only upperclassmen were club members; freshmen were not even allowed to walk on the avenue. Several of the clubs represented the wealthier elements of society—Ivy (1879), Cottage (1886), Tiger Inn (1890), and Cap and Gown (1891).

In 1906 the quadrangle plan was formally introduced. The plan immediately set off a storm of protest. Professor Andrew West, who taught Latin, became the most vocal opponent. Although the president had the majority of the faculty behind him, the board of trustees voted against the proposal. Wilson wrote a letter of resignation, but did not send it. Ironically, the quad plan is now being implemented at the university.

Grover Cleveland's House (private)

15 Hodge Road (corner of Hodge Street), Princeton, NJ

Professor West invited President Grover Cleveland to the Princeton Sesquicentennial (1896) and so charmed the man that the president decided to settle in Princeton upon retirement. In 1897 the Clevelands moved here to a house just three blocks from Wilson's house. They named their estate Westland in honor of Dean West.

The ex-president had no regular occupation, but he did become a member of the Princeton Board of Trustees. In 1904 he became the chairman of the trustees' committee on the graduate school. In this position he could help his old friend West.

For the last two years of his life, Cleveland was very sick. As his medical problems increased, he came to side even more with Professor West. He came out against Wilson during the quadrangle-plan fight. The ensuing conflict left the Clevelands and the Wilsons bitter personal enemies. Even after his death in 1908, Cleveland's wife, Francis, sided with the West faction.

Graduate College
College Road and Springdale Road, Princeton, NJ

Would you believe that the location and, indeed, the very existence of this graduate college was the subject of intense conflict? The conflict resulted in a second major defeat for the Princeton president, which shoved him into the world of nonacademic politics.

In 1900 Andrew West was elected dean of the new graduate school. Wilson felt that the man was not suited for such a position: he was elitist; he had done no graduate work himself; and he knew nothing of science or research. Instead of challenging the man's leadership, the president chose to delay building the school by fighting over its proposed location. In 1909 one of the college trustees came to an agreement with a donor of funds that the graduate school would be located on the golf links, situated a mile off campus. As a delaying tactic, Wilson proposed the building of two graduate colleges, one on campus and another at the golf links. Calling his bluff, the trustees accepted the idea. Wilson had to back down, virtually admitting that Dean West's abilities rather than the location of the graduate school was the real issue.

Meanwhile, West gathered another donation for the graduate school, this finally forcing his enemy to concede. Wilson acquiesced in the golf links site. Tears streamed down his face at the 1910 graduation exercises. He continued to have nightmares concerning the dean even when he was in the White House. In the twilight of his age, he still remembered his old enemy as being one of the most astute politicians with whom he had ever clashed. At the graduate college is the Cleveland Tower. In the inner courtyard is a statue of Dean West, first graduate school dean, 1901–1928.

Sometimes out of defeat come new triumphs. And this is what happened to Woodrow Wilson. The Presbyterian minister's son saw his college battles in terms of democracy against elitism and snobbery. This spirit had appeal in these progressive times and helped propel him to success in the race for the governorship of New Jersey. Boss Smith of New Jersey nominated him for the governorship to an unenthusiastic convention in September 1910. In November, the voters elected him to the governorship.

Wilson House (private)

25 Cleveland Lane, Princeton, NJ

While Wilson was governor of New Jersey, the Wilsons lived here. In the 1912 election campaign, the country was looking for a progressive president—a decent man who would smooth over some of the rougher edges of the giant corporations. Woodrow Wilson was such a man. His rise from his defeats at Princeton in 1910 to his election to the presidency of the United States in 1912 appears mercurial. Nevertheless, before giving him too much credit, it should be remembered that his election received considerable help from Theodore Roosevelt's third-party candidacy, which split the Republican vote. His speaking ability proved an invaluable campaign asset. Curiously, he resembled Richard Nixon in at least one sense. He could perform well before large groups, but was shy and awkward in small groups of strangers.

Other Sites to Visit

See the section on the Battle of Princeton.

29

The Du Ponts of Delaware

Wilmington is a great place to visit if you are interested in interior decoration and horticulture. The three mansions of the Du Ponts are absolutely sumptuous. Winterthur Museum specializes in educating people about interior decoration styles through the ages and is highly recommended. Make this one of your first visits, for a little knowledge of furniture styles will make house touring more enjoyable. The lifestyle evident at the Nemours Mansion seems more appropriate to a French aristocrat than an American industrialist. The reception at this palace is the most elegant you will receive in the entire travel area. The third Du Pont mansion, this one at Longwood Gardens, is much simpler in style, because it was designed to harmonize with the original Quaker house. If you take the time to tour the gardens in addition to the mansions themselves, the visit to Wilmington will take at least one and a half days. Please note that these are no ordinary gardens. They are some of the best in the region and in the nation.

The three mansions belonged to what may have been the richest family in the United States. We first met the Du Ponts when discussing the Industrial Revolution. Pierre Samuel Du Pont and his family came to the United States as immigrants from France, fleeing the aftermath of the French Revolution. Eleuthère Irénée Du Pont, one of Pierre's sons, established the gunpowder mills along Brandywine Creek. From these mills today's massive Du Pont conglomerate gradually developed.

Alfred (Eleuthère's oldest son) became the president of the firm in 1837. He was not suitable for this position, so his two younger brothers, Henry and Alexis, and a nephew, Eleuthère Irénée II, took his place. Henry took control from the other two and became sole head of the company. In later years, people referred to him simply as the General. Under the General, the company established the trust that fixed gunpowder prices. Needless to say, this greatly boosted the company's position in the industry.

Winterthur Museum and Gardens

From I-95 take the exit for Route 141 north, left/north onto Kennett Pike/Route 52, turn right shortly after the intersection with Route 82), Wilmington, DE (Open Tues–Sat 10–4, Sun 12–4, all year)

In 1839 Henry's sister, Evalina, and her husband, James Antoine Bidermann, bought land along the Kennett Pike and there built a Greek Revival house.

They called it Winterthur after the Swiss town where Antoine's mother had been born. The General bought the house from the only son of the couple. He, in turn, gave the house to his son, Henry (a colonel in the Civil War), who eventually wrested full control of the company from his detested brother/partner William. Henry, Jr., made extensive alterations to the house.

Henry Francis, the son of Henry, Jr., took over the house and tripled its size when, in 1929, he added a huge wing to contain his collection of American antiques. He took entire rooms (including floors, ceilings, and paneling) from various houses around the country and installed them in the museum. In 1952 his museum of interior decoration opened to the public. There are more than fifty thousand treasured objects in 196 rooms and display areas.

Take the Two Centuries Tour, which is an excellent one for history buffs. Each room illustrates a different style of decoration. American interiors are traced from the early (1640–1690) period to the Empire style of 1815–1840. The Port Royal Tour is also organized chronologically. The Georgian rooms are on the first floor, and the Federal and Empire styles are on the second.

Be sure to tour the gardens. Henry Francis specialized in wildflowers and shrubs, and there are many beautiful varieties here. He lived in the house in spring and fall. Consequently, there are many plants that look particularly beautiful at these times of year. In the spring the showy crab apple tree with its mountains of flower clusters is especially dazzling.

By 1902, power was shared by three Du Pont cousins: Coleman, the president; Pierre S., the treasurer; and Alfred I., the vice-president and general manager. Under this troika, the company became master of the United States gunpowder industry. Pierre was primarily responsible for changing Du Pont from a company of explosives manufacturers into a modern chemistry combine.

Without informing cousin Alfred I., Coleman decided to sell his stocks and Pierre purchased the majority of them. Pierre did not care for Alfred because of the latter's shady personal conduct (while still married himself, Alfred was having an affair with a married woman, Alicia Bradford Maddox, whom he later married). This created a feud between Pierre and Coleman on the one side and Alfred I. on the other. The conflict damaged both sides.

Longwood Gardens

From Wilmington take Route 52 north, which runs parallel with Route 1 for a short distance near the gardens, and then take Longwood Road, east of Kennett Square, PA (The gardens are open daily 9–6, all year; the Peirce–Du Pont house is open from 11–3)

These are the gardens of the onetime home of Pierre S. Du Pont. In 1700 a Quaker named George Peirce purchased from William Penn the grounds on which Longwood Gardens now sit. In 1709 his son, Joshua, built a log house on the property. This house was replaced by a red-and-black brick building in 1730. Joshua's son, Caleb, expanded the structure in 1764. Caleb's twin sons, Joshua and Samuel, had a great interest in botany, and it is they who in 1798 started to build an arboretum, which later became known as Peirce's Park.

In 1899 the property and house fell into the hands of an owner who contracted with lumber companies to cut down the trees. When Pierre learned that the area was to be sold to lumber interests, he purchased the property (1906). In 1914–1915 the great industrialist expanded the house but left the Quaker farmhouse as he had found it, thus preserving a historical home for future generations. The owner spent most of his leisure time here, running the house and gardens like a business. The estate's agricultural tradition continued with cattle, poultry, field crops, and orchards until 1951, when farming was halted.

The house itself has twenty-seven rooms, fifteen of which can be toured. The Peirce sections contain many items that once belonged to that family. One of the more interesting features of the house is the Conservatory, which was created by covering the forecourt with glass. The side windows can be lowered to the basement and replaced with screens in the summer. The Du Ponts liked to receive and entertain guests here. The library of the house is a huge room—large enough for the family to use it as a living room.

Pierre, who had a great interest in horticulture, expanded the gardens into the Longwood Gardens of today. These outstanding gardens rank with the New York and Brooklyn Botanic Gardens as among the best in the nation. The gardens employ 180 full-time employees and serve nearly 800,000 guests per year.

Nemours Mansion and Gardens

Rockland Road between Routes 141 and 202, Wilmington, DE (Open Tues–Sat 9–5, Sunday 11–5, May–Nov) (Visitors must be over sixteen years of age; bus tour available)

Alfred I. Du Pont was jealous of his cousin's house and gardens at Longwood and so he decided to build his own mansion. The Nemours estate is modeled after Versailles and rivals the mansions of Newport in lavishness. Nemours is the district in France from which the Du Ponts came. The seventy-seven-room French chateau was designed by Carrere and Hastings and built in 1909–1910. In the front are six two-story-high columns. The walls have pinkish colored stucco with concrete gray (Indiana limestone) framing. The house actually looks small from the front entrance, but this is deceptive. The mansion extends back into various wings.

The owner moved into the mansion with his second wife, Alicia Bradford Maddox. Alicia lived in the mansion for ten years until her death in 1920. Alfred then married Jessie Ball, a woman much younger than him. She proceeded to remove all portraits of the second wife from the mansion. There are many portraits of family members in the house: Alfred's maternal grandfather Henderson, who was a commandant of the Marine Corps; Jessie Ball; and the children. The only youngster to actually grow up at Nemours was an adopted child, Denise.

The industrialist was fond of music, and there are music motifs throughout the mansion. He was also quite an outdoorsman (on the tour you will see some of the weapons from his rifle collection). Located downstairs are a two-lane bowling alley made of cypress, a billiards room, an exercise room, and a photo lab. Also here is bottling machinery, enabling the owner to produce carbonated water if so desired. The house even has special ice-making machinery. In the kitchen, cork tiles made it easier on the servants' feet. In the dining room are portraits of King Louis XVI of France and Marie Antoinette. On the stairs is a bust of Lafayette, who was a family friend, and overhead is a chandelier that once hung in the general's home. Upstairs is a portrait of Alfred's three dogs, which had the run of the house. One dog came from Egypt, so they named him Mummy. An additional attraction is the terrace connected to Jessie's bedroom, which overlooks the beautiful gardens.

Following the owner's death in 1935, the estate became a hospital for crippled children. A tower with a carillon is erected over the spot where Alfred I., Alicia, their two children, and Jessie Ball are buried.

Tour the gardens that stretch almost one-third of a mile along the main vista from the mansion. These gardens are very different from those of Longwood and Winterthur. There are only a few identifying labels on the plants. The emphasis is on display, not education.

The bus tour stops at the garage (complete with iron grillwork that reminds one of New Orleans). Here are a number of Du Pont cars: a 1924 Cadillac limousine, a 1921 Renault, two Rolls-Royces, and a 1933 Buick roadster with a rumble seat.

Other Sites to Visit

See the sections on Swedish settlements, the Battle of Brandywine, and the Industrial Revolution. When in Wilmington, look for the Hotel Du Pont. For tax purposes, Pierre kept a permanent suite at the hotel and registered himself and his wife, Alice, as Delaware residents. The Du Ponts built the hotel in order to use up some of the surplus cash of the family. It opened in 1913.

30

Labor Troubles at Paterson

The Botto House in Haledon, a suburb of Paterson, New Jersey, is a real jewel. After all, there are so precious few sites connected with the history of American labor. While we often celebrate the contributions of the great industrialists, we tend to forget the sacrifices made by the millions of decent, ordinary men and women who helped establish more humane working conditions. Without their sacrifices, the workplace environment would be much worse today. Visit Paterson to catch some of the spirit of the movement for better working conditions. If visiting all the sites listed below, this trip will definitely take all day.

The section of this book on the Industrial Revolution and transportation covered the early history of Paterson, America's first planned industrial city. Paterson was an important industrial center producing such goods as locomotives and silk. Indeed, the latter activity earned Paterson the nickname Silk City.

Besides being the first planned industrial city, Paterson is well known in American history for the 1913 Silk Workers' Strike. Visiting the city provides the opportunity to view the conflict from the perspectives of the different sides involved. We see the working conditions of the silk employees, the house of an immigrant family that supported the 1913 strike, and the mansion of one of the silk factory employers.

Between 1881 and 1900 there were nearly 140 strikes in Paterson, but in labor history the city is best remembered for the strike of 1913. The conflict began in January of that year, when eight hundred workers walked off their jobs to protest the decision that employees would work four looms instead of two—a decision that would have eliminated many jobs and increased the workload. Within a month, nearly 300 mills were closed and twenty-four thousand employees were on strike.

The workers demanded a minimum wage of twelve dollars a week and an eight-hour day. Management thought this unreasonable and fought the strike with constant and massive arrests. On one occasion, hired detectives fired into the crowd to frighten the strikers. One of the bullets struck and killed an innocent bystander by the name of Modestino Valentino. He had been standing on his porch holding one of his small children and watching the day's excitement.

The Industrial Workers of the World, founded in Chicago in 1905 and better known simply as the IWW or the Wobblies, was a syndicalist organization that tried to change American society through direct economic action via a revolutionary labor movement. Fresh from a victory in the Lawrence, Massachusetts, strike of 1912, IWW members and supporters trooped into Paterson.

Among the so-called outside agitators were Big Bill Haywood (one of the organization's founders), Elizabeth Gurley Flynn (hero of many free-speech fights), Carlo Tresca, and Patrick Quinlan (president of IWW). Across the street from the Phoenix Mill on Van Houten Street in Paterson, the leaders would meet to discuss the strike. This building is now the Question Mark bar. Other left-wingers who came to Paterson included journalist Jack Reed (about whom the movie *Reds* deals) and writer Upton Sinclair. Greenwich Village radicals such as Walter Lippmann, Max Eastman, Henrietta Rodman, and Margaret Sanger also made pilgrimages to the city to lend their support.

Paterson Museum

2 Market Street, between Spruce and Main streets, Paterson, NJ (Open Mon–Fri 10–4:30, Sat–Sun 12:30–4, all year)

The earlier section on Paterson contains a description of this museum. Among other items of interest, it has displays on the various stages of silk making. These displays give the visitor a better idea of the labor conditions of the silk workers. Considerable information about the city's industrial history can also be found here.

The Botto House (American Labor Museum)

83 Norwood Street (from the Paterson Museum, take Main Street north, go north on West Broadway over the Passaic River, turn right on Belmont Avenue, and left onto Norwood), Haledon, NJ (Open Wed–Sun 12–4, all year)

The strikers found sanctuary from the constant arrests in this 1907–1908 Queen Anne house in the suburb of Haledon, where the mayor was a German socialist. Pietro and Maria Botto and their four daughters, immigrants from northern Italy, owned the home. They had lived in Union City, New Jersey, for fifteen years. They operated their Haledon house as a local resort, serving as many as one hundred people on Sunday trips to the country. There is a boccie ball court by the side of the house. They also took in boarders, who lived upstairs. In the backyard they had a chicken coop with twenty chickens as well as pigeons and rabbits. (They still have rabbits here, much to the delight of the children.)

The strike leaders met at the house every Sunday to map out strategies. The surrounding area formed a natural amphitheater, and from the balcony on the second floor the labor organizers would speak in different languages to huge crowds.

The Botto House (American Labor Museum), Haledon, New Jersey

During the strike, the silk factory owners sent much of the daily work to Pennsylvania where it was done by the wives of mine workers. The American Federation of Labor was fighting the IWW and therefore supported the strike-breaking action. As mentioned previously, given the conservative nature of the United States compared to European labor organizations, the American labor movement had to be very cautious. Many of the strikers were recent immigrants from countries that had socialist traditions. They naturally followed these traditions when they came to the United States. This created a real problem for the nonsocialist American labor leaders.

At the house the visitor sees a video on the background and history of the strike. In addition, the house tour enables the curious to learn about the way of life of a northern Italian immigrant family near the turn of the century. The tour also helps explain why socialism never gained massive support from American workers. Through very hard work, an immigrant family could obtain a share of the good things in life and have a chance for upward mobility.

Catholina Lambert Castle (Belle Vista)

Valley Road (from the Paterson Museum, travel south on Route 20N and turn right onto Valley Road), Paterson, NJ (Open Wed–Sun 1–4, all year)

The contrast in lifestyle between the factory workers and Catholina Lambert, one of the silk factory owners, is one reason for the 1913 strike. The employer was himself an immigrant from Yorkshire, England. He came to Paterson because a former colleague moved here to start a silk factory. The firm of Dexter, Lambert, and Company ran a successful ribbon-weaving business with mills on either side of Straight Street.

In 1893 Lambert built the mansion known as Belle Vista on Garret Mountain. The woodwork at the house is outstanding, especially that over the corner fireplace. The owner designed the main staircase to appear as if it were framed, because he said Mrs. Lambert descending the stairs was as pretty as a picture. Don't miss the gaudy E. Cornu clock made of onyx and bronze and embellished with ormolu, which was exhibited at the Paris Exposition of 1867. The industrialist had a gallery of over 350 paintings. To show off his pride and joy, he once gave a party for eight hundred people, who were brought to the house on private trains from New York City.

Three years after the mansion was built, the silk employer erected the observatory tower on the crest of the hill above the castle. A path leads up to the tower. There are also good views of Paterson from the castle terrace.

The strikers saw Lambert as the epitome of the industrial tyrant. Indeed, he was one of the key opponents of concessions. The industrialist eventually had to mortgage his estate and sell his art collection to meet his debts, only part of which stemmed from the labor troubles. He died in 1923 at nearly ninety years of age.

The strike hurt everyone involved. The struggle dragged on for seven months, but the employees eventually returned to their jobs. The workers were obviously hurt economically. The employers were also injured, because the strike badly damaged the silk industry. The silk industry in Paterson would have eventually died anyway, but the strike certainly hastened its collapse. The IWW was also damaged, because it had failed to accomplish its mission. Following the strike, the organization decided to concentrate future activities in the West.

The park commission tore down the mansion's north wing, saying it was too costly to maintain. Only some of the furniture remains in the castle today, so it cannot be seen in its original splendor. Nevertheless, the great discrepancy in wealth between Lambert and his workers is still apparent.

In the castle is a room devoted to Paterson's Garret Hobart, vice-president of the United States during President William McKinley's first term in office. The Hobarts and the McKinleys got along so well that if Garret Hobart had not died during the first term, he would have been the vice-president, instead of Theodore Roosevelt, when President McKinley was assassinated in 1901. Hobart's mansion, Haledon Hall, is now the campus nucleus of William Paterson College.

Other Sites to Visit

See the section on the early history of Paterson for other sites in this interesting city. Be sure to notice the old post office building (1889), now a part of the Passaic County court complex (located at the corner of Loop Road and Hamilton Street, by the county courthouse). It is a copy of a twelfth-century guild hall in Holland and is absolutely stunning. Notice the building's crow-stepped Dutch gables.

P A R T

ELEVEN
The Jazz Age

After the end of World War I, as is usual following a war, the people of the United States turned away from world affairs to concentrate on personal and family concerns. Fortunately, the immediate postwar period was one of considerable affluence (brought about in part by the new technology of mass production). Disenchantment with world affairs, combined with money to spend, produced an era of disillusioned play called the jazz age.

President Coolidge eased up on the progressive income tax. Consequently, the wealthy could afford to continue building huge mansions. Tours of some of these fantastic homes are included in the chapter on Long Island's Gold Coast.

With the return to "normalcy," Americans increasingly began to worry about the recent tide of immigration. The last chapter in the section describes sites connected with several ethnic groups in Philadelphia.

The most important trends in architecture centered around the building of skyscrapers. Corporations had the money for such expensive projects during this period. The architectural style most congruent with the jazz age was the sleek modernity of art deco. The name came from l'Exposition des Arts Decoratifs, a decorative-arts show held in Paris in 1925. In art deco the emphasis is on the geometric and the vertical, and Aztec and Egyptian art are frequently incorporated. Such famous skyscrapers as the Empire State and Chrysler buildings are examples. Art deco was also incorporated into interior decoration with an emphasis on sleek, shiny chrome.

31

Long Island's Gold Coast

If you are a nature lover as well as a history enthusiast, you will enjoy visiting the sites in this chapter. The grounds of many of the mansions once owned by Long Island's rich and famous have been turned into wonderful parks or arboretums. Many of the mansions are themselves fascinating places to visit. Especially noteworthy are the Phipp's mansion at Old Westbury Gardens, Falaise at Sands Point Park and Preserve, and the Vanderbilt mansion in Centerport. It will take at least one day to see Sands Point Park and Preserve and two more to see all the other mansions.

During the jazz age, the north shore of Long Island was known as the Gold Coast—haven for millionaires, writers, artists, and movie and theater personalities. This area stretched from Manhasset to Huntington and south to Old Westbury. Men such as William K. Vanderbilt, F. W. Woolworth, J. P. Morgan, Harry P. Whitney, Otto Kahn, and Daniel Guggenheim built great mansions here in the days before heavy income taxes took their toll. Among the entertainment personalities were Eddie Cantor, Ed Wynn, Jane Cowl, Leslie Howard, Basil Rathbone, and George M. Cohan.

Into this world stepped a young writer, Francis Scott Fitzgerald, and his wife, Zelda Sayre. Zelda was a very colorful person, and she is often cited as the very embodiment of the spirit of the age. In October 1922 they moved into a rented house (still a private residence today) at 6 Gateway Drive, Great Neck. They lived there until May 1924, when they moved to Europe.

Born in 1896 in St. Paul, Minnesota, the future author fast-talked his way into Princeton. He was a poor student and did not graduate. Even without a degree he became a second lieutenant in 1917. While stationed at Camp Sheridan near Montgomery, Alabama, he met his wife-to-be.

At the age of twenty-three, he published his first novel, the widely acclaimed *This Side of Paradise*. Not long afterward, he married Zelda Sayre at New York City's St. Patrick's Cathedral. In 1922 they moved to Great Neck. The area became the setting for his novel *The Great Gatsby*, published in 1925. When he wrote about East Egg and West Egg, he was really writing about Kings Point and Sands Point, Long Island.

The author became good friends with Ring Lardner, the short-story writer, who had a home on East Shore Road in Great Neck. From his place, Lardner could see the neighboring estate of Herbert Bayard Swope, executive editor of the *New York World*. From the porch of Swope's mansion, known as Land's End, Fitzgerald wrote parts of his most famous work. He used the house as the model for the home of Daisy Buchanan. The book's lavish parties were modeled after similar parties the writer attended at the estate.

Gatsby in many respects was Fitzgerald, being of two minds about the affluence of the jazz age—wanting to share in it but feeling disdain for its opulent vulgarity. Both Gatsby and his creator, like the nouveau riche, strove to be accepted into society. And yet they were bitter about the obstacles that the older, richer families put in the way of the newly rich or successful.

The Fitzgeralds entertained such guests as writers Edmund Wilson and John Dos Passos (fellow Princetonians) and actresses Laurette Taylor and Ina Claire. While living on the island, the writer suffered from insomnia and engaged in drinking bouts. The theater production of his play *The Vegetable* failed in its performance at Atlantic City—a defeat that sobered him into working harder. Writing in his room above the garage, he produced ten short stories. He eventually left Long Island, saying that the atmosphere would kill him creatively if he stayed.

Sands Point Park and Preserve

95 Middleneck Road (exit 36 off the Long Island Expressway, north on Searingtown Road, which becomes Port Washington Boulevard, then Middleneck Road), north of Port Washington, NY (Open Sat–Wed 10–5, May–Nov)

You can see three mansions on this preserve: Hempstead House, Mille Fleurs, and Falaise, but make the first stop the Visitors' Center.

Visitors' Center (Castle Gould)

Sands Point Park and Preserve, Port Washington, NY (Open Sat–Wed 10–5, May–Nov)

The area that now constitutes Sands Point Park and Preserve was once known as Castle Gould when Howard Gould, the son of robber baron Jay Gould, owned it. The Visitors' Center (presently referred to as Castle Gould) was once the carriage/stable complex, built in 1902. Purchase tickets here to visit Falaise, which is reachable only by bus.

Hempstead House

Within walking distance of the Visitors' Center, Sands Point Park and Preserve, Port Washington, NY

In 1909 Howard Gould commissioned Hunt and Hunt to build this medieval English manor. While it was being built, he separated from his wife.

In 1917 Daniel Guggenheim, the "Copper King," bought the entire estate. He named the mansion Hempstead House in reference to the harbor nearby. The new owner was one of seven sons of Meyer Guggenheim, the father who dreamed of obtaining one million dollars for each of his sons. This dream came true with the acquisition of one-third ownership in two lead-and-silver mines outside Leadville, Colorado. A big strike provided the money to buy copper mines. With these purchases he laid the basis for the entire United States copper industry. The big companies, such as Kennecott, Braden, and Anaconda Copper, all had their start in Meyer's operations.

Daniel, the most ambitious son, pushed to create a monopoly over the entire copper industry. In a fight with Rockefeller's American Smelting & Refining Company, the Guggenheims sold their interests to that company, but still managed to control it. Daniel was chairman of the board, while four of his brothers held board seats.

The mansion is presently being restored. It is often used by local organizations for various shows. Highlights include the palm court (one of two left on Long Island) and a foyer with beautiful woodwork and a vaulted ceiling over sixty feet high. A guide told us that the space scientist Werner Von Braun conducted experiments while at the house.

Mille Fleurs (by appointment only)

Sands Point Park and Preserve (reachable only by bus), Port Washington, NY

After Daniel's death in 1930, his wife built a smaller mansion, Mille Fleurs, because she felt the castle was too big for her. This French country mansion is U-shaped around a central enclosed garden. Mille Fleurs means "thousands of flowers" and, true to its name, the grounds' terraces are planted with a myriad of flowers. Florence Guggenheim died in 1945. Her bedroom and dressing room both have green paneling made of pickled wood, which is unappealing to many guests.

Falaise

Sands Point Park and Preserve (reachable only by bus—stop at the Visitors' Center), Port Washington, NY

In 1923 this manor house was built for Daniel's son, Captain Harry F. Guggenheim. He was ambassador to Cuba and president of the Solomon R. Guggenheim Museum. He also developed the daily newspaper *Newsday.*

Captain Harry Guggenheim promoted aviation. He became close friends with Charles Lindbergh after the latter's famous solo flight across the Atlantic Ocean. Indeed, the world-famous pilot often stayed in the

Sound Room. In 1927 he wrote his book *We* here. One page of the book's manuscript is framed on the wall outside the room. The captain was also a supporter of Dr. Robert Goddard's rocketry experiments. Another frequent visitor was the financier Bernard Baruch. Alicia Patterson, Harry's third wife, was from the famous *Chicago Tribune* family. She too was interested in aviation, making a solo flight from New York to Philadelphia.

The Morning Room is really beautiful, with great views of the Long Island Sound on three sides. After touring the mansion, take a stroll in Sands Point Park and Preserve, which has 216 acres with many nature trails.

Old Westbury Gardens and Mansion

71 Old Westbury Road (exit 39S off the Long Island Expressway, to Glen Cove Road, follow service road east 1.2 miles, turn right onto Old Westbury Road, one-quarter of a mile to the gardens), Old Westbury, Long Island, NY (Open Wed–Sun 10–5, May–Oct)

The traveler enters Old Westbury Gardens and Mansion through an early eighteenth-century gate on a road lined on both sides by European linden trees with their lower branches bent toward the road. It is an impressive beginning for a visit to the former home of entrepreneur John S. Phipps. He was the son of Henry Phipps, who was a partner in the Carnegie Steel Company. John married Margarita Grace of the Grace shipping line family.

The Phipps were definite Anglophiles. In 1909 the London architect George Crawley designed the Georgian manor here in the style of King Charles II's manor house. The house also maintains the English theme inside with many paintings by English artists of the late eighteenth century: Gainesborough, Reynolds, Raeburn, Downman, Morland, and Wilson. During the Second World War, the Phipps invited thirty English children to stay with them for the duration of the conflict.

There are beautiful views of the gardens from the ballroom and the upstairs. If you like houses that use decorative wood, this is the place to see. In Mr. Phipps's dressing room, there is outstanding woodwork on the four-poster canopy bed, wardrobe, chairs, and mirror. The Red Ballroom with its colorful walls and spaciousness now serves as a music room and lecture hall. A room not to be missed is the West Porch with its walls of glass—nine hydraulic windows that can be lowered to the basement and replaced with screens. The room blends in with the gardens on the outside. Notice the oak ceiling composed of coffers and beams.

Visit the luxurious gardens as well as the mansion. Many of the trees and other plants are labeled, making this a particularly educational place to tour. An especially lovely spot is by the gossamer-domed Temple of Love, which stands by the lake. The gardens are highly recommended.

Coe Hall

Planting Fields Arboretum, Planting Fields Road off Oyster Bay Road, Oyster Bay, Long Island (Open Mon–Fri 1–3:30, all year)

A prominent New York City lawyer, James Byrne, built a large house on this property in 1906. Planting Fields was the original Indian name for the area. In 1913 the property and house were purchased by William Robertson Coe and his wife, Mail Rogers Coe. William Coe was a successful insurance executive; Mail Coe was a daughter of Henry Huttleston Rogers, one of the founders of Rockefeller's Standard Oil Company. William Coe collected memorabilia of the American West for over forty-five years. Presently, Yale University has the collection.

The house burned down in 1918. The present house is a combination of English medieval and Elizabethan. Known as Coe Hall, the home was finished in 1921. Many of the items used in the construction came from English Tudor homes. For instance, the stained glass-windows are from Hever Castle, where Anne Boleyn, one of the eight wives of Henry VIII, lived. The interior is also Elizabethan in style. The house contains many of the antiques the owners purchased in Europe.

Be sure to see the grounds of the arboretum. The owner delighted in improving his collections of rhododendrons, azaleas, and camelias, but there are many other species here also.

Nassau County Museum of Fine Arts

Northern Boulevard near its intersection with Bryant Avenue, Roslyn Harbor, Long Island, NY (Open Tues–Fri 10–4:30, Sat–Sun 1–5, all year)

Ogden Codman, Jr., designed this mansion, originally known as Clayton, for a distinguished author of the late nineteenth century, Lloyd Bryce. In 1917 Charles Frick, the son of Henry Clay Frick (one of the founders of U.S. Steel), bought the estate. Frick made major changes to both the mansion's exterior and interior. The grounds include five miles of bridle paths, a lake, and a "pinetum," which contains 190 species of rare pine trees.

Caumsett

Caumsett State Park, Lloyd Harbor Road on Lloyd Neck, Huntington, Long Island, NY (Open daily 8–4:30, all year)

John Russell Pope designed this fifty-room mansion in classic brick Georgian style for Marshall Field III, a grandson of the Chicago mercantile multimillionaire. The name of the mansion is the area's original Matinecock Indian name, which means "place by a sharp rock." The estate was self-supporting with its own farm. Eighty-five men maintained the grounds.

Field died in 1959. The estate is now owned by the Long Island State Park Commission. The mansion, racing stables, dairy barn, and other structures are deteriorating, but the magnificent grounds can be toured.

Vanderbilt Museum

180 Little Neck Road at the tip of the Little Neck peninsula that juts into Northport Bay (Exit 42 off the Northern State Parkway, north on Deer Park Road West, changes name to Park Avenue after crossing Jericho Turnpike, right/north onto Greenlawn/Broadway/Centerport/Little Neck Road), Centerport, Long Island, NY (Open Tues–Sat 10–4, Sun 12–5, all year)

Children like to tour this estate with its many displays of animals, fishes, and seashells. William K. Vanderbilt II built the mansion, known as Eagle's Nest. He was the son of the infamous Alva Smith Vanderbilt, who was one of the triumvirate ruling Newport society.

Alva's son was a great auto enthusiast. In 1904 he won the Automobile Association Cup. In the same year, he created the Vanderbilt Cup Race, which ran until 1910. Moreover, he was responsible for building the Vanderbilt Motor Parkway, which covered forty-eight miles from the Queens-Nassau border to Lake Ronkonkoma in Suffolk County. This highway was one of the country's first modern paved parkways.

In 1899 he married Virginia Graham Fair, whose father had obtained great wealth from the silver and gold of the famous Comstock Lode in Virginia City, Nevada. The couple apparently did not get along, for by 1907 William began building a six-room Japanese-style bachelor retreat. By 1910 they were no longer living together. The cottage gradually expanded over the years through 1936 into the present twenty-four-room Moroccan and Spanish Revival mansion.

On his yacht during a fishing trip in 1926, he met and later married Rosamond Lancaster Warburton. This bit of happiness was followed by tragedy. In 1933 he lost his son in an auto accident. In 1936 the devoted father added the Memorial Wing to the mansion, filing it with mementos from his son's life. William Vanderbilt died in 1944. Taxes took thirty million of his thirty-six-million-dollar estate. Rosamond died in 1947.

The interior of the house is very eclectic, reflecting more the collecting trips of the Vanderbilts than a unified design. For instance, while the dining room has a tiled floor, carved wooden ceiling, and Moorish wall decorations in harmony with the house's architecture, the twelve carved walnut side chairs are seventeenth-century Flemish pieces and the carved-walnut table is seventeenth-century Florentine. Actually, this is one of the more harmonious rooms. William Vanderbilt's bedroom is furnished in the Empire style with items from eighteenth- and nineteenth-century France. However, on the floor is a carpet from East Persia, and the lamps are from China.

In the mansion are several display rooms dealing with natural history. On the grounds there is a planetarium, as well as a Hall of Fishes with an outstanding display of marine species. Vanderbilt himself collected and named many of the species on display. He loved to golf and would tee off from the roof of the building housing his fish collection.

Bailey's Arboretum

Locust Valley–Bayville Road, corner of Feeks Lane, northwest of Planting Fields Arboretum, Lattingtown, Long Island, NY (Open Tues–Sun 9–4, mid Apr–mid Nov)

In 1968 Nassau County obtained this forty-two-acre estate, the former summer home of Mr. and Mrs. Frank Bailey. The house was built in the mid 1800s, but was purchased by the Baileys in 1912. It is now used as a meeting place by the garden club. Frank Bailey was particularly fond of trees and collected more than six hundred different kinds.

Other Sites to Visit

See the chapters on Theodore Roosevelt and Walt Whitman. What the historian Frederick Lewis Allen has called the "big change" started at this time. This change was partially fueled by new inventions, the most important of which was the automobile. (This is appropriate considering that automobile manufacturer Henry Ford constructed the world's first factory designed for mass production.) The automobile gave people greater freedom to escape the watchful eyes of parents and neighbors. Visit the Boyertown Museum of Historic Vehicles (Reading Avenue and Warwick Street, Boyertown, not far from Reading, Pennsylvania). One of the pioneers of the automobile, Charles Duryea, owned an auto factory in Reading. The museum has many excellent early automobiles made in Berks County. The Saturday before Labor Day in Boyertown is Duryea Day, at which time antique and classic cars from the local area and adjoining states are shown.

The airplane was another invention that became increasingly important during the jazz age. The Mid-Atlantic region, more specifically, Long Island and Teterboro, New Jersey, was home to an astounding number of aviation firsts. Learn more about aviation by visiting the Cradle of Aviation Museum (Museum Lane, Mitchel Field, Garden City, Long Island) and the

Aviation Hall of Fame and Museum at Teterboro Airport (off Route 46, Teterboro Airport, Teterboro, New Jersey). The children will really enjoy these museums. Another airplane museum is available at Old Rhinebeck Aerodrome (north of Rhinebeck at the intersection of Norton and Stone Church Roads, off Route 9, Rhinebeck, New York). This one specializes in early biplanes and has a good air show.

32

The Ongoing Immigrant Experience

As everyone knows, the United States is a nation of immigrants. While we share certain key values, we differ on others according to recency of immigration and our particular ethnic heritage—where ethnicity is defined in its broader sense to include national origin, race, and religion. In this chapter we celebrate both the diversity of our ethnic heritage (by visiting various museums and areas devoted to various immigrant groups) and the blending of these heritages (as in the Mummers Museum). To see all the places listed below would take more than a day, so carefully choose the sites. The Mummers Museum ranks as one of the most enjoyable museums in the region.

The great ethnic diversity of the United States is a relatively recent phenomenon. For most of American history, from the period of settlement to the 1880s, groups from northern Europe dominated the country. Immigration is never easy, but it was relatively easier for the country to assimilate the pre-1880 immigrants because they were mostly Protestant in a mostly Protestant country; they dispersed widely across the nation; and they settled in rural as well as urban areas.

Following the Civil War, immigration started to increase, but it was not until the period after 1880 that the rate dramatically jumped. The number of immigrants from 1880 to 1889 was 5.2 million and from 1900 to 1909, 8.2 million. Before 1880 the highest decade figure was only 2.7 million.

Even more dramatic than the increase in the number of immigrants was the change in their ethnic composition. By 1896 over half of the total immigration consisted of groups from Italy and the Russian and Austro-Hungarian empires. It was more difficult to assimilate these new immigrants because they came in greater numbers in a short period of time; they had been primarily peasants and laborers in their countries of origin; many were Catholics and Jews settling in a predominately Protestant country; and the new immigrants congregated in the urban areas of the East Coast (in part because the cities had a great demand for low-paid, unskilled labor).

As the new Americans poured in, anti-immigration feelings mounted. The result was the restrictive immigration acts of 1921 and 1924. The anti-foreigner feeling was especially reflected in the 1924 law, which restricted immigration to no more than 150,000 persons per year (or 1.5 million per decade). It also set quotas whereby the number of immigrants allowed into the United States from any one foreign country was to be 2 percent of the number of foreignborn Americans of such nationality based on the 1890 census. Need one point out that the ethnic composition of the United States was quite different in 1890 compared to 1924?

During this period of heavy immigration, the gap between the rich and the poor was never wider. The great expansion of the nation's industrial might created many millionaires, while heavy immigration provided millions of poorly paid household, construction, factory, and sweatshop workers.

Through the post–Civil War period to the Progressive Era, we have described many places where America's rich lived and played. There are not as many places to visit when it comes to immigrants. The outstanding monuments to American immigration are, of course, the Statue of Liberty, Castle Garden, and the recently renovated Ellis Island in New York City. If you have not already done so, you should visit these places to better acquaint yourself with an important period of American history. Or you can take an ethnic tour of Philadelphia. The rapid influx of immigrants can be shown with a few statistics. The city experienced a 33 percent increase in population between 1901 and 1905, due primarily to the influx of new immigrants. One of the most dramatic increases was the jump in the number of Jewish residents from 100,000 in 1905 to 200,000 in 1918.

Afro-American Historical and Cultural Museum

Corner of Seventh and Arch streets, Philadelphia, PA (Open Tues–Sat 10–5, Sun 12–6, all year)

Strictly speaking, African-Americans are not an immigrant group, because they were brought to this country as slaves. However, these involuntary immigrants have certainly enriched the nation's cultural heritage. The museum traces some of this influence. The emphasis in the five galleries is more on black art than on black history, but you do get some sense of the many contributions made by African-Americans. At the museum is a video on the life of Martin Luther King, Jr., along with the suit he wore when he met President Johnson in March 1966 to urge full implementation of the Voting Rights Act.

Balch Institute for Ethnic Studies

18 South Seventh Street, next to the Graff House at the corner of Market and Seventh streets, Philadelphia, PA (Open Mon–Sat 10–4, all year)

This small museum has both permanent and changing exhibits dealing with the history of immigration and ethnic cultures. Children are intrigued by the ethnic history display. The youngster places a little red ball in the slot for his/her ethnic group and pushes down the appropriate yellow button, thereby adding the ball to the ethnic tabulation board.

National Museum of American Jewish History

55 North Fifth Street, corner of Commerce Street off Independence Mall, Philadelphia, PA (Open Mon–Thur 10–5, Sun 12–5, all year)

In front of this museum is a statue of a woman symbolizing religious liberty. It is dedicated to the people of the United States by the order B'nai Brith and the Israelites of America. Officials rededicated the statue on May 4, 1986.

A permanent exhibit entitled The Jewish Experience does an excellent job of tracing the history of Jews in the United States. This museum is especially interesting because the visitor sees the United States from the perspective of one of its minority groups. Note the attitude of the museum curators toward the restrictive immigration laws of 1921 and 1924. They make the telling point that "by the time Hitler came to power, the New World was closed to massive European Jewish immigration."

Mikveh Israel Cemetery

Eighth and Spruce streets, Philadelphia, PA

This is the burial ground of the Sephardic Congregation Mikveh Israel (1740). In 1783 John Penn granted the land to Rabbi Nathan Levy. There are twenty-one Revolutionary War soldiers buried in the cemetery. Some sources say that, during the occupation of Philadelphia, the British firing squads used the cemetery walls to execute British military criminals. The most famous grave is that of Rebecca Gratz, a tireless worker for social welfare organizations. She was a friend of Matilda Hoffman, the fiancée of Washington Irving (see the section on Irving for more information).

Mummers Museum

Second Street and Washington Avenue, Philadelphia, PA (Open Tues–Sat 9:30–5; Sun 12–5 all year)

You will have a great time here. Every New Year's Day there is a mummers parade in Philadelphia. At the museum you can watch videos of the best of the mummer bands. It is a real treat to hear the music and be dazzled by the costumes. After seeing the video, examine some of the actual parade costumes, displayed on mannequins. This museum is particularly interesting because it illustrates the mixing of cultures to produce something

Costumes from the Mummers Museum, Philadelphia, Pennsylvania

uniquely American. Therefore, the history of the Mummers will be presented in some detail.

The word *mummers* comes from the German *mumme,* which means disguise. In medieval Europe, the mummers would enter homes to dance or play dice. During the colonial period, English and Welsh settlers in Philadelphia would visit neighbors' homes to recite rhymes and be rewarded with refreshments, and at New Year's, Swedish and Finnish settlers would shoot off guns. Paraders used to be called New Year's Shooters because of this practice. Needless to say, the city elders frowned on this activity and repeatedly banned it.

During the 1860s, there was a great influx of African-Americans into the city. The Shooters adopted the minstrel show tradition, which became popular in the late 1800s. The mummers often use a distinctive walk called the Philadelphia Strut, which evolved from the old cakewalk.

By 1901 the parades had become a city-sponsored celebration. Five years later, they were divided into three separately judged divisions. The two largest divisions are those of the string bands and the fancies, with the comics in the minority. The string bands emphasize music, drill, and costume. The bands blend the accordion, saxophone, drums, violin, banjo, bass fiddle, bells, and clarinet to make a unique sound. The fancies are composed of the fancy brigades (displaying elaborate themes) and the fancy clubs. The latter use traditional frame suits made of plywood, which rest on the wearer's shoulders. They also put on novelty presentations. And, finally, the comics cavort as clowns.

Other Sites to Visit

You can have lunch or dinner in Chinatown, which is only two blocks from the Afro-American Historical and Cultural Museum. Or you may want to eat in Philadelphia's Little Italy. The Italian Market runs on Ninth Street from Christian Street to Washington Avenue in South Philadelphia. Another museum to visit is the American Swedish Historical Museum (see the section on the Swedish settlers).

PART

TWELVE

The Modern Era

The modern era includes not only the post–World War II period, but also the Great Depression. The stock market crash of 1929 and its aftermath seriously weakened the optimistic faith of the Progressives and conservatives that the economic system could automatically balance itself if just left alone. In response to the ugly reality that one-third of the nation's work force was unemployed, legislators created ad hoc measures, such as unemployment insurance, social security, welfare, and food allotments, that eventually laid the foundations for the modern welfare state. The welfare state is committed to intervening in the economic sphere to insure that individuals are guaranteed at least a minimum standard of living and comfort.

To capture the spirit of the modern era, we visit the Hyde Park home of the man most responsible for combating the Great Depression and forging the early American welfare state: Franklin Delano Roosevelt. We also visit the home of Eleanor Roosevelt, who was a very important person in her own right. The next chapter in the section describes President Eisenhower's Gettysburg farm to capture the feeling of the 1950s.

33

The Roosevelts of Hyde Park

There are two main reasons why travelers will enjoy visiting Hyde Park. The first is the natural beauty of the grounds—one estate set by the Hudson River and the other by a peaceful stream. The second is the great respect all Americans should feel for the owners of the two houses. Franklin and Eleanor Roosevelt were the most influential couple of the modern era, because the American welfare state took shape under their leadership. Moreover, their joint concern for the less fortunate has never been equaled in another presidency. Precisely because they were such decent, caring people, the two Hyde Park homes are an inspiration for both adults and children. The two tours together will take more than half a day. And if one is especially interested in this period of history (some visitors, after all, have lived through it), seeing all that is available could take an entire day.

Franklin's father, James Roosevelt (1828–1900), led a life of leisure at his thousand-acre Hyde Park estate. The home he purchased in 1867 was called Springwood. It has been modified many times. The oldest section, the central part, dates from the early 1800s. James Roosevelt transformed the family home into an Italianate villa of seventeen rooms. In 1915, after her husband's death, Rebecca Howland Roosevelt changed the house into a Georgian Revival mansion of thirty-five rooms.

After the death of his first wife, in 1880 James married Sara Delano (who was half his age). Some two years later, Franklin Delano Roosevelt was born in the blue room on the second floor of Springwood. His father died when Franklin was just approaching his teenage years.

Eleanor Roosevelt was born in 1884. She was the niece of President Theodore Roosevelt and the daughter of Theodore's brother Elliott. Franklin was her fifth cousin.

The future married couple had very different childhoods. Franklin's mother doted on him and he had a happy boyhood. In contrast, Eleanor's mother died in 1892, and her father died two years later. This left the shy, solemn girl orphaned at the age of ten. She was raised by her grandmother, Mrs. Valentine Hall, who had an estate at Tivoli on the Hudson River. Left by herself a great deal, the young Eleanor spent many hours reading.

Franklin went to Groton for his preparatory studies for Harvard University. He had a hard time adjusting because he arrived at the age of fourteen, instead of the usual age of twelve. This left him feeling an outsider and also gave him sympathy for the underdog. Eleanor had a better experience, going to England to study at the Allenswood School. The headmistress there took the young woman under her wing, and the future first lady blossomed.

At age eighteen she came home for her coming-out party. Shortly afterward, she met Franklin again, even though the two had known each other since childhood. During his last year at Harvard, the future president fell in love with her. He proposed and she, nonplused and disbelieving at first, accepted. Her future mother-in-law tried to prevent the marriage. Failing in this, Sara attended her son's wedding on St. Patrick's Day 1905—the bride was given away by President Theodore Roosevelt. Relations between Eleanor and her mother-in-law remained strained. Eleanor meekly submitted to the older woman, while deeply resenting it.

Franklin studied law at Columbia University and in 1907 joined a law firm. He participated in politics, and his subsequent rise was quick. In 1910 he ran for state senator from Columbia, Dutchess, and Putnam counties and won easily. In Albany he became the focus around which anti-Tammany forces rallied, giving him a statewide reputation.

He supported Woodrow Wilson in the 1912 election campaign and was rewarded with an appointment as assistant secretary of the navy. While in Washington, he and his wife began to drift apart. They were, after all, such very different people. He liked to mingle socially, while she preferred a more quiet life. This gulf widened when Franklin had an affair with Eleanor's part-time social secretary, Lucy Mercer. When the relationship came to full light in 1918, it devastated Eleanor. She was never really the same after that—there was always that deeper sadness in her. She demanded that her husband either stop seeing the woman or get a divorce. He agreed to stop seeing her. However, he did not keep this agreement. Lucy Mercer frequently visited the White House when Eleanor was out of town.

Disagreeable as the confrontation was, it marked the beginning of a beautiful professional relationship between the two—one that greatly benefited the nation as a whole. In 1921 Franklin contracted polio, which left his legs paralyzed. His wife served as his stand-in and became an important political figure in her own right.

While his legs were paralyzed, his mind certainly was not. His 1924 "Happy Warrior" speech helped Al Smith, the governor of New York, in his bid for the Democratic nomination for the presidency of the United States. Although Smith lost, Roosevelt's political reputation soared. His campaign adviser, Louis Howe, encouraged his wife's political activity. At this time she became close friends with New York Democratic committee co-workers Nancy Cook and Marion Dickerman.

Eleanor Roosevelt had been looking for a way to get out of the Hyde Park house, which she had always considered the home of her mother-in-law. The opportunity arose when Franklin offered to build for her and her two Democratic party co-workers a cottage at the family's favorite picnic spot at Val-Kill on Hyde Park estate grounds. Cook and Dickerman settled into the cottage when it was completed in 1925 and made it their residence until 1947. In 1926 the three women ordered the construction of a larger building to house a factory designed to teach local farmers craftsmanship by making furniture, pewter, and weavings.

In 1928 Al Smith succeeded in becoming the Democratic candidate for the presidency. Although he lost the election to Herbert Hoover, Roosevelt narrowly won the governorship of New York. With the onslaught of the depression, in 1932 the voters chose the man from Hyde Park to be president of the United States. They elected him again in 1936, 1940, and 1944. He was the only president to serve more than two terms.

Franklin D. Roosevelt National Historic Site

Route 9 (Route 55 exit of the Taconic Parkway, travel west on Route 55, turn right onto Market, left onto Washington, which leads into Route 9 north), Hyde Park, NY (Open daily 9–5, Apr–Oct; Thur–Mon 9–5, Nov–Mar)

For the president, Hyde Park remained a wonderful retreat from the cares of Washington. Via the radio he gave his famous fireside chats to the nation from the family living room. In the room are two highback leather chairs used by FDR when he was governor of New York. He always sat in the one on the left. On the second floor is the Blue Room where Franklin was born and which was later used as a guest room. His adult bedroom was directly over the living room. In the room are naval prints, family photos, and his dog Fala's chair, leash, and blanket. One of the funniest stories from the White House years, and one that illustrates the president's sense of humor, involved the black Scottish terrier. Speaking at a news conference, Roosevelt noted that even his dog was now getting press coverage. He commented that the reporters had criticized him, had criticized his wife, and had even criticized his children, but that now they were picking on poor Fala. He added that he did not mind the criticism, Eleanor did not mind the criticism, nor did the children mind. "But Fala . . . Fala minds!"

At the site is a museum with exhibits tracing the life stories of both Franklin and Eleanor Roosevelt. It has many of their belongings, including the White House desk FDR used at the time of his death. It looks like a child's desk, covered with knickknacks, photos, and mementos. After the museum, tour the house itself. Leave enough time to walk around the grounds. Roosevelt loved the view from the southern terrace, where the family would often gather.

Eleanor Roosevelt National Historic Site, Val-Kill

You can only visit Val-Kill by purchasing tickets at the Franklin D. Roosevelt National Historic Site in Hyde Park. Access to the site is by bus only. (Open daily 9:30–4:30, Apr–Oct; weekends, Nov–Dec, Mar)

Eleanor had a falling-out with Nan Cook and Marion Dickerman, who felt they had not received enough recognition for being the first lady's politi-

Eleanor Roosevelt's office and her secretary's sitting room, Val-Kill, Hyde Park, New York

cal mentors. Instead of asking the two women to leave the cottage, she had the factory building (the factory folded in 1936) converted into living quarters. Speaking of Val-Kill she said, "I knew this was always to be my home." With her lived her secretary, Malvina "Tommy" Thompson.

FDR died in Warm Springs, Georgia, on April 12, 1945, just before Germany surrendered to end the European part of the Second World War. (Ms. Mercer had been with the president when he died, but was whisked away before Eleanor arrived.) He is buried next to the Hyde Park mansion.

Eleanor returned to Val-Kill. In 1946 President Harry Truman appointed her a member of the American delegation to the United Nations. In this position she helped draft the Universal Declaration of Human Rights, which she felt was her most important work. Following this, she again returned to Val-Kill and wrote two autobiographies. She died in 1962 at the age of seventy-eight. She is buried beside her husband.

Visitors to Val-Kill are shown an excellent and inspirational film on the former first lady's life. They then tour Eleanor's home, the converted factory building that still resembles a factory. The simple lifestyle revealed within the house speaks volumes about Eleanor Roosevelt. Even her furniture was mostly made at Val-Kill. The cottage used by Eleanor's friends is not open to the public.

Other Sites to Visit

While in Hyde Park, you might want to eat at the restaurant of the Culinary Institute of America (reservations: 914-471-6608), located on Route 9 just south of the FDR home. Tour the Vanderbilt and Mills mansions just north of Springwood or see the Samuel F. B. Morse home just south of Poughkeepsie.

34

Eisenhower at Gettysburg

The Eisenhower farm is adjacent to the Gettysburg battlefield, making it possible to see both sites in a day. The Eisenhower house tour will be a unique pleasure for many visitors because it will be the only site in the travel area that is contemporary with their own lives. They can tell their children that they or their family owned something similar to that owned by the Eisenhowers. There are also fond memories associated with the general. The name Ike brings back pleasant associations because, for most children of the 1950s, he was the most popular figure (next to Elvis Presley) in their grade-school world. Eisenhower probably would have been elected to a third term had terms not been limited to two. The man with the sunny, optimistic disposition seemed to match the very spirit of the decade.

When thinking about Eisenhower's army career, what really stands out is that he had no actual battle experience. This illustrates just how vast a bureaucratic machine the army had become. The future leader of all the Allied forces in Europe rose to the top through graduate education, experience in planning peacetime battle maneuvers and then actual war plans, and through his likable personality.

Eisenhower's biography is a true American success story. He was born in Denison, Texas, in 1890, the third of seven sons of a railroad worker. Shortly after his birth the family moved back to their home territory of Abilene, Kansas. Growing up in poor circumstances, he had an unremarkable childhood and adolescence, even staying in Abilene following high school graduation. Then a friend told him about the service academies and his life forever changed. He reported to West Point in 1911.

His first assignment as an officer was to Fort Sam Houston, near San Antonio, Texas. There he met Mamie Doud in October 1915. The two became engaged on Valentine's Day in 1916 and married the following July.

When the United States entered World War I, the Kansas officer desperately sought action, but the army brass ordered him to remain stateside. During the war years, he briefly worked at Camp Colt near Gettysburg. The Eisenhowers lived at the still-standing, but private, 263 Springs Avenue.

While stationed at Camp Meade in Maryland, his friend George Patton introduced him to Brigadier General Fox Conner, who became Eisenhower's mentor. The young officer went to Camp Gaillard in Panama to serve with Conner (and to escape the painful memory of the death of his three-year-old child—a tragedy that placed a great strain on his marriage). Another son, John, was born in Panama.

During the period between the two world wars, Eisenhower furthered his education in army tactics by attending the army's equivalent of graduate school. He served as an aide to General Douglas MacArthur, even accompanying him to the Philippines. The aide admired the general, but found the American Caesar to be arrogant and conceited and soon returned stateside. Once back, his brilliant planning of wartime exercises as chief of staff, Third Army, brought him some well-deserved recognition. Following the Japanese bombardment of Pearl Harbor on December 7, 1941, he was assigned to the War Plans Division of the army general staff to work with Chief of Staff George Marshall.

He worked with Marshall to plan the Allied assault on German forces. He was so impressive in this role that the chief of staff selected him over 366 senior officers to command all American forces in the European theater of operations.

His commander made the right decision. The army needed someone capable of working with the different national goals and competing egos. Eisenhower was this someone, for two of his outstanding qualities were his general affability and willingness to compromise for the larger good. Can you imagine what would have happened had a Patton-type been given this position?

Under his leadership, the Allies invaded North Africa in November 1942; Sicily and Italy in July and September 1943; and France on June 6, 1944 (D-day). The European war ended in May 1945.

During the war, Eisenhower may or may not have had an affair with Kay Summersby, his Irish driver and later personal secretary and military aide. The evidence is sketchy. President Truman has been quoted as saying that he destroyed correspondence between Eisenhower and Marshall wherein the senior officer wrote that if Ike divorced his wife and married Kay, he would bust him out of the army and do all he could to ruin him.

Following the end of the war, Ike became the new chief of staff. He retired in 1948, but soon accepted an offer to become the president of Columbia University in New York City. While serving in this position, he and his wife began to search for a summer place. A friend who had just purchased a home in Gettysburg persuaded the couple to investigate the area.

The Gettysburg Farm

Tickets may be purchased at the Visitors' Center, Gettysburg National Military Park, Taneytown Road (from Lancaster take Route 15 south, Route 140 north, turn right onto Hunt Avenue, turn left onto Taneytown Road) Gettysburg, PA (Open daily 8–5, Feb–Dec)

Traveling to Gettysburg, the couple fell in love with a century-old brick farmhouse on 189 acres of land. They purchased the place in early

1951. Use of the farm had to be delayed, however, because President Truman appointed the old soldier commander of the North Atlantic Treaty Organization (NATO). The Eisenhowers proceeded to Europe.

Republicans pressured Ike to run for the 1952 nomination for president. He resigned from NATO in June of that year, and in July was unanimously chosen as the Republican candidate with Richard M. Nixon as his running mate. They won the election with 55 percent of the vote.

Once in the White House, Mamie decided to fix up the Gettysburg farm as a retreat and future home. The main part of the new house was built over the remains of a two-hundred-year-old log cabin. Therefore, major remodeling was necessary. While waiting for this, the new president was busy handling McCarthyism, the truce ending the Korean War, and the fight over desegregation set off by the 1954 landmark Supreme Court decision in *Brown v. Board of Education.*

In September 1955 the president suffered a heart attack while in Denver, Colorado. Workers finished the house remodeling just in time for him to use it for further recuperation. Mamie had transformed the place into a two-story Georgian farmhouse with two new wings built around the original brick section. In all, there were now fifteen rooms and eight baths. The couple referred to the house as the only home they ever owned.

Eisenhower recovered his health and, with running-mate Richard Nixon, won the 1956 election by the biggest plurality in twenty years. During his second term, he had to face many crises. In the fall of 1957 he used federal troops to enforce school integration in Little Rock, Arkansas. Also in the fall of that year the Soviet Union shocked the Americans by launching the first satellite, *Sputnik,* into outer space.

Despite continuing political concerns, many visitors came to the Gettysburg farm. Among the famous names in the guest book on the hall table are Winston Churchill, Charles de Gaulle, Konrad Adenauer, Jawaharlal Nehru, and Nikita Khrushchev. The host enjoyed giving his guests a tour of the adjacent Gettysburg battlefield.

In the 1960 presidential election, John F. Kennedy defeated Richard Nixon. The Eisenhowers left the White House in January 1961 to retire to their farm. The former president was still very much in demand, however, and on many occasions advised both Presidents Kennedy and Johnson.

In the spring of 1968 the ex-president suffered another heart attack. Admitted to Walter Reed Hospital, he remained there until his death in March 1969. Mamie resided in the Gettysburg house until her death some ten years later.

At the house don't miss the Sun Porch, which was the Eisenhowers' favorite room. Here they entertained guests and watched television—and at times Ike would paint. Upstairs you can see two of these paintings. On the outside of the house the visitor will find a barbecue, a putting green, skeet range, and a Crosley runabout (a golfcart used to drive guests around the Gettysburg battlefield).

Presbyterian Church of Gettysburg
Baltimore and High streets, Gettysburg, PA

The Eisenhowers attended this church. President Lincoln worshiped here when he came to Gettysburg to give his famous address.

Eisenhower's Office
Corner of Stevens and Carlisle streets, Gettysburg, PA

Ike had an office here in the former home of the president of Gettysburg College. He used it from 1961 to 1967. Here he wrote his memoirs. Next to the office stands a statue of this very popular man.

Other Sites to Visit

Be sure to tour the Gettysburg Battlefield. You may also want to take the train ride available in the downtown area (see the chapter on railroads.)

Suggested Readings

The following books on regional subjects are particularly interesting.

On early settlements, see Clare Brandt, *An American Aristocracy: The Livingstons* (Garden City, N.Y.: Doubleday, 1986); and C. A. Weslager, *New Sweden on the Delaware: 1638–1655* (Wilmington: Middle Atlantic Press, 1988).

On later settlements, see Fredric Klees, *The Pennsylvania Dutch* (New York: Macmillan, 1950).

On the struggle for the continent, see Isabel Thompson Kelsay, *Joseph Brant, 1743–1807: Man of Two Worlds* (Syracuse: Syracuse University Press, 1984); and Douglas Edward Leach, *The Northern Colonial Frontier: 1607–1763* (Albuquerque: University of New Mexico Press, 1966).

On the American Revolution, see James Thomas Flexner, *Washington: The Indispensable Man* (New York: Signet, 1984); Edward S. Gifford, Jr., *The American Revolution in the Delaware Valley* (Philadelphia: Pennsylvania Society of Sons of the Revolution, 1976); Richard Ketchum, *The Winter Soldiers* (Garden City, N.Y.: Doubleday, 1973); and Russell F. Weigley, ed., *Philadelphia: A 300-Year History* (New York: Norton, 1982).

On the federal period, see Jeffrey Simpson, *Officers and Gentlemen: Historic West Point in Photographs* (Tarrytown, N.Y.: Sleepy Hollow Press, 1982).

On the age of Jackson, see Gay Wilson Allen, *Walt Whitman* (Detroit: Wayne State University Press, 1969); and Barbara Babcock Lassiter, *American Wilderness: The Hudson River School of Painting* (Garden City, N.Y.: Doubleday, 1978).

On industry and transportation, see Timothy Jacobs, *The History of the Pennsylvania Railroad* (New York: Bonanza Books, 1988); Aaron E. Klein, *The History of the New York Central System* (New York: Bonanza Books, 1985); and Arthur D. Pierce, *Iron in the Pines: The Story of New Jersey's Ghost Towns and Bog Iron* (New Brunswick: Rutgers University Press, 1957).

On the Civil War, see Bruce Catton, *Never Call Retreat* (New York: Washington Square, 1967); and Historical Times, *Gettysburg* (Harrisburg: Eastern Acorn, 1968).

On the post–Civil War period, see Architectural League of New York & The Gallery Association of New York State, *Resorts of the Catskills* (New York: St. Martin's, 1979); Brooklyn Museum, *The American Renaissance, 1876–1917* (New York: Pantheon, 1979); Robert Conot, *A Streak of Luck: The Life and Legend of Thomas Alva Edison* (New York: Seaview, 1979); and Matthew Josephson, *The Robber Barons* (New York: Harvest Books, 1962).

On the Progressive Era, see Edmund Morris, *The Rise of Theodore Roosevelt* (New York: Ballantine Books, 1979).

On the jazz age, see Monica Randall, *The Mansions of Long Island's Gold Coast* (New York: Hastings House, 1979).

On the modern age, see Joseph P. Lash, *Eleanor and Franklin* (New York: Signet, 1971).

Geographic Cross-Reference

Boldface page numbers indicate illustrations.

Delaware

Wilmington Area

Greenbank: Wilmington and Western Railroad, **215**, 216

Pea Patch Island (Delaware City): Fort Delaware, 240–242, **241**

Wilmington: Fort Christina State Park, 11; Hagley Museum, 173–176, **174**; Hendrickson House, 12; Nemours Mansion and Gardens, 298–299; Old Swedes' Church, **11**–12; Winterthur Museum and Gardens, 296–297. *Other sites*: Brandywine Village, 176; Hotel Du Pont, 299; Old Town Hall, 15

New Jersey

Central and Northwest

Flemington (Hunterdon): Black River and Western Railroad, 217

Menlo Park (Middlesex): Edison Memorial, 254

Princeton (Mercer): Bainbridge House, 86–87, 290; Drumthwacket, 87; Graduate College, 294; Grover Cleveland's House, 293–294; Morven, 86; Nassau Hall, 84–85; Paul Robeson House, 86; President's House, 85; Princeton Battlefield, 81–84; Princeton Battle Monument, 84; Princeton Cemetery, 86; Prospect Avenue, 293; Prospect House, **292**–293; Thomas Clark House, 82, **83**; Wilson House(s), 291–292, 295; Witherspoon Hall, 291

Trenton (Mercer): Battle Monument, 77; Douglass House, 80; Old Barracks, 78–**79**; St. Mary's Cathedral, 78; St. Michael's Episcopal Church, 78; William Trent House, 80–81. *Other sites*: New Jersey State House, 81; New Jersey State Museum, 81; Washington Crossing State Park, New Jersey (Mercer), and Washington Crossing Historic Park, Pennsylvania (Bucks), 81, 204

South

New York

Kingston-Rhinebeck Area

Long Island (Nassau County)

Long Island (Suffolk County)

Mid–Hudson River Area

Catskill (Greene): Thomas Cole House, 155–**156**

Germantown (Columbia): Clermont State Historic Park, 24–25. *Other sites*: Clermont Mansion, 153, 159

Haines Falls (Greene): Kaaterskill Falls, 156; North-South Lake Public Campground, 157

Hudson (Columbia): Olana, 158

Kinderhook (Columbia): Martin Van Buren National Historic Site (Lindenwald), 151–153, **152**. *Other sites*: James Vanderpoel House, 153; Luykas Van Alen House, 153

Other Sites in the Area: Coxsackie (Greene): Bronck House Museum, 159

Newburgh Area

West Point (Orange): Commandant's Quarters, 129; Fort Putnam, 127; Great Iron Chain, 127–128; Kosciuszko's Monument, 127; Old Cadet Chapel, 129; Superintendent's Quarters, 129; Sylvanus Thayer Monument, 128; Visitors' Center, 126; West Point Museum of Military Arms, 126

Other Sites in the Area: Garrison (Putnam): Boscobel, 130; Cold Spring (Putnam): Foundry School Museum, 130; Stony Point (Rockland): Stony Point Battlefield Reservation, 112; Vails Gate (Orange): New Windsor Cantonment, **111**, 112

Port Jervis Area

Barryville (Sullivan): Roebling Suspension Bridge, 204. *Other sites*: Zane Grey House, 204

Cuddebackville (Orange): Delaware and Hudson Canal Park, 205

Minisink Ford (Sullivan): Minisink Battleground Park, 61–62

Narrowsburg (Sullivan): Fort Delaware, 60–61

Poughkeepsie-New Paltz Area

High Falls (Ulster): Delaware and Hudson Canal Museum, 205

Hyde Park (Dutchess): Eleanor Roosevelt National Historic Site, Val-Kill, 325–**326**; Franklin D. Roosevelt National Historic Site, 325; Vanderbilt Mansion National Historic Site, 250–252

New Paltz (Ulster): Lake Minnewaska, 265; Mohonk Mountain House, **264**. *Other sites*: Huguenot Street Houses, 9, 265; Jean Hasbrouck House, 9

Philadelphia—Northeast (Bucks County)

Philadelphia—Northwest

Philadelphia (Southwest and Southeast)

Prospect Park (Delaware): Morton Homestead, 14

Other Sites in the Area: Chester (Delaware): Caleb Pusey House, 39;
Philadelphia Airport area: Fort Mifflin, 100

Reading Area

Birdsboro (Berks): Daniel Boone Homestead Site, 58

Elverson (Berks): Hopewell Village National Historic Site, 186–**187**

Newmanstown (Lebanon): Zeller's Fort, 58

Temple (Berks): Blue Mountain and Reading Railroad, 213

Womelsdorf (Berks): Conrad Weiser Park, **56**, 57

Other Sites in the Area: Boyertown (Berks): Boyertown Museum of Historic Vehicles (Duryea auto museum), 58, 313; Cornwall
(Lebanon): Cornwall Furnace, 187–188; Cornwall Village, 58, 187–
188; Reading (Berks): Union Canal Towpath Tour, 58, 203

Scranton Area

Honesdale (Wayne): Stourbridge Lion, 212; Stourbridge Line Rail Excursion, 212

Scranton (Lackawanna): Steamtown U.S.A., 212–213. *Other sites*: Anthracite Museum, 199

Index